THI
ULTIMATE
GUIDE TO BOOK
MARKETING

THE 80/20 SYSTEM FOR
SELLING MORE BOOKS

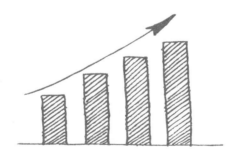

NICHOLAS ERIK

www.nicholaserik.com

The Ultimate Guide to Book Marketing/ Nicholas Erik. —1st ed.

CONTENTS

GET THE FREE MARKETING

NEWSLETTER

For more in-depth book marketing information like what's in this guide, subscribe to my free book marketing newsletter at **nicholaserik.com/newsletter**.

ONE

PRINCIPLES

Welcome to the *Ultimate Guide to Book Marketing*, **a complete step-by-step marketing system that gives you the tools to sell more books with less effort and time.** It aims to be the most comprehensive book marketing resource in existence—better, even, than high-dollar paid courses.

I'll let you be the final judge of whether I hit that mark.

Marketing is not an arcane art; it is a learnable skill based upon well-established, time-tested principles. But if you're anything like I was a few years ago, you have a random collection of bookmarks, scribbled to-do lists, Excel sheets, and notes all pulling you in twenty different directions. Whether you're an experienced author or just starting out, this guide cuts through pages of nonsense to focus on one thing: getting you results.

The marketing system detailed within is founded upon thousands of hours (and many dollars) of personal testing that spans 50+ titles, multiple pen names/clients, and a variety of genres.

We'll cover every essential piece of book marketing, from strategy to blurbs to newsletters, complete with action exercises so you can apply this info to your own books. These exercises are not busywork, but are specifically designed to help you implement the most important aspects of this guide. If you do them, by the end you'll have created a marketing plan *specifically* designed for *your* books.

I occasionally reference articles or resources from my site. These dive into more depth on a specific topic. The reason they're not integrated into the guide itself is simple: keeping them separate allows me to continually update them as the need arises.

A final note: each part of this guide was written to stand alone. So you can either read it in order, or select which sections are most relevant to you.

Enough preamble. In this section, we'll cover:

- Who I Am (And Why I Wrote This)
- Three Core Principles
- The Trifecta of Indie Success

A BRIEF BUT IMPORTANT CAREER NOTE

Marketing is a skill.

Or, rather, a set of many sub-skills.

Much like writing itself, marketing demands time and experience to master. While this guide features step-by-step exercises designed to quickly sharpen your skills, do not be discouraged if your first marketing efforts yield less than spectacular results. Being disappointed by this would be akin to going to the gym once and then lamenting that you weren't immediately in immaculate shape. That's not how anything challenging works, and while legions of super-long internet sales pages might suggest the book business is exempt from this rule, allow me to dissuade you of that notion before we travel any further. Accepting that this will be difficult will free you from the tyranny of unrealistic expectations and might stop you from quitting too early.

This is a long game (five, ten, twenty years). Plan accordingly.

But much like any other area, if you're patient and put in the time, you will improve.

So let's get started, shall we?

WHO I AM (AND WHY I WROTE THIS)

This guide isn't about me; while it draws heavily upon my experiences, I'll spare you the anecdotes and focus on the data. That's because this is all about getting *you* results. But you might be wondering why you should invest multiple hours reading a very lengthy guide that you perhaps stumbled upon at random. So here are the basic broad strokes of who I am:

1. I'm a sci-fi and fantasy author who's written 20+ novels.
2. My micro press has sold 100,000+ books and published 50+ titles.
3. I've hit the *USA Today* Bestseller list.
4. I've spent $100k+ of my own money refining these principles.
5. I've consulted and/or run marketing campaigns for multiple six-figure authors.

6. I've worked in a variety of genres, including crime/mystery/thriller, romance, action adventure, horror, fantasy, and sci-fi.

7. I've personally tested and implemented almost everything in this guide (in the rare instances where I mention something I haven't tried, I try to note this).

As for the *why*: writing this guide has helped me structure my own marketing ideas and strategies into a usable format. If I can't explain something, it means I don't fully understand it—or it's actually BS. And we all know far too well that BS spreads like wildfire. I've kindly omitted it from this guide.

I've torn down and rebuilt this guide multiple times since writing the initial version way back in 2017, with each iteration featuring new strategies, principles, and the latest marketing info. Each revision has helped me refine my principles and strategies.

In short, writing and rewriting this guide over the past three years has been an indispensable learning tool for me. It has helped me get significantly better at marketing. I hope you find it helpful as well.

And since learning more about me won't help *you* get better at marketing, let's switch gears and talk about the three core principles this guide is built upon.

CORE PRINCIPLE #1: THE 80/20 RULE

I'm big on streamlining and simplifying everything to its absolute essentials. In this information-rich world, **curation is 100x more valuable than information (which, thanks to the internet, is now essentially infinite)**. Amidst the noisiness of this spiraling complexity, it's refreshing to know that, in any discipline, there are probably less than a dozen core principles that you must master to get results.

Often, it's even less.

The 80/20 rule, also known as the Pareto Principle, is the reason why. For the uninitiated, this rule states that 80% of your results come from just 20% of your actions. The numbers vary (e.g., 1% of your actions can produce 99% of the results). The key takeaway is this: **a select few actions have a disproportionate impact on your outcomes**. You cannot do everything, nor should you even try; most tasks are worthless. **Small, marginally effective tactics are, in fact, liabilities, as they thieve time from high impact, ultra-valuable tasks.**

Doing everything is not a recipe for overachieving; it is a recipe for ruin.

While the 80/20 rule may sound like a BS business term or productivity hack, the math behind it is fairly robust (economist Vilfredo Pareto first observed the principle in relation to land ownership in early 20th century Italy, where 20% of the population owned 80% of the land) and can accurately predict/model input-output relationships in a range of disciplines.

80/20 is what's known as a **power law**. This means these core actions aren't marginally better than their superfluous counterparts; they're literally 100x or 1000x more potent.

Focus on the wrong things and you'll get poor results. While hustling is a staple of entrepreneurial culture, hustling produces *negative* effects if the core 20% essential to progress is ignored in favor of garbage. One hour of work spent on these essentials obliterates 100 hours of "work" spent changing the fonts on your website.

At its heart, the 80/20 rule is really about identifying the fundamentals and leverage points in any discipline, then relentlessly working on them until you achieve your desired outcome. Focusing only on what matters allows you to simplify and streamline your entire schedule—saving you time and energy while massively increasing your results.

How do you identify the key 20%? A few sections from now, we'll go over the three core areas (productivity, craft, and marketing) critical to your success. But *within* each area, identifying the core 20% is an exercise in trial and error. The truth is, it's impossible to identify what matters and what doesn't when you're new to a discipline. You simply don't have enough experience or skill to understand what truly matters (yet). BS, unfortunately, doesn't announce itself as such; it is often packaged in plausible explanations and enticing case studies.

What you need to do, then, is use a technique I call **shotgun, then narrow.** To find out what works and what doesn't, you need to consume multiple quality resources and then start putting promising ideas into practice as soon as possible (rather than sitting on vast quantities of notes). The last part is critical: most people devour information, get excited by the possibilities, then never execute. You either need to take action or eliminate it. To be clear, even with good resources at your disposal, **there is a lot of trial and error involved in identifying what works**. Narrowing your focus too soon usually leads to focusing on the wrong things.

Try an array of techniques, then eliminate what doesn't work or doesn't make sense, and double down on what does. Then **iterate and optimize** to further improve those things that work the best.

When you find principles that work, you should always continue testing new ideas while iterating on your current process to find ways to improve. Don't remain stagnant and assume your way is the best. The learning process should never stop. Because you either keep evolving, or your business dies.

For much more on the 80/20 rule, check out Perry Marshall's excellent *80/20 Sales and Marketing*. It is one of the Top 10 books (not just business books) I've ever read and is well worth your time.

CORE PRINCIPLE #2: LIFE IS DICTATED BY EVOLUTION

Success in indie publishing—and, presumably, life at large—is *not* about being the strongest, fittest, smartest, or quickest. Success is a product of being the best *adapted* to the current environment. That means **life is dictated by your ability to evolve**—that is, your willingness to try new, uncomfortable things. This business constantly changes. **You can adapt, or you can die**.

Evolution essentially boils down to asking yourself two core questions.

(Ɪ) *How do I get better?*

(ꞮꞮ) *How do I leverage my core strengths?*

A fish is well-adapted to water; a human is not. While many self-improvement or how-to books suggest the metaphorical solution to this problem would be growing gills, I've found that to be a poor strategy.

A human is a land creature.

No amount of wishing otherwise is going to change that.

A better strategy is finding an environment that suits your strengths.

Your strengths are what give you a competitive advantage.

It is better to hone what *you* do uniquely best.

Focusing on strengths, of course, can be an excuse for stagnation. Humans used their problem-solving abilities to conquer the seas with boats.

Such is the art of evolution: **adapting your strengths to solve the problem at hand**. This sounds all well and good, and perhaps fairly obvious. But it still fails to answer the burning question at hand.

How does one evolve?

Simple: 80/20.

Devote 80% of your time and budget toward things you *know* work. Fundamentals. Proven ads. Strategies that reliably make money. Principles that haven't changed for decades.

Devote 20% of your time to testing new ideas. This number can actually be anywhere from 5% – 20% (or even beyond 20%) of your resources, depending on how much risk you want to assume. These shouldn't just be random ideas; they should be good ideas. Your *best* ideas. Why? Because even your hit rate on seemingly good ideas will be annoyingly low.

But the hits? They become part of your core 80%—improving your bread and butter tactics and strategies.

And if you don't have *anything* that works yet? Flip the script: 20% to principles that you're almost certain are true (according to successful authors and experts) then 80% on testing.

Remember, **shotgun and narrow**. You evolve by testing new ideas and putting in the hours, honing your skills while slowly eliminating what doesn't work. **Persevere, but iterate**. You can't simply grind away at the *exact* same things for the next ten years. Best case scenario, you've found something that works, but will eventually change. Worst case scenario, you haven't found *anything* that works, and you're spinning your wheels in a mud pit.

Ultimately, evolving is a question of mindset. Once we find something that produces results, or assume a core belief as part of our identity, change becomes difficult. To adapt, we must have **strong beliefs loosely held.** That means having the confidence to double down on what's working right now while still being able to pivot the instant the market renders our current strategies or tactics obsolete.

CORE PRINCIPLE #3: COMPOUND INTEREST RULES THE WORLD

You've probably heard of compound interest.

But even those well-acquainted with its impressive effects often underestimate its jaw-dropping power.

Compound interest applies to everything from money to newsletter subscribers to skill acquisition. For example, if we **get 5% better each month,** compounded over five years that's a more than 18x increase. Initial progress is modest—until you hit critical mass (an inflection point), which people mistakenly call "overnight success."

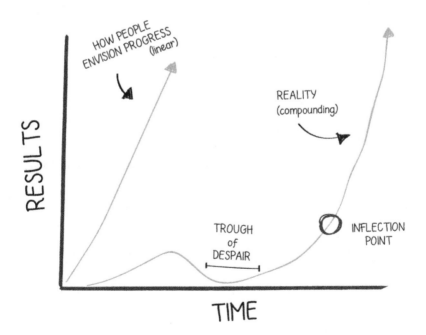

Compounding is one of the reasons the 80/20 rule works mathematically—success tends to automatically consolidate. When an individual gains an edge over their competition, they gather more fans and receive more revenue. At the beginning, these advantages over the competition might be small; over time, however, these small deposits compound into massive differences between the most successful authors and the midlist hopefuls.

Note that compounding assumes you're *iterating* and *putting in the time*, as outlined in the discussion on evolution above. If you're not making constant deposits into your skills account, so to speak, there will be nothing to build upon.

It's easy to quit long before you reach the inflection point. The initial burst of motivation and feel-good energy from changing your life or embarking upon something new quickly wears off. And after peaking much lower than you originally thought, things crash (the valley of despair). The situation might even appear worse than when you started: when you start exercising, investing time in your writing, or doing anything with a long-term payoff, you often end up seeing *negative* short-term results.

If you exercise, you're sore. You can't eat all the foods you want. And you see no discernible results for *months*. In the short-term, everything is negative.

Compounding demands time. Expect this to take five years.

This doesn't mean *waiting* five years. It means putting in the time and effort into the core 20%.

The inflection point won't announce itself. Suddenly, you'll look at your sales charts, your productivity, your craft, and realize *Damn, I've elevated my game to a whole new level.*

Compound growth is fractal. A fractal is something where the part is similar to the whole. That means the line you see on the right-hand side, where everything goes vertical? If you zoom in, really, the same sequence will play out over a shorter time frame:

you'll plateau. Relinquish some of those gains you fought so dearly to acquire as you test new stuff to replace the shop-worn old ideas that can't get you any further. And enter the valley of despair once more.

But once you've been through the process, you'll understand that despair is fleeting. And you'll be off to the races again. For the person who hasn't experienced this cycle, however, you must keep pushing. Much like finishing a novel irrefutably proves to your brain that you can be a writer, pushing through the valley and meeting with success on the other side proves to your brain just how powerful compound interest can be.

THE TRIFECTA OF INDIE SUCCESS (THE CORE 20%)

80/20 sounds great and all, until you realize that finding the essential 20% can be a harrowing odyssey in trial and error. I'm not going to pretend that you can completely avoid this process; trial and error is an absolutely crucial part of discovering what works for you (e.g., the core 20% within each of these three areas). I won't leave you to discover the *main* areas on your own, though, which are productivity, craft, and marketing. These can be arranged in a handy pyramid:

We can add business principles such as money management and strategy as the soil upon which the pyramid rests. If your understanding of business is shaky, the rest of the structure will teeter.

⚹ Marketing is relatively simple if you regularly produce books that your target audience enjoys.

Marketing is remarkably difficult if you fail on the consistency or quality fronts. For those concerned about writing every day, consistency in this business is measured in *years*, not days or months. If you write four books a year, but it only takes 40 days to do so, that's not better or worse than dividing that workload up over 365 days.

The main takeaway is you need to be publishing good books. ⚹

Yes, it's possible to push a sub-par book up the charts via clever marketing. However, a long-term career is built on sellthrough—that is, readers purchasing and reading the next books in the series (or your backlist). If your books are bad, then they won't buy the others. And if your backlist is nonexistent because your work habits are poor, then readers will have nothing else to purchase from you and be forced to move on to another author. Should you go long enough between releases, the fond memories of your book will likely fade from their consciousness altogether.

All three elements are vital to your success; none is more important than the other. And each of these elements act as a multiplier; they're not additive. 10 + 10 + 10 doesn't equal 30; 10 x 10 x 10 = 1000. You must be strong in *all* three areas to maximize your chances of success.

You will notice, however, that productivity is the foundation of the pyramid. That is not a mistake: without the ability to do the work, it's impossible to improve your craft and deploy marketing campaigns.

Both productivity and craft are beyond the scope of this guide. However, if you have weaknesses in either area, it pays to shore them up—doing so will massively amplify the effectiveness of your marketing efforts. There are many approaches to applying the information in this guide, but the simplest is to do **one marketing task per day OR dedicate up to one hour per day to marketing**. That could be as simple as reading a chapter in this book, or as complex as setting up your first launch. For more, check out the *Ultimate Guide to Author Productivity*.

MANAGING PROBABILITIES AND VARIANCE: PLAY POKER, NOT ROULETTE

Many of us hold an inherent belief that skill should be rewarded. Over time, this is true. But even when you do *everything* at a high level, you can't *guarantee* a win. In fact, you will *still* fail (or come up short of expectations) more often than you'd like.

This can feel shockingly unfair and uncomfortable in the moment.

One of the hardest things to come to terms with in self-publishing is **variance**. As that word likely suggests, that means results in this business are not constant; they vary. Even with a good process and marketing strategy, a book can still flop. And when we put a dollar into our marketing expecting two, but instead get zero, it can be a jarring experience.

Indie publishing is ultimately a **probabilities** game. By improving your skills in the core three areas—productivity, craft, and marketing—you can significantly raise the probability that each book you release will be successful. But that probability will never reach 100%.

Our brains aren't great at intuitively grasping probability. They're pattern recognition machines tuned to look for cause-and-effect. This is a basic hard-wired survival instinct: if Bob ate the red plant in the forest and died, we avoided eating red plants, too. This cause-and-effect relationship is later reinforced by society: we do good work, we receive a reward (grade, job, promotion, praise, etc.).

Being able to identify these types of cause-and-effect relation-ships is a big reason why we've survived for thousands of years.

But complex systems don't work like that. Yes, there are many books and articles promising explanations to massive problems. These are alluring precisely because we want answers to big questions. The problem?

Simple explanations to complex issues are almost always fiction.

Self-publishing—and marketing in particular—doesn't follow set patterns that work all the time. Often what looks like a pattern is, in fact, noise. Or the cause of a marketing campaign's success or failure can be totally opaque, offering no lessons at all. Or, most confusingly, it can be completely random: perhaps Amazon picked the book up for a deal we didn't know about, or a popular author shared our title, thus blasting it into the ranking strato-sphere.

Thus, even marketing campaigns designed using the same strategy and principles can produce wildly different outcomes. Because human behavior is hard to predict.

This leads some authors to oscillate to the other extreme: that skill hardly matters at all, and that self-publishing is all **luck**. That conclusion, however, would be incorrect.

Instead, this game is a *combination* of luck and skill akin to poker.

A pro-level poker player will win more often than he loses against amateur players. That is because he has an **edge**—his skills are superior, therefore his probability of winning is higher. But because of variance (e.g., the inherent randomness of the cards he's dealt and the unpredictability of the people playing), it's entirely possible for a novice to beat the best player in the world at a hand. It's even possible (though not likely) for them to win an entire *game*.

This is much like someone's first novel becoming a lightning strike success with minimal marketing. These stories get a lot of ink and internet traffic *precisely* because they're so uncommon. That can make this path seem like the norm (or even *likely*). It isn't.

A counter-argument might be that such a method is not impossible. I wouldn't disagree. You can, after all, also head over to the roulette wheel, bet it all on black, and emerge a wealthier individual. But this isn't a strategy; it's a wish. A losing wish, over time, given the probabilities.

And what people often ignore is that your career is not defined by a single temporary success, but successfully surviving (and thriving) long-term. $100,000 a month in royalties can turn into $1,000 as that surprise success is overtaken on the charts by next month's breakout hit. The real measure of skill, then, is whether the percentages remain in your favor after playing thirty games of poker—or publishing your thirty-seventh novel.

That's because only time—and playing enough hands—can smooth out variance and reveal our actual skill in games where variance is a factor. If we are truly skilled, we will come out ahead. If we are not, then we won't. But we must **publish enough books** and **do enough marketing** to find out.

And the best part of this approach? With each progressive book and marketing campaign we create, we further tilt the odds in our favor by improving along the way.

KEY TAKEAWAYS

- **The Indie Trifecta of Success**: productivity, craft, marketing
- **3 Key Principles:**
  - **80/20**: a few key actions have much more impact on your results than anything else
  - **Compound interest**: it takes time to build momentum and hit critical mass; most of today's work doesn't truly pay off for months or years
  - **Evolution: shotgun and narrow** (trial and error to find the core 20%, then iterate and optimize the core 20%) to adapt and evolve in a changing environment
- If you're overwhelmed, **implement one thing at a time**. It's far better to master a couple strategies and principles than be trash at 50 different things.
- Build your marketing and craft skills over time to increase your chances of success.

ACTION EXERCISE

1. **Devote time to taking action.** You can go through the guide exercise by exercise—they're specifically designed to help you apply the keystone points—or pick and choose whatever is useful based on your current situation. A simple system is doing one marketing task a day OR up to one hour of marketing each day.

TWO

BUSINESS FUNDAMENTALS

If you've been publishing for more than a couple months, you've no doubt come across someone telling you to **treat your writing like a business**. It's good general advice, but it's almost always offered without any sort of explanation about *how* one goes about doing this.

First, let's talk about what business is *not*: it's not about wanting to make a lot of money or appearing successful (e.g., hitting a bestseller list or getting an award). Having lofty aspirations is fine, but it doesn't make you a savvy business person.

Instead, running an effective business involves **five primary administrative tasks:** knowing your numbers, knowing your monthly burn, saving a solid percentage of your profits, getting a good accountant, and never running a credit card balance.

In this section, we'll talk about:

- What you need to get started
- The five primary administrative tasks required to run your business
- Strategy & Execution

GETTING STARTED

Before we launch into numbers, strategy, and all that, we need to take a step back and make sure our administrative ducks are in a row. It's easy to get caught in the weeds when you're just getting started instead of doing actual work, spending all your time making business cards or getting a custom logo that won't sell any books. After careful consideration, I believe **there are only two absolute necessities** every part-time or full-time author must have:

1. An email newsletter service provider like MailerLite (**mailerlite.com**; free up to 1k subs) or ConvertKit (**convertkit.com**; $29/mo for up to 1k subs).
2. An author website, which requires:

   - A domain ($12/yr from Google; **domains.google.com**)
   - Hosting (rock-solid WordPress hosting from FlyWheel ($15/mo) or Pressidium ($25/mo); **getflywheel.com** and **pressidium.com**)
   - A WordPress theme (use the free Astra Theme with the Elementor page builder; **wpastra.com** and **elementor.com**)

That's it. While you can get away with not having an author website, I believe this is a long-term oversight. A website acts as a hub for your author brand, and while it's unlikely to get a ton of traffic, readers can visit the site to learn about new books, sign up to your newsletter, and also explore your backlist. A website may seem like an expense in the short term, but the long-term benefits are well worth the nominal costs. You can hire someone for under $500 to build a basic WordPress site if you don't have the technical skills to create it yourself.

While these two items are the only mandatory ones, here are a few more things that can prove helpful as your business grows:

1. **BookFunnel (bookfunnel.com**; $20 – $150/yr): necessary if you're using a reader magnet (e.g., free novella or starter library) to build your email list, as BookFunnel provides seamless instant delivery of EPUB/MOBI/PDF files to your readers' reading devices of choice. Also used to participate in cross promos.

2. **StoryOrigin (storyoriginapp.com**; beta): used to participate in cross promos, along with a host of additional useful features. Run by an excellent developer who consistently rolls out updates.

3. **Vellum (vellum.pub**; $250 one-time purchase; Mac only): easily format your book in 15 minutes and generate beautiful print and eBook files with a single click. A contender for best program I've ever used in any industry.

4. **A custom email address** (i.e., name@yourauthorname. com; $50/yr from Google GSuite; **gsuite.google.com**): having an email address from your own domain instead of a free email service helps increase the deliverability of your newsletters.

This isn't an exhaustive list, but those are the most useful things I've found. For more, visit my resources page at **nicholaserik. com/resources**.

1: KNOW YOUR KEY NUMBERS

Every author needs to know their key numbers inside and out. Most don't.

For how to calculate these metrics (other than net profit), visit the Appendix.

The two main KPIs (key performance indicators) I track in a simple Excel sheet are **NET PROFIT** (royalties – expenses) and **ORGANIC SUBSCRIBERS** (people who sign up to your newsletter from the front and back matter of your books).

Net profit is the whole purpose of being in business. It's the money in your pocket after all the covers and marketing and formatting expenses are paid for. I calculate this on a weekly/monthly/quarterly/yearly basis.

You must track net profit. It is not optional.

Tracking **organic subscribers** may seem unnecessary, but I've found it's the best single metric to predict future success for three reasons: one, it's an indication of how much marketing you're doing and how many books you're selling. If you're not getting your books into people's hands (or you're not releasing any books at all), then people can't sign up for your newsletter. Two, it's the ultimate engagement metric, in that people only sign up to your newsletter if they like your books. If people aren't signing up, then your books aren't resonating.

Finally, organic subscribers massively amplify any other marketing you do for a launch or promotion. A few hundred fans can catapult your book up the Amazon charts and make all your other efforts much, much easier.

Note that organic subscribers are extremely slow to accumulate; less than 0.5% of people who read your book will sign up for the list if you're only offering updates on new releases (you may hit 1% if you offer a free novella, which is why I recommend doing so later in the guide). This is *not* cause for alarm. Growth here will be slow, but each of these subscribers is like gold. Treat them well, and make sure you're getting a steady stream of them.

I track organic subscribers on a weekly/monthly/yearly basis.

If you want to stop here, you can. These aren't the only metrics I track, however. **Before I run ads to a series, I'll usually calculate:**

- **SELLTHROUGH**: the % of people who go on to read Book 2, Book 3, etc., after reading Book 1. In my experience, normal is around 35% – 40% for a full price Book 1 > Book 2 sales; 50 – 60% for Book 1 > Book 2 KU reads. Higher is possible, but anything more than 10% above is either a unicorn book, or, more likely, an error in the calculations. Sellthrough is primarily a *troubleshooting* metric. It can tell you why your ads aren't profitable (that's the primary use); if it's too low, then advertising that series is generally a non-starter. But beyond that, drawing concrete conclusions (e.g., the series is bad/writing is bad/the characters are wrong, etc.) is impossible. Reading too much into it (positive or negative) can drive you to madness.
- **REVENUE PER SALE**: the total revenue a sale of Book 1 generates when factoring in sellthrough to the other books in the series.

While I'm running ads or doing a launch or promo, I'll track these:

- **Sales and page reads**: found on the KDP Dashboard. You can track these weekly/monthly as well if you'd like, but it takes significantly more time once you have a lot of books.
- **Conversion**: the % of clicks that end up producing a download or sale.
- **Cost per sale**: the number of dollars it takes to produce a download or sale.

A few general tips for making tracking a fifteen-minute affair instead of a multi-hour one:

- **Instant**: I recommend logging expenses in your Excel sheet *the minute they're charged*. This gives you a clear, real-time snapshot of money going out the door, and prevents a mad scramble to do your taxes.
- **Daily**: I track numbers daily under two circumstances only: for books I'm currently advertising via pay-per-click ads (PPC), or during a big promo or launch (I track the first 30 days of the launch or promo).
- **Weekly**: With a small backlist, I'll track sales and reads by individual book, along with organic subscribers and net profit weekly. With a larger backlist, I'll either track sales and reads by series, or eschew that all together in favor of solely focusing on net profit and organic subscribers.
- **Monthly**: same as for weekly.
- **Quarterly and Annually**: I use the monthly net profit reports to calculate quarterly and annual net profits for tax purposes.

If you don't have your own system yet, you can use that as a starting point. From there, you can—and should—experiment with different tracking methods and intervals to suit your own needs. Generally, when you're starting out, it makes sense to track more data. This gives you a better feel for what's important and what isn't. It's also much easier to track sales for individual books when you have five versus fifty. It's also possible to track more data if you're handy with Excel, because you can set up sheets (or pay someone) to automatically import data from various sources.

Regardless of how much you track, the main metric and your core focus should always be on **net profit**. While startups might pursue growth at the expense of current profits (to the point of running at a substantial loss), their goal is selling the business to outside investors (or going public). The purpose of a small business is to turn a profit (i.e., put money in *your* pocket). If you are incinerating dollars, this is a red flag that something needs to be fixed.

As a final note, know that, when it comes to taxes, you can *usually* write-off most of your publishing-related business expenses such as covers, formatting, advertising, web design costs, business services, and so forth. Properly expensing eligible items will substantially lower your tax bill. Talk with an accountant to confirm which items you can expense for your business; it may vary by country and based on your business structure. Doing so, however, is well worth your while: it can save you hundreds of thousands of dollars over the course of a long career.

2: KNOW YOUR MONTHLY BURN

To know how much money you can invest in your publishing business, you first need to know how much money it takes just to keep the lights on. This is known as your **monthly burn**. As a company of one, your burn rate is typically going to start with your living expenses. If you employ other people, it will include their salaries. Your monthly royalties need to cover your monthly burn if you want to be a full-time author (and don't have any other sources of income). Calculating monthly burn as a solo-preneur is a simple matter of adding up all mandatory expenses, which include:

- Rent or mortgage
- Health insurance (if you have health insurance through your current day job or spouse, include the approximate cost of replacing this yourself)
- Car payments
- Utility bills
- Food and essential supplies like toilet paper/soap (average this over three months)
- Mandatory business expenses

If you have children or employees, your monthly burn may include:

- Tuition
- Employee salaries
- Employee health insurance
- Employee retirement plans

Don't ignore bills that occur regularly, but not monthly (e.g., dentist visits, vet bills, etc.). Amortize such costs over 12 months and add it to your monthly burn. For example, if it costs $240 to go to the dentist once a year, you'd add $20 to your monthly burn.

Finally, you'll also want to identify *optional* expenses that recur monthly. These are often excellent places to start cutting if your burn rate exceeds your monthly royalties:

- Personal subscriptions (Netflix, Spotify, spa memberships)
- Business subscriptions

Knowing your burn rate is especially critical in the nascent stages of your business, but it's also important as you grow.

I don't have a set schedule for calculating this. If you're struggling to pay bills or free up cash for your books, this should be the first thing you calculate, though. And it's good to check in every few months, even if things are going well. Lifestyle creep is very dangerous, in that your earnings in this business tend to be volatile. If your burn rate gets too high, that limits the amount of money you can reinvest in activities to grow your business while also exposing you to significant risk if your earnings fall.

3: SAVE

Rough rules of thumb for saving money break down as follows:

1. **30% of profits for taxes**. This might sound excessive, but self-employment taxes are often higher than employee tax rates. If your country's self-employed or corporate tax rate is higher than 30% (don't forget state and local taxes), you'll need to set aside more. Consult with a good accountant for more precise figures.

2. **10% of profits for savings**. You want an emergency cash fund, because as a self-employed author you don't get paid time off or sick days.

3. **10% of profits for retirement.** As a self-employed individual, you're responsible for funding your retirement. US residents should look into tax-friendly retirement planning options designed for self-employed individuals like SIMPLE, SEP IRAs, and the Solo 401(k).

4. **The rest**. Most of what doesn't go to key business investments, living expenses, and the areas above I'd recommend keeping in cash—as outlined below, having steady cash flow allows you to capitalize on good opportunities when they arise. Cash reserves also act as a buffer against unexpected down months (or overall economic downturns). Your month-to-month royalties *will* fluctuate wildly. Don't spend freely during boom months only to be caught without funds during the inevitable lean ones.

Yes, I understand setting aside 50%+ of your profits is a lot. You can get away with putting away 0% for retirement or a rainy day fund—for a bit. Eventually, you'll have a bad month, or you won't be able to release a book due to injury, or a new release will flop, and your business will be toast. This is all about surviving—and thriving—long term. If you're currently blowing through everything you earn each month just to pay the bills, saving this much might appear ridiculous, to the point of impossibility.

I've been there.

You have three options.

The first: **start with the full percentages**. This is usually only viable if your business is doing well (or you have a full-time job already). Consult with an accountant on how much you specifically need to put aside for taxes and any benefits regarding specific retirement accounts.

The second: **put away 1% or 2% in *one* area this month**. It's easiest to save when you immediately transfer the money to a *separate* account right after Amazon/the other retailers deposit it. If you wait until the end of the month, quarter, or year, the tendency for most people—myself included—is to find it's already long gone. When it's immediately out of sight, you don't miss it. This also frees you from any complex budgeting systems or focusing on eliminating hundreds of small transactions (e.g., coffee, candy bars, lunch) to save money—five minutes per month, and a couple clicks, and you're ready to go. Your lifestyle will automatically adjust with little pain.

Bump up the percentages on a monthly or quarterly basis. You *don't* want to notice any change in your day-to-day lifestyle—other than the fact that you can now pay your taxes on time and are no longer worried about money thanks to having a nice nest egg, of course.

The third: **start when you get a windfall**. If you're making $500 a month, then one month pull in $7,000 because a new release hits it out of the park, start at the full percentages (paying off any credit card debt you may have accrued first). And then keep your lifestyle the same so you can reinvest most of the free cash leftover back into your business so you can keep that revenue momentum going.

Waiting for a windfall can be a dangerous game. That windfall may never come. And the taxman doesn't wait. Make sure you're at least saving money for taxes.

As a final note, **make sure you have health insurance**. This can be expensive, so if you're going full time, factor this in—and don't "self-insure," because that's playing with extreme fire.

4: GET A GOOD ACCOUNTANT

A good accountant is not an expense; they can save you thousands of dollars and hundreds of hours with your local tax authority. Most offer free consultations to prospective new clients. This allows you to ask them questions, see if their services are a good fit for your business, and find one that suits your needs without spending money upfront.

Take this step. Don't hypothesize about how much it's going to cost you. This is why many people never get an accountant; they assume it costs way more than it does. Explain your situation and *ask*. You'll likely be surprised by both the price and the service you receive for that cost.

If you already have an accountant, many offer year-round tax advice. Thus, if you have an accounting-related question, don't consult random internet forums or Google; ask the tax professional who you pay every year. Your accountant should also be able to tell you what corporate structure is right for your business, which can save you additional money and provide other benefits once your earnings grow to a certain amount.

A good accountant might be the best financial investment you can make in your small business. Don't skip this.

5: NEVER RUN A CREDIT CARD BALANCE

Never charge anything that won't be paid off at the end of the month. There are zero exceptions to this rule.

Business owners often try to paper over poor cash flow management or unsustainable monthly burns with credit cards. This *will* come back to bite you in the form of excruciatingly high interest rates (ask me how I know).

If you cannot pay cash, find an alternative to acquiring the services you need: barter, save, sell old stuff on eBay/Amazon, start a book-related side hustle (formatting, proofreading, cover design, consulting, working as an assistant, etc.), or simply go with a cheaper/no-frills option. And should none of these options prove appealing, then search for another way (while not optimal, you can catch most of the typos in your books by reading it out loud, line-by-line, for example), or *wait* if there's no viable way to fund your publishing business right now. You don't necessarily have to publish right away; you can stockpile books and then release them later. They don't go stale.

It's also worth considering that many things you might think are mandatory are not. There's always the option of going without and just pressing publish.

Whatever you do, do not rack up debt; it is a noose that most small businesses cannot escape.

If you take just *one* tip from this entire guide, please make it this one. And if you're already in debt, things are not bleak. Just formulate a plan to start paying it down. (Not tomorrow. Not in a month. Now.)

YOUR STRATEGY FLOWS FROM YOUR OBJECTIVES

Beyond administrative tasks, **business** boils down to two core elements: **strategy** (your system—the specific steps you're going to take to achieve your core objective) and **execution** (actually implementing your strategy).

At the heart of this is, of course, your **core objective**. This guide assumes that you want to make a part-time or full-time income. There are many other objectives to pursue in this game; just know that they are often at odds with one another. Writing whatever you want without any regard for genre conventions, for example, is a fine objective; just know that it rarely reconciles with making money unless your tastes align with the market's.

Most authors stumble in establishing a clear objective. Someone who wants to make a million dollars a year will need to adopt a vastly different strategy than the person who wants a small side-income that maintains work-life balance. Every choice comes with a trade-off.

As an alternative example, a non-fiction author might be using their book as a client generation tool, rather than trying to profit directly from the book's sales. Their marketing strategy would look substantially different from the fiction author trying to make a full-time living directly from the books.

Further, your strategy should be framed around your **signature strengths**. Maybe you can write fast. Maybe you can run ads well. Maybe you're a social media maestro.

Whatever the case may be, you want to work *with* your strengths rather than against them. Too many authors want to be something they are not; the fast writer wishes they had more time for ads. The author deep within their spreadsheets envies the person who can crank out a book a month.

Don't worry what other people are doing.

Double down on what you do best.

This is why the framework of this guide is designed to be flexible. There's an old proverb that says *chase two rabbits, catch none*. Unsurprisingly, trying to chase sixty-five rabbits at once is not a secret way to hack this and turn things into your favor.

Thus, your objective, whatever it is, must be **crystal clear**. You then **eliminate** all choices, options, and tasks that will *not* help you achieve that objective by making key strategic decisions in the following areas:

- **Indie or trad**: whether you'll self-publish your work or pursue a traditional publisher (or do both as a "hybrid" publisher)
- **Kindle Unlimited or Wide**: whether you'll be exclusive to Amazon or publish on all retailers (or a mix of both)
- **Release frequency**: the number of books you'll release per year
- **Genre, series, and length**: what genre will you write in? Will you remain in one sub-genre, or branch out into many? Will your books be in a series? What will the approximate word count be?
- **Formats**: eBook and print only, or will you release in audio as well? If so, do you plan on doing a royalty share, pay upfront, or seeking an audio-only deal?
- **Newsletter**: how are you going to generate new subscribers?
- **Marketing**: what platforms do you plan to focus on—e.g., you could focus on paid Facebook Ads, creating a reader magnet to grow your newsletter, or building up your BookBub followers
- **Production budget**: will you purchase professional covers, editing, proofreading? How much will you invest?
- **Advertising budget**: will you advertise? Where and how much?

If this seems daunting, don't worry; this guide will help you answer these questions. By the end, you'll be able to design a strategy specifically tailored to your personal strengths and core objective.

All the components of your strategy should be pulling in the same direction. To use an analogy, imagine a team of sled dogs. When they pull as one toward a common destination (the finish line), they make consistent progress. Perhaps they win; sometimes they lose. Sometimes the elements come into play, and wreak havoc. But they make *progress*.

However, if a few of the dogs stop pulling their weight, progress is slowed significantly. The team is now at risk of running out of resources or energy before reaching the finish line. And if a few of them start running in the opposite direction to chase a deer they spotted, then the whole operation stalls, and everyone dies of frostbite.

Thus, it pays to streamline your strategy to its absolute essentials. Remember the importance of 80/20: if the BS crowds out the core 20%, your results are going to be very poor indeed.

After you have a basic plan of attack mapped out, you need to actually put it into play.

Execution is the art of doing what you planned to do (and doing it well).

Most people blame poor discipline for their execution problems. But the root cause is often a bad, unrealistic strategy. It is easy to design a strategy that does not align with your existing skills and resources. Jumping beyond your current capabilities or employing overly complex methods are both tempting. An effective strategy that dovetails with your strengths is far better than an ultra-optimized one you cannot implement.

Great execution flows from great strategy—which in turn flows from a clear objective.

Which leads us to the ultimate takeaway: do not worry about what other people are doing or saying. Only worry about what *you* can do. **The optimal strategy is the one you can execute**. The end.

If you build a strategy around monthly releases, but can only write four books a year, that's a *strategy* problem which results in poor execution.

If you plan to run thousands of dollars in ads, but have no plan in place to secure those funds, this is a *strategy* problem that inevitably leads to poor execution.

It should be noted that your strategy is not a fixed document; it is a living organism that evolves as the marketplace changes and your skills grow. This is a feedback loop: you start with a strategy, execute, use lessons you've learned to revise the strategy, and then rinse and repeat.

Finally, every aspect of your strategy does not need to be written out in pinpoint detail. **This is not a business plan**. Strategizing can quickly turn into procrastination. You cannot divine the future; you just need to reflect on the best way for you to achieve your core objective, then get to work.

KEY TAKEAWAYS

- You only need two things as a full-time author: a mailing list provider and your website. A personalized email address is recommended once you have a few thousand subscribers to increase deliverability of your emails.

- Other services can be useful, but it's easy to rack up unnecessary charges. Save most of your money for covers, editing, and advertising.
- Treating your publishing endeavors like a business entails five things:
  - Knowing your numbers
  - Putting minimum amounts aside for taxes (30%), savings (10%), and retirement (10%)
  - Knowing your monthly burn so that you know how much you have to earn each month, royalties-wise
  - Getting a good accountant
  - Never charging money to your credit card
- Your goal as a small business owner is money in your pocket, better known as **net profit** (royalties - expenses).
- If you're going full time, make sure you earn enough to cover **health insurance**.
- Your **strategy** is your system and the specific steps you'll take to achieve your **core objective**. **Execution** is about actually doing these tasks. Great execution flows from great strategy—which in turn flows from a clear objective.
- **The optimal strategy is the one you can execute.** This means making sure it dovetails with your current resources and signature strengths.

ACTION EXERCISES

1. Make sure you have a website and mailing list.
2. Calculate your net profit for the past year.
3. Calculate your average monthly burn over the past year.

4. Set up a spreadsheet and start tracking your net profit and organic subscribers on a weekly or monthly basis.

5. Set a timer for 10 minutes. Then map out a rough draft of your strategy for the next year by writing out the following on a sheet of paper:

- Your core objective
- Whether you'll launch your books wide or in KU
- Whether you'll write in a series and, if so, the planned # of titles
- What length they'll be: novels, novellas, serials, or short stories
- The number of new titles you'll release over the next year, with approximate word counts
- The sub-genre(s) you plan to write in
- The format(s) you plan to publish in
- Your core three traffic sources
- How you plan to build your newsletter
- Your production budget for each title
- Your advertising budget for each title

Answer as best you can, but *don't* spend hours deliberating, researching, or otherwise worrying about making it perfect. This document is not set in stone. Rather, it's something you'll update as you learn more about marketing.

If this guide does its job, by the end you'll have the necessary tools to confidently answer *each* of these questions, thus giving you a personalized marketing strategy to work from going forward.

THREE:

THE ULTIMATE BOOK MARKETING FORMULA

The core of the *Ultimate Guide to Book Marketing* is a simple rule of thumb called **The Ultimate Book Marketing Formula**. This distills everything you need to focus on when it comes to selling books into a heuristic that fits on a single 4 x 6 note card. There are no secrets, of course; the true power, if there is any, of the formula lies in its simplicity. It's 80/20 embodied: it focuses on the 20%—the 1%, really—of vital tasks that will produce 99% of the results in your indie career. If you focus on these areas and execute them well, you can make huge strides quickly.

Before we hop into the main formula, though, I have another, more general, formula to share that explains the basic framework of internet marketing. If you've found that selling books is a confusing, labyrinthine process, this should hopefully give you some clarity on how it works. It's remarkably simple, but some marketing books massively overcomplicate things with arcane theories and buzzwords. We'll cut through that and focus only on what matters (it's just three things).

In this section, we'll cover:

- The Internet Marketing Formula
- The Ultimate Book Marketing Formula
- A Marketing Flight Check

THE INTERNET MARKETING FORMULA

The **Internet Marketing Formula** is well-known and used to sell everything from soap to shoes to online courses. Here, I've adapted the terminology specifically to books:

(1) **TRAFFIC**: directing the right potential readers to your book page via paid ads, your mailing list, social media, Amazon's algorithms, and so forth. Commonly referred to in the indie world as "generating visibility." Often thought of as advertising, although there are multiple ways to generate free/ semi-passive traffic, too. This would be handled by an organization's marketing team.

(2) **CONVERSION**: convincing readers to buy your book with a stellar blurb and cover, competitive price, hook-filled first few pages, and so forth. Later, you convert them into fans by directing them to the next book in the series from the back matter or offering them something of value to join your mailing list. This would be handled by an organization's sales team.

(3) PROFIT: did you make money? Track your numbers to determine which traffic and conversion efforts have been effective. After analyzing the numbers, you have two options:

(3a) If you made money, you repeat the process or, if you have additional marketing funds, you can slowly scale up your ad spend to grow your business.

(3b) If you lost money, you typically need to troubleshoot one of the following problems:

TRAFFIC: the advertising was too expensive or it was ineffective (e.g., you advertised to the wrong audience, or the promotional method didn't work).

CONVERSION: your cover or blurb are weak, or your price is too high. Or you sent the wrong traffic to your book—i.e., you advertised your gritty, serious, hyper-realistic thriller to readers who like snarky urban fantasy with talking animals.

CRAFT: sellthrough (the percentage of readers purchasing the next book in a series) is the lifeblood of your career. You can send a bunch of high quality, reasonably priced traffic to your Book 1 and get these people to buy with a great cover/blurb/price...but if the story doesn't deliver, no one's coming back for Book 2. At which point you're DOA, because it's very hard to make a profit promoting a single book. The three best ways to increase sellthrough, in order, are:

1. Cliffhangers (when used properly, otherwise can irritate readers; not appropriate in all genres, e.g., crime/thriller/mystery)

2. Improved craft (scene and plot structure influence pacing the most)

3. Limiting the number of CTAs on the same page as THE END to two (link to next book with one sentence teaser and newsletter sign-up link).

Anyway, that's all marketing is: you need to direct targeted readers to your book's page, and then you need to convince them to buy it; and you need to do these two things at a low enough cost to turn a profit. Then you **double down on whatever makes you money and immediately stop or fix what doesn't.** Rinse, repeat in a cycle of trial and error and iteration and optimization.

Simple. Not easy.

Note that, as authors, we're responsible for both marketing *and* sales which, in a big organization, are traditionally split between separate teams. The marketing team finds leads and prospects, which are then turned over to the sales team to "close." These require different skillsets, which is why internet marketing can be tricky: you have to wear both hats. A third hat, too, if you consider that crunching the numbers is often the purview of the accounting or analytics department.

I refer to (and think of) all of these components simply as "marketing," rather than separating them into their traditional silos. They're symbiotic and interlocked to such a degree that it makes much more sense to think of them under one umbrella, rather than independent entities. Long term, it's a *benefit* that you're forced to do them all, as this gives you much more insight into why readers buy. In the beginning, however, the sheer volume of information can certainly be overwhelming.

Wondering how this traffic-conversion-profit cycle applies to book marketing specifically? Let's talk about The Ultimate Book Marketing Formula.

THE ULTIMATE BOOK MARKETING FORMULA

As discussed in Part 1, your career hinges on three core components which I call The Indie Trifecta of Success: **productivity + craft + marketing**. Your job as an indie author comes down to honing these three areas through repeated practice. When your skills in one of these areas is weak, achieving success becomes difficult to the point of de facto impossibility.

But this concept, while useful, isn't an actionable strategy. What benchmarks should an author aim for when it comes to "marketing" or "productivity" to be successful?

And how do we integrate this trifecta of skills with other important items we've discussed, like **The Internet Marketing Formula** and creating a personalized **strategy**?

Enter the **Ultimate Book Marketing Formula**. This heuristic is the 80/20 rule in action—the key stuff that you *must* do, with zero padding. There are ten thousand more things you *can* do in this business. **But if you consistently execute well in these six areas over 3 – 5 years**, you'll have a good shot at making it. How can that be, you say? This formula forces you to focus on keystone tasks—and, most critically, get them done. **It is designed to maximize your odds of succeeding in a highly competitive business.**

Ready? Here it is:

THE ULTIMATE BOOK MARKETING FORMULA

MARKET RESEARCH + 3 TRAFFIC SOURCES + PRO COVERS + GREAT BLURBS + NEWSLETTER + 4-6 NOVELS PER YEAR

CONSISTENTLY FOR 3-5 YEARS

FULL-TIME AUTHOR

(1) Market research: researching what books are selling in your sub-genre—both consistently and what's hot right now. Understanding the core tropes and audience expectations of your sub-genre. Finding the overlaps between what *you* can write long term and the audience's preferences. Then incorporating these genre elements into everything: the book, its cover/blurb, and your advertising so that your target audience knows that your book is specifically for *them* with a single glance.

(2) Three targeted traffic sources: mastering three marketing channels that provide consistent visibility to your books instead of splitting focus and being mediocre at ten of them. You can use more; this isn't a set number. The idea is to narrow your focus.

(3) Pro covers: using your market research to commission genre-specific, professionally designed covers that attract the right readers to your work at a one-second glance; branding your covers so that readers can easily tell they're in the same series and by the same author.

(4) Great blurbs: writing an engaging blurb that convinces your target readers to buy.

(5) Newsletter: building your email list so that you can directly contact fans about new releases, updates, and other book-related news; keeping them engaged between projects so they remain interested in your upcoming books.

(6) Consistently publish 4 – 6 quality novels a year: releasing four full-length (40,000+ word) novels a year provides readers with a steady stream of new books. Readers prefer full-length novels and will generally pay more for them than shorter works. Longer books also have a longer shelf life, which makes your backlist more effective.

Amazon's algorithms reward new releases, and readers like them as well. Consistent releases smooth out your earnings, making your cash flow more stable. Once you have good covers, good blurbs, and some effective traffic sources, **your best marketing is a new, quality book.**

If you release consistently over a period of 3 – 5 years, you'll build up a substantial backlist. It's possible to succeed with fewer than four annual releases in certain genres (e.g., epic fantasy and psychological thrillers), but it means your craft or marketing chops must be significantly better to compensate.

Writing in a series massively decreases the difficulty of marketing profitably and thus increases your chances of success. A certain percentage of readers who buy Book 1 will also pick up Books 2, 3, and so forth. An author with a long series of books with high sellthrough can spend more on advertising and still be profitable versus an author who writes standalones/has poor readthrough. There are very few genres where you can write profitable standalones (psychological thrillers being one of the few).

You can hopefully see how there's significant overlap between the three core skill areas (productivity, craft, marketing). Market research is a marketing skill, but it also requires an understanding of structure, tropes, and other craft-related elements. Publishing 4 – 6 novels a year appears to be primarily a productivity-based skill, but it's perhaps your most powerful marketing tool—and figuring out how to execute at this speed while maintaining quality is often a matter of refining your craft to a fine point.

Play with the variables **in accordance to your personal strengths and weaknesses**; some people are productivity monsters, writing 12+ books a year. They constantly tap into the massive boost Amazon grants new releases (covered in Part 5), instead of doing stuff like Facebook Ads. Other authors only release a couple times a year, but build a huge mailing list that reliably launches them into the Top 100. Which lever(s) you pull should be dictated by your strengths and overall strategy.

HOW MANY BOOKS DO I NEED?

Frontlist is the ultimate marketing tool. Each new book you release brings in new readers and visibility to your backlist. Do whatever you can, even if it means ignoring most of this guide, to ensure that you're publishing consistently.

Whatever that means for you.

It's no surprise the biggest sticking point in the formula is the last piece: **publishing 4 – 6 quality novels a year.** This is where many authors say *there's no way I can do that.*

But do not give up if you can only publish, say, two or three books a year. It's a recommendation, not a requirement; it's also genre-dependent. Cranking out four 200k epic fantasy novels a year would be an insane pace and is not expected from that reader base. Putting out four 60k urban fantasy novels per year will likely see you get buried and forgotten in the ranks.

The optimal release pace is largely dictated by the sub-genre's expectations. Voracious readers want more content; if you're a slower author and want to publish successfully in such sub-genres, that is doable. Just understand that your books must be at a significantly higher craft level, and your marketing chops must be on point.

You must also be willing to accept more variance. Fewer bites at the apple leaves you more susceptible to a bad release or two significantly impacting your year.

The main principle behind my recommendation is **consistency**. Whatever pace you write at, make sure the books are coming out regularly and on time. It's very easy for two books a year to become one book every two years. That's not tenable; realistically, I'd put two books a year as the minimum viable number. Any fewer than that, and you're essentially at the whims of variance, even if you're an excellent writer and marketer.

CRAFT IS NOT THE ONLY THING THAT MATTERS

Content is king, the old saying goes. Put out good work, and readers will notice. Marketing is only for subpar titles or those that couldn't rise above the fray based on their artistic merits.

Therefore, some authors conclude that the best strategy is *I'm just going to write good books and ignore marketing.*

This doesn't work.

The formula doesn't ignore the importance of writing good books. It's critical to your long-term success—just not in the way most authors think. Unfortunately, "write good books" is a uselessly vague piece of advice, often proffered with a not-so-subtle undertone: if you're not selling, your books are crap. This might be the case, but marketing shortcomings are far more common, especially among creative types. We've all encountered fantastic TV shows, movies and books that died from lack of exposure. And there are plenty of wonderful stories, too, that are simply too niche to make much commercial impact.

Writing good books is not a reader acquisition strategy. No one can tell if your book is good from the cover or blurb (or even the sample, which I strongly suspect most readers don't read prior to purchasing). They *assume* they'll enjoy it if your presentation hits the correct notes. But it is not until they are deep within the book some hours later that the final verdict is known. Thus, writing good books—particularly strong, satisfying endings—is a **reader retention** strategy.

Ultimately, all business is built on repeat business (which for us means readers who become fans). **Without penning compelling books that your target audience LOVES to read, you will never have a career**. But publishing a good book will do nothing by itself, either (with rare exceptions that I can assure you are not you), *until you make it visible to the world through competent marketing.*

BASIC FLIGHT CHECK: THINGS TO DO BEFORE WE BEGIN

We're almost ready to jump into the actual book marketing. Before we do that, however, let's make sure the groundwork is laid down. If you already have an Amazon Author Central account, Amazon Affiliate account, and your Amazon series pages all in order, you can skip this section. Rest assured: if you're already a part-time or full-time author, there's plenty of more advanced stuff coming.

You'll want to make sure you have the following Amazon items squared away:

1. **Create an Amazon Author Central (authorcentral. amazon.com) account.** This is so you can claim all your books under your author profile (making it easy for readers to browse your backlist). It also allows you to have a bio, author photo, and link to your website. You do not need to enter a bio, picture, or website if you do not have one; many authors simply use their logo or their latest cover for their photo. You don't have to sign up in all of the regions; just make one in the US (unless your books are super popular in another part of the world) and make sure you claim all your titles.

2. **Create an Amazon Affiliate (affiliate-program.amazon. com) account.** While you can't use Amazon Affiliate links in your newsletter, your actual books, or pay-per-click (PPC) ads (it's against the affiliate TOS), you can use them on your website. Some promo sites will also allow you to use your affiliate code when you book a promotion. None of this will make you rich, but it can earn you a few hundred to a few thousand dollars extra a year (depending on how many books you sell) with zero additional effort. Much like the Author Central account, just create a US affiliate account—don't worry about the other regions unless a huge portion of your fanbase is located there. I also wouldn't bother signing up for affiliate programs on non-Amazon retailers unless you sell in huge numbers there.

3. **Link your Kindle, audio, and print editions**. This is supposed to occur automatically, but sometimes the automated system drops the ball, leaving your book's various formats

floating around in isolation. If all your versions aren't linked, login to your KDP account and contact support to link your books.

Finally, you want to **make sure your books are linked in a series on Amazon and have a corresponding series page**. Amazon often does this automatically, but the automated systems can sometimes fail to add your latest release to the page. They're properly linked when you see this on your book's page:

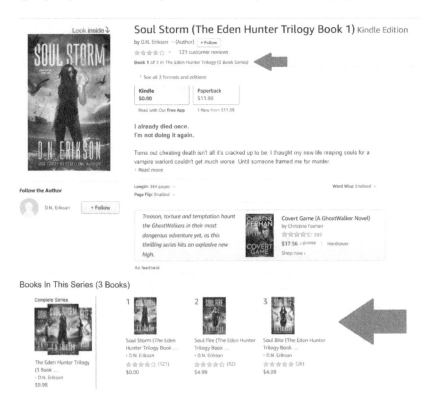

When you click on the series name—The Eden Hunter Trilogy, in this case—you land on what's known as a series page, which, as its name would suggest, displays the entire series on one page:

Linking the books in a series serves four important functions:

1. Amazon's automated systems will market Books 2, 3, 4, and so forth more aggressively to readers who have bought the previous volumes, since the system knows the books are related. On many devices, an automatic pop-up will trigger at the end of the book with a direct purchase link to the next volume in the series. This increases sellthrough.

2. It clearly indicates on the book's Amazon page that it's part of a series with multiple books, rather than forcing the reader to hunt through your website/all your books to find out.

3. Readers can one-click buy the *entire* series from the series page.

4. The series page has relatively few ads or distractions, which means directing paid advertising traffic can be very effective when you're running discounts on multiple titles in the series.

Some romance authors choose to keep their series unlinked so that readers know each book stands alone. I believe you're better off with the series linked, due to the factors above, but if you find that the numbers have dropped, you can always request for the books to be unlinked.

I won't pretend doing these things is fun; if you've put them off, it's probably because they're boring. But spending a couple hours to tick off these administrative tasks will dramatically amplify the effectiveness of *all* your marketing efforts going forward.

KEY TAKEAWAYS

- **The Internet Marketing Formula: generate traffic** to your Amazon book page (via paid ads, mailing list, PPC, and so forth), **convert** potential readers into buyers by having compelling covers/blurbs; later, convert readers into fans by having a compelling mailing list offer, and then crunch the numbers to see if your efforts are profitable. Finally, **double down on things that make you money** (i.e., repeat the cycle again) and **immediately stop stuff that doesn't.**
- **The Ultimate Book Marketing Formula**: market research + 3 targeted traffic sources + newsletter + great covers/blurbs + consistent new series novel releases of 40,000+ words (4+/year) = full-time author
- A new release is the ultimate marketing strategy once you have the other four elements working. Until then, publishing a good, new book is *not* a reader acquisition strategy; it is a reader retention strategy. To acquire readers in the

first place, you need to generate targeted traffic and have compelling packaging (covers/blurbs/price).

ACTION EXERCISE

1. Make sure your Amazon Author Central account, Amazon Affiliate account, and your Amazon series pages are all in order.

FOUR

MARKET RESEARCH

In this section, we'll be examining the first, and most important, component of our Ultimate Book Marketing Formula: **market research**.

First, a little refresher on our formula:

MARKET RESEARCH + 3 TRAFFIC SOURCES + PRO COVERS + GREAT BLURBS + NEWSLETTER + 4-6 NOVELS PER YEAR

CONSISTENTLY FOR 3-5 YEARS

FULL-TIME AUTHOR

Yes, market research sounds boring. But it tends to be enlightening and interesting. And even if you hate it, market research is mandatory. An hour up front can save you hundreds of frustrating hours on the back end. That's a pretty good deal.

Alas, this critical marketing step is the one that most writers skip. For a first novel, or a third, this is okay: at the beginning, it's more important to start (and finish) than it is to get things *exactly* right. But if you want to go full-time, you must deeply understand what your readers want. This is what good market research entails: diving into *why* your readers pick up certain books, their expectations, the covers they respond to, and more.

Some authors learn this by osmosis: they've read heavily, and have commercial tastes themselves. As such, understanding what their target readers want is easy, because it's what they themselves also seek. Most have to dig a little deeper, and actively uncover just what their target reader expects.

This section will *not* examine which genres are hot right now; such information would be outdated within the month. Instead, it supplies you with the tools and framework necessary to perform your own market research. This way you'll be able to analyze any market with ease and generate your own up-to-the-minute analysis whenever you so choose. Best of all, market research can be performed for free, right on Amazon.

We'll cover:

- The two types of "writing to market" (and why it's not a new concept)
- Reader expectations and how to identify them
- Why positioning your book properly is critical to standing out in a crowded marketplace
- How to start building a sustainable, long-term author brand

MARKET RESEARCH = WRITING
TO MARKET, RIGHT?

Yes and no.

"Writing to market" is a dirty phrase to some, so we should take a moment to go over what it is (and, perhaps more importantly, what it is *not*).

For the uninitiated, writing to market means actively writing your book's story and designing its packaging to fit a specific sub-genre's expectations. This may sound like a wildly new internet-age concept. But it's really just **writing commercial fiction to a preexisting audience**. This has long been known as "genre fiction."

The bulk of novels sold fall under genre fiction. Think romance, thrillers, cozy mysteries, urban fantasy, military sci-fi, and so forth. These genres and sub-genres all have established fan bases that want certain things from their books. These core expectations are known as tropes. As a professional author, your job is to deliver this expected experience in a satisfying way. You're providing a service (entertainment) to readers. And what *you* want matters far less than what *they* want.

As a brief thought experiment, imagine ordering a lobster in a restaurant, only to be given flounder. Would you accept the chef's "innovation" or explanation that they're both "seafood"? Absolutely not—you'd never eat there again. **This is what an author is doing when, say, they don't include a happily ever after (HEA) in a book marketed as a romance**. A reader ordered lobster, but the author delivered flounder. Maybe the flounder was delicious. Doesn't matter; they broke the implicit promise their cover/blurb made.

Market research—or writing to market, if you prefer—is all about learning your genre's tropes and expectations so that you understand what makes a thriller different than, say, a romance. And also learning why leaving out key elements is a recipe for disaster.

The major genres are as follows:

- Romance
- Thriller
- Mystery
- Crime
- Sci-Fi
- Fantasy
- Horror
- Westerns
- Literary

A genre, however, is *not* homogeneous. This means that your research must extend beyond the umbrella genre and dive into specific sub-genres. Beneath the umbrella of sci-fi, for example, lies a variety of sub-genre readers seeking different experiences. Cyberpunk (*Blade Runner, Snow Crash, The Matrix, Deus Ex*) is a different sub-genre than space opera/military sci-fi (*Battlestar Galactica, Star Trek, The Expanse, Dune, Foundation*). It's important to study what makes *Snow Crash* (cyberpunk) a different reading experience than *The Expanse* (space opera), despite sharing some tropes—or a billionaire romance different from a bad boy rock star one.

Often, this is an emotional feeling, rather than simply "include tropes X, Y and Z."

For example, James Bond, Jack Reacher, and Jason Bourne are all trained killers, but they *feel* different. The reading demographic has significant overlap, but the takeaway experience from each is different. James Bond has an aristocratic, escapist elegance; Jack Reacher is an imposing physical presence and eternal wanderer; Jason Bourne is an adept improviser and master of his environment.

These distinctions might strike you as granular, but they're critical—not just for selling books, but for writing *good* ones that resonate with readers. Aim to understand the principle behind why a hero is dark and brooding, or a wanderer, or an aristocrat—what emotional hot button that presses in your target demographic—rather than blindly copying a trope.

You can identify reader expectations by reading the reviews, studying the blurbs, and analyzing the covers—but the best method is reading books from your sub-genre's Top 100 list.

That's all there is to understanding your genre.

Still not convinced this process is necessary?

Selling authors have done this for over a hundred years. They will do it for a hundred more, long after your books are forgotten. If you are going to write a romance, understand what readers expect. Thriller? Understand what *those* readers expect. Want to mash up the two genres into romantic suspense? Fine—understand which elements must be present to craft a satisfying cocktail.

There are two basic approaches to successfully writing genre fiction:

Writing to market: writing a book in a well-defined genre/sub-genre, using the tropes, expectations, and common characters within. E.g., disaster fiction, urban fantasy, or paranormal romance.

Writing to trend: writing a book in a well-defined sub-genre that's currently hot & selling well, using all of the tropes, expectations and common characters within. Trend books are often laser-targeted toward a very specific sub-genre (in a popular larger genre) that has suddenly grown to a size that outstrips normal demand. Often they're simply sub-genre books that are enjoying a sudden swell of popularity. E.g., LitRPG or reverse harem.

Most genre fiction falls into the **writing to market** category. While certain genres ebb and flow in popularity over the years, the major ones have been around for upwards of a century or more. They're not disappearing any time soon.

Writing to trend takes market research to an extreme, where authors identify hot genres and then write tropes *exclusively* the way people like them now. This is often what authors envision when you mention "market research": checklists of tropes, recycled characters and generally indistinguishable books. Such titles are mostly churned out as pulp commodities to capitalize on a sudden (and brief) spike in reader interest. People's broader tastes don't change much (romance has been around for almost two centuries), but niche sub-genres can fall in and out of favor rapidly. By focusing only on these tropes, your book will sink when that sub-sub-genre is no longer hot.

Weigh the pluses and minuses and factor in your writing speed when deciding. Writing to trend demands fast releases, but it's the quickest way to go from zero to making a living. Once you step off the book-a-month writing treadmill, however, your earnings are likely to nosedive. Writing to market allows more creative latitude and is a better path to building a long-term, non-commoditized brand. I think you're best off somewhere in the middle (although hewing toward the "write to market" end of the spectrum): where you're writing in a genre with current commercial appeal, but which has also held readers' interest for, say, longer than the past ten minutes.

And, finally, find an intersection between what you enjoy writing—and write well—and what readers will buy. Because consistent production is impossible when you dread visiting the keyboard.

F*** That, I Want to Be Original

Let's address the elephant in the writing room. Because authors often dismiss market research before they even try it by saying things like *I want to write anything I want. This is for my soul. This is for fun.*

All that is perfectly fine, but focusing on what *you* want is a fundamental mindset error if you want to make a living writing fiction. Perhaps money does not interest you; cash is hardly the sole reason why people publish books. But for even the most intransigent artiste, however, I'd suspect that having an *audience* matters a lot. And haphazardly writing whatever you want is unlikely to connect with readers—no matter how good your book is—unless you have commercial tastes. Most successful authors who tell you to write what you love—to pen the book of your heart, and that readers will connect with that passion— were fortunate enough to love a super commercial sub-genre.

Passion means nothing.

Quality means little if you miss genre conventions.

Let me be clear: a book that misses the market faces an uphill climb at best. Most commonly, your book is dead in the water the instant you press publish. **Fight reader expectations at your own peril**.

This is not a binary situation like some authors believe. It's a continuum, where on one side we have "writing to trend" and on the other side, "writing whatever the hell I want and not following anything."

There is almost certainly overlap between at least one genre's key tropes and what you like to write. Most genres probably have elements that you can work with.

You don't need to follow *every* trope.

That is a surefire way to become a commodity.

You do not even have to follow *most* of the tropes.

You just need to understand your genre.

The core emotional experience readers are seeking.

Then find a way to deliver it.

For a long-term career, you also need a voice and a unique angle. Some trope-heavy books have them. Most don't. Because the authors are concerned that too much deviation from the formula will turn off some readers.

Which is a very valid concern, because it's definitely true. Readers who select books based on an extremely specific set of tropes are usually not author loyal. They'll bounce from author to author, looking for whoever can deliver exactly what they want.

That's fine.

As an author it's hard to make a long-term career that way, though.

Make sure your stuff has *you* in it.

Because *that* is what draws fans to your work.

This is somewhat inevitable the further away you get from a lot of the tropes. That's not necessarily a good thing; many books are weird for no good reason, and don't really work.

But when done correctly, this uniqueness can be a tremendous long-term advantage. Because it means you're offering a reading experience people can't get anywhere else.

If you don't like most of your sub-genre's tropes, the easiest way to maintain marketability is identifying the **One Big Trope**.

In romance, this is the happily ever after (HEA) or happily for now (HFN).

In a mystery, the crime gets solved.

You can get away with a lot of creative license in between if you deliver on the One Big Trope. Will your books take off as quickly as something more tightly tuned to the market's expectations?

Probably not.

But the biggest part of marketing is not the marketing at all.

It's being able to show up and consistently publish books.

If you hate what you write, you won't be able to do that.

So calibrate the level of tropey-ness to your taste.

Some authors can incorporate more tropey stuff, even if they personally don't like it that much.

Some can't.

Some authors love the tropes and love hitting them in their books.

Some authors hate them all.

If you love all the tropes, great. There are thousands of readers that do, too. Cannonball into that pool and start swimming.

Just don't forget to incorporate *your* voice and style.

If you like the broad strokes of a genre, but can't stand 90% of the smaller things in it, cool. Forget all that stuff and nail big picture. Then get to work building your audience book-by-book.

Subverting or lampshading tropes is an excellent way to "avoid" using the ones you dislike, while still acknowledging to the reader that you understand the genre's expectations. It's often a better route to go than simply avoiding everything entirely, because you're *surprising* the reader by nodding to the familiar and then deviating from it, which makes them go *what's gonna happen next?*

This requires a respect for your chosen sub-genre.

Careful study.

In the immortal words of Charlie Parker: *Master the instrument, master the music, and then forget all that shit and just play.*

But mastery comes *first*.

Skip the research process at your own peril.

HOW TO FIND YOUR TARGET SUB-GENRE

You may have already written a book (or three) without much commercial success. If this reflects your current situation, then your first order of business is simply identifying a viable sub-genre in which to build a career. Perhaps it's the genre you're writing already; or maybe a significant change in approach is necessary to achieve your main goals.

Whatever the case, this research process will help you figure things out. This process is still useful if you've already written a book, as it can help troubleshoot why a title is under-performing.

Identifying potential sub-genres to write in involves the following steps:

1. Research your sub-genre on the Kindle Bestseller charts (**nicholaserik.com/top100**).
2. Assess the level of competition—how well are the Top 100 books selling/ranking?

3. Write down the ranks of the #1, #5, #20, and #50 ranked books.

- Everything in the Top 50 ranked between 1 – 25,000 overall in the Kindle Store? That's enough of a reader base to carve out your niche and make a living. Expect competition, however, from plenty of other books.
- 1 – 5,000? Big reader base, really good money, but very competitive.
- 1 – 2,000? Voracious reader base, potentially huge money, but hyper competitive.

4. Determine whether this sub-genre can meet your financial goals.
5. Determine whether your writing style and production level are a good fit for the audience's expectations.
6. Determine whether you're actually willing to write in this genre on an ongoing basis.
7. Determine whether you can realistically "break into" the Top 50/100 of this sub-genre's bestseller list with your current resources (time/money).
8. Write down 10 indie authors and 10 traditionally published authors in the sub-genre.

A key limitation of this approach: many popular sub-genres don't have their own bestseller list—e.g., LitRPG and paranormal academy romance will often appear on the Kindle Bestseller for cyberpunk and urban fantasy, respectively, but they don't currently have their own charts. To further assess the viability of such niches, click on one of the most popular titles, then click on the books that appear in its also-boughts to check their ranks.

It's important to note that Amazon's charts are skewed toward the preferences of Kindle Unlimited subscribers, since a KU borrow counts the same as a sale when calculating your Amazon sales rank. Amazon rank is largely an irrelevant metric for determining how well a wide book is doing. Thus, if you're going wide, you should repeat this exercise on each bookseller as well.

The eight steps above are just rules of thumb to eyeball a genre/sub-genre and determine how well it's currently selling—and if there's ample opportunity for your own work to find a niche. Obviously it's possible to make huge money in a smaller sub-genre.

Breaking into a sub-genre's Top 100 charts is *not* the be-all, end-all goal. Nor do you have to hit it with your first book (or at all). But it's a good gauge of competitiveness. A sub-genre like contemporary romance—which has a Top 100 chart featuring a ton of books ranking below 1,000 in the Kindle Store—demands substantial resources to establish a readership.

After you've done the exercise above, you should have some viable sub-genre candidates. But let's drill into this on a deeper level.

I find that many authors simply emulate what others have done or gravitate toward what's hot. When I wrote a previous edition of this guide in 2018, one could launch a LitRPG book with a substandard cover and minimal advertising into the Top 5,000, simply because the readership was voracious and the supply of LitRPG was still (relatively) low. In marketing terms, this was an "under-served niche." LitRPG has since become much more competitive, and this is no longer possible.

I've seen the same cycle play out in other sub-genres since.

In mid-2019, paranormal academy romance was extremely popular.

Then supply outstripped reader demand, and by 2020, many of these titles—save for the most popular authors' books—disappeared from the charts. And even the popular authors' books didn't hit as high as when the academy trend was at its peak.

Yes, you can make a lot of money if you strike while the iron is hot.

But these books are rarely long-term backlist assets.

After the trend ends, they tend to make very little money.

That's because most of them are written as commodities.

If your only advantage is that a genre is "hot," then you're sitting on thin ice. Eventually competition enters the market, and the quality level rises. If your books do not meet this new threshold or are completely interchangeable with any other, they'll drown.

It pays to sit down and work out the *principles* behind why certain things work. Then put your own spin on them. This helps you build a long-term brand and stand out in a crowd of lookalikes.

IF YOU ALREADY HAVE AN
ESTABLISHED PEN NAME

Even if you already have a book available, market research pays big dividends. You'll often find that your book is under-performing not because it sucks, but because your cover and blurb are off-base. Or you've placed it in the wrong category.

If you're struggling to sell, the exercise outlined in the previous section should be completed before moving forward. It's possible that the sub-genre you chose is simply unpopular—or it's so popular that the amount of money you're currently investing isn't enough to compete.

But once you've found a solid, viable sub-genre and have an established pen name, ongoing market research involves the following process:

1. Research your sub-genre on the Kindle Bestseller charts (**nicholaserik.com/top100**).

2. Analyze your fellow authors' covers, blurbs, and categories. What's popular? What's working? What's not?

3. What are they pricing at?

4. Read their reviews. What did readers like? What did they not enjoy (this represents a potential open niche for your books to fill)? Look for commonalities and patterns—if one person mentioned something, that's often just an opinion. If ten people say it, it's worth diving deeper.

5. Sign up for their newsletters and skim their websites. Look at their social media profiles. How are they building a platform? How do they interact with readers?

6. Scan Amazon and other sites: are they running ads? If so, what does their copy look like? Click through the also boughts. Are there authors selling books who don't appear on the bestseller lists? Are there other tropes or takes on the sub-genre that might make good angles for your own ads, blurbs, or other marketing elements? Are there any new marketing techniques or trends?

All of this takes time. But over the months and years, you should have a clear picture of what the biggest names in your sub-genre are doing (and aren't). And you should be using everything you learn to improve your own books.

WIDE OR KU: WHICH TO CHOOSE?

Deciding whether to make your book(s) exclusive to Amazon (frequently called "being in KU") or publish them on all retailers (called "going wide") is one of the most hotly debated topics in all of indie publishing.

For those curious as to why you'd make your book exclusive in this new age of publishing, the answer is simple: Amazon offers exclusive authors perks. Here's what you get in exchange for making your book Amazon exclusive for 90 days:

- Enrollment in Kindle Unlimited, which is a library of 1,000,000+ titles that Kindle Unlimited subscribers (an all-you-can-read eBook service that's essentially Netflix for books) can read for free. You, in turn, get paid per page read for these borrows (usually around $0.0045, but that number fluctuates on a monthly basis). If someone purchases your book, you still get paid as you normally would.
- 5 promotional free days per 90 day exclusivity term to use whenever you'd like.
- Access to Kindle Countdown Deals, where you can discount your book to $0.99/$1.99 in the US/UK markets (other regions aren't currently eligible) for up to 7 days and still receive 70% royalties.

Note that you do *not* have to enroll your entire catalog in Kindle Unlimited to participate; you can have some titles wide and others exclusive. Indeed, you'll probably find as your backlist grows that certain titles perform better wide than they do exclusive. You should, of course, choose the same distribution option for all the books *within* a series—having Books 1 and 3 exclusive, and Book 2 wide, will only frustrate both KU *and* wide readers.

One of the biggest perks of being exclusive is the visibility you can generate through a combination of your own effective marketing + free runs and Kindle Countdown Deals. These two tools are very useful for promotional purposes, and their effectiveness is enhanced by Amazon's algorithms which, as noted earlier, counts each borrow by a Kindle Unlimited subscriber the same as a sale when calculating a book's sales rank.

Thus, a Kindle Unlimited title does not need to sell nearly as many copies as one of its wide counterparts to rank high on the bestseller charts.

When you're performing your initial market research, you can identify a sub-genre's relative popularity in Kindle Unlimited by skimming through the Top 100. If most of these titles are enrolled in Kindle Unlimited, putting your own titles in KU will likely give them the best chance of success.

You'll find that **Kindle Unlimited's popularity varies widely by genre**. This is one of the many reasons why market research must be done on a series-by-series basis if you write in multiple genres. What is true about mysteries may not apply to contemporary romance. Some genres (e.g., LitRPG and urban fantasy) have huge Kindle Unlimited audiences. Their Top 100 charts are dominated by Kindle Unlimited titles. Going wide in such situations usually makes less financial sense, although it's good to explore alternative waters when your books aren't killing it in KU.

Other genres are far less Kindle Unlimited dependent.

Another bonus of exclusivity is **simplicity**. You only have to upload your books to one store, then track the numbers for Amazon. If you make an update, it's a simple matter of changing something on Amazon—rather than doing it in five or six locations. This cuts down on administrative time.

Wide, of course, allows you to publish to all retailers, thus getting your book in front of readers on Apple Books, B & N, Kobo, Google Play, and a host of other smaller stores.

Advantages include not being as dependent on Amazon for income (although Amazon will still likely produce the majority of your sales) nor being subject to fluctuations in the Kindle Unlimited payout rate. Finally, if you sell a significant number of copies overseas, other retailers have a larger foothold in those markets—Kobo, for example, is actually the most popular eBook retailer in Canada.

Which to choose, then?

I generally recommend for new authors—regardless of genre—to put their titles into Kindle Unlimited. There are exceptions to this, but it streamlines the publishing process, and the visibility tools are useful for building a bit of momentum.

Ultimately, whichever option you choose, I don't think this decision is all that controversial if you follow a simple rule: do what works best for your books and genre.

WHEN SHOULD I SWITCH GENRES?

Those struggling with their initial publishing efforts and considering a genre switch might be wondering when to make the jump.

On the one hand, doubling down on a sinking ship is not advisable. Waiting too long wastes valuable writing time and money on a lost cause.

On the other, if you're constantly hopping genres, it's hard to get a feel for what truly matters to a genre's fans. You never develop a mastery of the sub-genre, nor do you hone a distinct voice. And much of the money in this gig is in the backlist. Without that, you'll have trouble making a living. Indeed, there have been surveys indicating most six-figure indie authors had more than 25 books available. If you have a solid author brand with a cohesive, quality backlist, even a modest hit can elevate your career to incredible new heights, as the visibility from that title spills over to your quite similar older ones. Each new reader is gently encouraged to pick up the others, because the writing, packaging, and other marketing elements suggest readers can expect a similar experience.

Far too many authors try to hop on what is hot at the moment, without any semblance of a long-term strategy. The problem with seeking quick hits is this: if you have a disjointed backlist, or no backlist (because you've started five or six different pen names), then even a single mega-hit does you little good. Readers who picked up your breakout will have nothing to read—either because your other books aren't similar, or simply because they don't exist. And when the spotlight fades, your platform and brand are right where they started, at flatline levels.

Backlist is where at least half the money is.

What, then, to do?

I wrote about 15 sci-fi novels under this name (Nicholas Erik) before I tried my hand at urban fantasy, which proved a much better fit for my voice and style. While I did hop on something that was a bit trendy at the time, this change made sense for two reasons: A) sci-fi readers weren't resonating with my books, and B) I'd given sci-fi a good run.

In fact, I probably waited a bit too long. Of course, it's incredibly easy to fall victim to shiny object syndrome and hop blindly into the latest hot trend. Subsequently, my suggestion is to **write**

a minimum of six novels in a sub-genre. That can be one series or two trilogies—but six novels gives you enough of a backlist and taste of the genre to know how readers are responding to your work.

This does *not* mean you should expect to make a huge income from just six novels. It will likely take anywhere from 10 – 20 to generate a consistent full-time income. But if the *potential* isn't there after six, you should reassess your publishing strategy.

How to assess potential? I'd make profit my main metric: are these books generating income? If you're in a sea of red ink, trying a different genre might be one fix (but, to be clear, it's not the *only* fix—or necessarily what's wrong). If, however, you haven't made any effort to promote your books (covered in Parts 6 and 7), that would be my first order of business.

POSITIONING: HOW TO BUILD
AN AUTHOR BRAND

Ultimately, the goal of market research is *not* to create a homogeneous, cookie-cutter product. Once you understand your audience, you can craft marketing materials that position your books uniquely within your sub-genre. Thus, proper market research allows you to craft a distinct author brand. However, we don't create our author brand using the same methods as Coca-Cola. We don't have millions of dollars for branding campaigns that go up in Times Square or air on prime time TV. In recent years, direct marketers have started to preach the "brand advertising is dead" mantra. I wouldn't go this far; the marketing people at Coke or Apple are not morons.

However, as indie authors, we do not have the funds for large-scale, mass-media awareness campaigns. But we can still develop our brand. What is a brand, after all? **A brand is a promise of a consistent customer experience**. Many authors and business owners mistakenly believe their customers want novelty. No; they want consistent quality. As Ray Croc, founder of McDonald's said, "People don't want the best burger in the world; they want a burger that's just like the one they had last time."

You know *exactly* what you're getting from Starbucks or McDonald's—whether it's located in London, Tokyo, Sydney, or Seattle. Such is the power of a great brand.

Likewise, your name on the cover implicitly promises a specific reading experience. But it's easy to shatter this promise by genre hopping or breaking expectations.

Thus, I recommend adhering to a simple rule: one pen name, one genre. This sets clear expectations for the reader and ensures that they will never be surprised (by the genre; the story can have twists and turns galore, of course). Many readers are more genre and sub-genre loyal than author loyal. There's unlikely to be a ton of crossover between your urban fantasy and techno-thrillers, even if they really, really like you as an author. Some readers read almost exclusively in a single *sub-genre*—they'll devour historical romances, but have no interest in contemporary or billionaire romances.

Certain genres are symbiotic; you can get away with writing science-fiction and fantasy under the same name, and enjoy some crossover. You can pull this off when you have a strong, distinct voice and style which have become a greater part of your brand than simply the sub-genre you write in.

But writing cross-genre can easily muddy your brand and confuse expectations; hence the elegant simplicity of the one pen name, one genre rule. This has the added benefit of *focusing* your efforts with laser-like precision; managing multiple pen names is a huge pain in the ass that I do not recommend. Each pen name is like a little sub-business that you're starting from scratch. Unless you can support each one with four annual releases apiece, stick with one and build a sizable, quality backlist of books.

The heart of your brand is your **unique selling proposition (USP).** A classic USP example is Domino's famous "30 minutes or less" guarantee. In the indie realm, a USP is something your books offer that no other author does.

In other words, getting to the heart of your brand is as simple (and difficult) as answering this question: **what makes your books distinct (while being familiar enough to appeal to that sub-genre's readers)?**

The USP operates on two levels:

- **AUTHOR**: What do you offer that no other author can? What makes your work distinct? This is often a matter of craft/voice, although it can be even more specific than that (i.e., Elmore Leonard's dialogue). Beyond your take on genre tropes and your voice/style, your brand is about delivering a certain emotional experience.
- **BOOK**: The hook, concept, or tagline for each individual book. Generally referred to as "high-concept."
  - *The Matrix*: what if reality was actually an elaborate computer simulation designed to enslave humanity?
  - *Groundhog Day*: romantic comedy where protagonist is caught in a time loop
  - *Her Last Tomorrow*: Would you murder your wife to save your daughter?

- *The Hunger Games*: children/teenagers fight to the death in a live gladiatorial arena for the entertainment of the wealthy
- *11/22/63*: a high school teacher travels back in time to prevent the assassination of JFK

Is a hook necessary to sell your book?

No. If you want to break out of your sub-genre and generate massive crossover appeal, it can be a big help, however. Thus, when you have what's known as a "high-concept" idea, it pays to sharpen that hook to a razor's edge.

Of course, it's wise to remember that mass appeal isn't critical to becoming a full-time author. Writing genre books that never break out beyond their core fandom is usually far more lucrative (even if no one outside your chosen genre knows your name). Most full-time authors are simply writing high-quality genre fiction for their target audience.

The majority of novels won't have hooks, especially in genres with well-established tropes and standard story structures like mystery or romance. The draw is rarely an earth-shattering concept.

A cop investigates a murder.

A girl and guy fall in love.

Indeed, much of the appeal here is the *familiarity*.

These are timeless stories that readers will still enjoy long after we're all gone. Your job is to present such stories in a distinct, but not too different way.

As such, these books rely on snappy taglines or well-written leads (the first few sentences of the blurb) to differentiate themselves from millions of similar titles. Much like the story itself, it's not so much the content of the tagline or the lead, but *how* you write it that proves to be the difference maker.

And why 80 – 90 words for the lead, specifically? That's the visible area "above the fold" on Amazon before a reader has to click read more. If readers don't like what they find here, they'll move on.

We'll discuss taglines and leads further when we dive into blurbs later in the guide. For now, if you're stuck coming up with taglines or hooks for your book, here are a few ideas:

- Analyze your favorite fiction, particularly whatever's stuck in your mind for months or years. The core elements drawing you to these books, movies, and shows are often strong hooks.
- Read other books in your sub-genre. Read their reviews/comments. How do your books differ?
- Read your reviews/comments to find out what readers found unique.
- Survey your readers.

This takes work and revision to get right; don't expect to come up with a great USP and brand in five minutes. It's a process of constant refinement that keeps evolving as you grow as a marketer and storyteller.

But it's worth keeping in mind, because a quality brand is one of the best ways to make your books and author name stand out in readers' minds. Then, next time they see one of your books, they'll say, *yeah, that author's the one who does [x].* And you'll have risen above the fray of similar titles into the realm of books that readers anticipate and remember long after the final page has closed.

KEY TAKEAWAYS

- Genre research is critical. If you mess up your book's genre/sub-genre targeting, it's often difficult to sell.
- **Writing to market**: writing genre fiction that follows an established audience's tropes and expectations (e.g., contemporary romance or urban fantasy).
- **Writing to trend**: writing in a hot sub-genre of fiction that's currently enjoying a spike in popularity that may not last for a long time (i.e., reverse harem).
- For new authors, enrolling your book(s) into Kindle Unlimited for at least one 90-day period is recommended—it's simple and has visibility tools that help you build momentum.
- Some genres are dominated by Kindle Unlimited; others aren't. Do market research to determine whether your title essentially needs to be exclusive, or whether wide is a viable (or even preferable) solution.
- **Brand:** a promise of a consistent customer experience.
- **USP:** what's your book's hook? What do you offer as an author that no one else can?
- Identifying potential sub-genres to write in involves the following steps:

1. Research your sub-genre on the Kindle Bestseller charts (**nicholaserik.com/top100**).
2. Assess the level of competition—how well are the Top 100 books selling/ranking?
3. Write down the ranks of the #1, #5, #20 and #50 ranked books.

- Everything in the Top 50 ranked between 1 – 25,000 overall in the Kindle Store? That's enough of a reader base to carve out your niche and make a living. Expect competition, however, from plenty of other books.
- 1 – 5,000? Big reader base, really good money, but very competitive.
- 1 – 2,000? Voracious reader base, potentially huge money, but hyper competitive.

4. Determine whether this sub-genre can meet your financial goals.
5. Determine whether your writing style and production level are a good fit for the audience's expectations.
6. Determine whether you're actually willing to write in this genre on an ongoing basis.
7. Determine whether you can realistically "break into" the Top 50/100 of this sub-genre's bestseller list with your current resources (time/money).
8. Write down 10 indie authors and 10 traditionally published authors in the sub-genre.

- Once you've found a solid, viable sub-genre and have an established pen name, ongoing market research involves the following process:

1. Research your sub-genre on the Kindle Bestseller charts (**nicholaserik.com/top100**).
2. Analyze your fellow authors' covers, blurbs, and categories. What's popular? What's working? What's not?
3. What are they pricing at?

4. Read their reviews. What did readers like? What did they not enjoy (this represents a potential open niche for your books to fill)? Look for commonalities and patterns—if one person mentioned something, that's often just an opinion. If ten people say it, it's worth diving deeper.

5. Sign up for their newsletters and skim their websites. Look at their social media profiles. How are they building a platform? How do they interact with readers?

6. Scan Amazon and other sites: are they running ads? If so, what does their copy look like? Click through the also boughts. Are there authors selling books who don't appear on the bestseller lists? Are there other tropes or takes on the sub-genre that might make good angles for your own ads, blurbs, or other marketing elements? Are there any new marketing techniques or trends?

ACTION EXERCISE

1. **Research your sub-genre on the Amazon bestseller charts (nicholaserik.com/top100).**

   - Write down the ranks of the #1, #5, #10, #20 and #50 book in two sub-genres that fit your series.
   - Write down ten indie authors and ten traditionally published authors who represent your target market (i.e., authors who can realistically complete the statement, **my book is for fans of [Author X]**).
   - Write down character names instead, if the character is more recognizable than the author.

- You'll use this list of authors and character names for PPC (pay-per-click) ad targeting, your blurb, cover inspiration and more down the line, so save it (Excel tends to work best).

FIVE:

CRACKING AMAZON'S ALGORITHMS

W e're about to take our first foray into traffic and promotion (you know, the stuff that usually come to mind when people hear the word marketing). But this part of the guide isn't about how to direct prospective readers to our book page—the various promotional and advertising options that you can use to drive readers to Amazon and other retailers will be discussed in the next section. Right now, however, we're going to dive into how you can amplify *all* your marketing efforts by leveraging the power of the Amazon algorithms (colloquially known as "the algos").

Now, if you've been an indie author for a bit, you've probably heard *a lot* about the importance of Amazon's algos. But *why* do they matter so much?

Simple: if you know how they function and what they reward, you can put Amazon's marketing machine to work for you. And Amazon is the most powerful bookselling force on the planet. Even if you spent $10,000/mo on Facebook, you couldn't match the power of Amazon's organic visibility. By understanding the algorithms, we can structure our marketing campaigns and launches to maximize the impact of every promo dollar.

WHAT *ARE* THE AMAZON ALGORITHMS?

Amazon is essentially a giant AI recommendation machine. When authors refer to the algos, they're really referring to a specific subset of the thousands of algorithms and rules currently running behind the scenes on the site. That is, they're talking about the **book recommendation algorithms**.

Unlike other retailers, almost *all* the merchandising on Amazon is regulated by automated mechanisms. This is one of Amazon's major retailing innovations. By taking staff members largely out of the merchandising equation, their system can update recommendations in near real-time, churning out millions of up-to-date, highly specific recommendations to Amazon's many customers. Not only do these occur without human intervention, the system often makes far more accurate guesses than a human can about what a prospective buyer likes based upon Amazon's massive stores of customer data.

First, it should be said that there is no single algorithm governing book selling. Amazon is a complex organism with a ton of code interacting in complicated ways. Technically, the main beast driving the show is called A9. Diving into the technical details of A9, however, isn't what this guide is about (after all, this is a guide to selling books, damnit, not an engineering white paper).

Instead, by analyzing patterns, trends, and how Amazon's site is constructed, we can peek behind the recommendation engine's curtain. And then we can use that information to sell more books—without an advanced degree in statistics or computer engineering.

So what we know about Amazon is this: the algorithms aim to show buyers what they want to buy *when* they want to buy it (or perhaps before the customer even knows he wants to buy it). Their engineers are constantly refining and updating the code that governs these recommendations, always trying to find new ways to generate more sales and increase customer satisfaction. The latter part is really the key: **Amazon's core drive is the customer experience**. This cannot be overstated and should not be ignored; it is built into the framework of their cultural DNA. They are obsessed with delighting customers because they know that providing the customer with an incredible experience is the key to repeat business, word of mouth, and dominating the retail landscape.

Thus, Amazon strives to recommend hyper-relevant items not only because customers are more likely to purchase them— relevant items have higher conversion, in marketing parlance— but because people appreciate finding *exactly* what they want without tons of legwork.

How does this apply *specifically* to books, then? Well, Amazon has a number of automatic recommendations triggered by factors we'll discuss shortly. But first, let's look at just a few of the places these recommendations appear:

- The Also Boughts
- Merchandising Emails

- The Bestseller Lists
- The Popular Lists (known as the "Pop" lists)

There are probably over a dozen of these merchandising spots located in nooks and crannies all over Amazon; this is merely a taste of how powerful the recommendation engine is.

And if you can convince Amazon that readers are buying and enjoying your book, they're happy to put this engine behind you as an author.

THE POPULAR LISTS

You've probably heard of the Pop Lists (short for Popular Lists) mentioned before. To check them out, you can hit this link (nicholaserik.com/pop) to see the cozy mystery pop list. Buyers don't really browse these (although they are the default on some devices, apparently), but they are a useful research tool. Because unlike the bestseller charts, which are simply a list of what's selling best, the popular lists are more reflective of what Amazon is pushing through via their automated recommendations and emails.

General rules of the pop lists (note: general hat tip to Phoenix S. and David Gaughran for doing most of the research here; any errors are my own):

1.   Rolling average of the last 30 days of sales and small sliver of free downloads (approximately 1/100), weighted by revenue with a four-day delay.

2.   Borrows are not counted toward pop list "rank."

3.   To navigate to the Pop List in your genre, head to the Amazon home page, type in your sub-genre (e.g., "urban

fantasy" or "thrillers") in the search bar. Then, along the left-hand side, under Kindle Books, click your sub-genre. Finally, make sure you're sorting the search results by "Featured" at the top right. Then go up the search bar, delete your search term, and hit enter. You'll see a list of regular Amazon search results within your sub-genre—this is that sub-genre's Pop List.

Great. This is extremely cumbersome to reach.

In other words, who cares?

I want to be clear: I rarely look at these lists.

Their most useful application is as a diagnostic tool (if a promo isn't going as well as planned). If you're not getting any juice from Amazon's recommendations, a quick perusal of the pop lists in your sub-genre can often tell you *why* that is. Because if you're nowhere to be found (you have to navigate through manually, and it's going to vary based on sub-genre how high you need to hit to get recommended), then you're probably not getting pushed by the algorithms.

And understanding how they work—particularly the four day delay in updating—is critical to understanding why, say, page reads often peak a week or two (or even longer) after a big promo, rather than the day of the largest advertising push.

Basically, the pop lists tell you which books have made the most money over the past 30 days. By contrast, the bestseller lists simply catalog those books with the most borrows and sales over the past few hours or days.

But marketing is not about sales or borrows.

It's about dollars. Profit.

No one knows the exact algorithm that goes into the pop lists. Without knowing exactly what's going on under the algorithmic hood, it's impossible to say for certain that spot #2 is making more than #3. But spot #2 is almost certainly making more than spot #20.

Don't obsess over these lists.

Don't obsess over *any* lists (especially the bestseller lists).

Just understand how they work.

THE KEY THINGS TO KNOW

What do Amazon's algorithms like to see?

Well, to reiterate: *no one* knows for sure. They're a black box, and obviously Amazon's not opening the doors to show everyone exactly how they function. Nonetheless, as mentioned earlier, we can examine patterns in the data to get a general idea of what they like, including a book's overall popularity, the buyer's purchase history, price (e.g. how much a product makes for Amazon), verified reviews (apparently; which goes against the grain of popular belief) and probably hundreds of additional factors.

In practice, most of this stuff doesn't matter when it comes to generating visibility via Amazon's recommendations, also-boughts, popularity lists (now referred to as "Featured" in Amazon's search options), or bestseller charts; ergo, variables like reviews, which are allegedly factored into the algorithm, don't mean jack when it comes to rank.

So let's talk about what *really* matters.

The three keys for tripping the algo wires are:

1.   **Sales volume & velocity** (this is the main factor) (key for pop lists/bestseller charts)
2.   **Sales consistency** (key for pop lists/bestseller charts)

3. **The sample of people who buy your book** (key for Amazon's automated emails, also-boughts, and on-site merchandising)

The algo also factors in:

- **Newness**: promotes new content more readily than old backlist
- **Sales history**: if a book has a consistent history of poor sales, it's harder to revive than one with a consistently solid sales history. Don't worry; if your book is in the cellar, you can market it. Just understand that a book with steady sales is easier to revive/boost up than one camping in the telephone number ranks.

This works for two reasons:

1. Amazon's algorithms treat consistent sales as organic buying activity, and will start to recommend your book if it sees evidence of this (provided you've targeted your book toward the right buyers).
2. You'll maximize the impact of those sales on your sales rank, generating visibility for you on Amazon's genre and sub-genre bestseller charts.

It's also important to know that Amazon counts each borrow via Kindle Unlimited (or Prime Reading) *equal* to a sale in the sales ranking. That's why Kindle Unlimited books tend to dominate the Top 100 in most sub-genres. Ranking, however, doesn't necessarily mean profit—Kindle Unlimited subscribers can borrow a book and never read it (thus not generating any sweet, sweet KU reads). Don't fall into a trap of chasing rank and sacrificing significant profits.

Sales volume and velocity are self-explanatory: **sell more books in a short period of time and you'll rank higher**. What's a little counter-intuitive, however, is that Amazon's algorithms also reward consistency, rather than massive spikes. As such, you want to spread out your marketing efforts to mimic the right-hand curve:

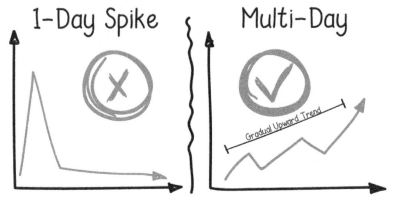

To be clear, sales will fluctuate, and you're not screwed if one day your sales dip slightly; the underlying principle is what's important. **You want your sales to trend upward over the course of your promotions to maximize your visibility and the tail.** To ensure this happens, simply to spread out your traffic over multiple days, instead of doing a "one shot" blast that results in a massive spike and then...nothing.

You can massively amplify the effect of those sales when you spread them out over multiple days, rather than firing all of your promo sites, newsletter, and social media efforts on a single day.

It's important to note that spikes aren't "penalized"—selling a lot of books in a day is *never* a bad thing. You're not hurting your book's long-term chances or anything like that. A spike without any follow-up, however, will drop right back into the sales cellar. Thus, the core reason we avoid spikes and focus on consistent sales is because the same amount of sales spread over a 4 – 10 days works better, both in the short term *and* for long term post-promo sales. I prefer 5 – 7 day promos and launches, for the record; that's enough time to show the algos consistency and establish a solid sales history, but short enough to generate the velocity/condensed sales mass required to really move the needle. It's also doable even if you have a modest (or practically no) existing platform.

Longer launches and promo pushes totaling 10 days or even more aren't uncommon, but they tend to have patchy areas where sales drop precipitously, thus killing momentum.

Curious about the math behind this? Let's dive into that and explore why we should strive so hard for a consistent upward trend.

WHY CONSISTENCY MATTERS: HOW TO MAXIMIZE YOUR SALES RANK (THE MATH)

This is the math that explains *why* you need to spread your sales over the course of a promo. You can skip the math, but working it out will give you a deeper understanding of what's actually going on behind the curtain.

First, two points of clarification:

- Sales rank (the # you see on every book page—**Amazon Best Sellers Rank:** #67,339 Paid in Kindle Store) is purely driven by sales + KU borrows.

- Each sales rank takes a certain number of sales + borrows to hit. It takes fewer sales/borrows, however, to *stay* there because of the math below. I refer to the combined number of sales + borrows as **rank points**.

Now, the math:

- For simplicity's sake, let's say it requires 40 rank points to rank at 5,000 in the Kindle Store.
- 1 sale = 1 rank point, 1 borrow = 1 rank point.
- Today's rank point score = 1/2 of yesterday's score + today's sales/borrows.
- Let's say, given our budget, available promo and mailing list size, we can reliably generate 80 total sales @ $0.99 over a 5 day promo window, after which the book will return to full price.
- How should we spread these out to hit the top 5,000 and maximize our visibility/ROI (return on investment)?

Sales	Day 1	Day 2	Day 3	Day 4	Day 5
Option A (start big, taper down)	30	20	15	10	5
Option B (start small, gradually trend up)	5	10	15	20	30

Rank Points	Day 1 RP	Day 2 RP	Day 3 RP	Day 4 RP	Day 5 RP
Option A (start big, taper down)	30	35	32.5	26.25	18.125
Option B (start small, gradually trend up)	5	12.5	21.25	30.625	45.3125

OPTION A (start big, taper down): At the end of our promo, we have our lowest score, lowest rank, and we didn't hit our goal of hitting the top 5,000. Our rank points peak at 35 on Day 2.

OPTION B (start small, scale up): At the end of our promo, we exit at peak rank (beating our goal), breaking the top 5,000. Our rank points reach 45.3. We return to full price at maximum visibility, and with our strongest rank point history, thus enhancing our chances of getting "sticky" at a higher rank even as sales naturally decline to an equilibrium point.

Remember, we're not spending more to deploy OPTION B, nor are we generating more sales: we're merely structuring the promotion differently. In fact, Option B is a perfect inverse of Option A. This is, of course, imperfect in practice; you can't know *exactly* how many sales you'll get from a certain traffic source beforehand. Using historical estimates, however, we can schedule our efforts so that they trend consistently upward, with the heaviest promo push at the end.

The general principle is simple: **backload your biggest promos toward the end of a promo, if possible, and create a consistently increasing sales curve**.

Why does sales rank even matter? Because readers browse the sub-genre Top 100 lists—so hitting your sub-genre's Top 20 is a source of free organic traffic.

Now that we've covered the first two key principles (volume & velocity and consistency) to leveraging Amazon's algos, it's time to address the third principle: the sample of people purchasing your book.

THE DATA SET: ALL TRAFFIC IS NOT EQUALLY BENEFICIAL

We've talked about how to rank higher on Amazon's sales charts.

We've even talked about the Holy Grail: a book selling on its own for weeks or months at a time, otherwise known as stickiness. Indeed, Amazon's recommendation engine can push far more books than you can ever hope to—and all for the low, low price of $0. Alas, however, stickiness is a fickle beast.

But what if we could increase our chances of getting sticky?

We can. To be clear, the algos are a temperamental, unpredictable beast under even optimal circumstances. But the more we can tilt the odds in our favor, even slightly, the better chance we have at winning this book publishing game.

And that requires understanding how to train Amazon's data set.

As we've previously discussed, Amazon's site is essentially one big machine learning organism. You can consider it a baby AI: it's constantly recording your actions and trying to predict what you'll buy next—before *you* even know. It does this via advanced statistical analysis of massive amounts of data. As it combs through all this data, Amazon's baby AI searches for patterns amidst the hundreds of millions of customers in the database, like a pig searching for truffles. Based on your browsing and buying history, it will then recommend things that other folks with similar data profiles purchased.

All this sounds well and good and has already been covered: Amazon works hard to recommend us shit we like to buy. So what?

By feeding Amazon the right data, you can get them to recommend your book. But not just *any* readers. Exactly the right readers—whether you write political thrillers or culinary cookbooks. Result? When your book is shown to the *right* readers, it produces a higher conversion rate, better reviews, and more sales. Best of all? Amazon's algorithms interpret this behavior as "customers enjoy this book"—so then the AI returns to its little data storage vault and recommends your book even more. This reinforcing cycle has massive upside, given Amazon's hundreds of millions of customers. Imagine them hand-picking customers who *love* urban fantasy or bad boy romance out of this database, then aggressively marketing to those people—i.e., your core fanbase—automatically and totally for free.

What does look like in practice?

In short: if you have an urban fantasy book, and you feed Amazon some voracious urban fantasy readers—who have purchased dozens of UF books on their Amazon account—Amazon's recommendation engine searches through the customer base to find *other* people who fit this "voracious urban fantasy reader" profile. (Hat tip goes to Chris Fox for putting these pieces together in *Six Figure Author*).

The rest is basically as easy as counting your money. Because when voracious urban fantasy readers are recommended new, cool urban fantasy books, what tends to happen? They buy. And boom: Amazon is now selling books to hardcore fans that you *never* could have reached on your own.

Let's dive further into the specifics of *how* to find the right initial readers to properly train Amazon's data monster.

HOW TO TRAIN AMAZON'S DATA MONSTER

If you're worried that getting Amazon recommending books to the right readers is going to be difficult, worry not.

You train Amazon's algorithms simply by selling books to your core readers. This means that if you have a first-person female main character urban fantasy mystery, finding 150 people who have bought lots of similar books will be more beneficial than

1,000 more general book buyers. Because those 150 sales will teach Amazon *exactly* who your target market is.

This is when the magic starts: Amazon sends out highly targeted recommendations to voracious urban fantasy readers. Your book sells well, they recommend it more, it sells, and so on, as previously outlined.

But what happens when you get a random or more general sample of 1,000 people to buy?

Well, this broader collection of buyers will also trigger recommendation emails. After all, your book is selling; and sales volume is a big factor in Amazon's algos. Let's say I like thrillers and purchased a UF book once—randomly. I might get an email from Amazon because I fit their vague, uncertain profile of people who *might* like your new UF book. Unfortunately, I don't buy, because I don't really like books featuring wizards. The result of these broader recommendations is catastrophic and also self-reinforcing: your conversion rate plummets due to your book not being relevant to a ton of the people it's been recommended to, review scores drop, customer interest metrics are low (clicks on the book in emails or in-store merchandising placements/bounce rate on the page). All of which leads Amazon's friendly neighborhood AI to an obvious conclusion after it sorts through the aftermath.

Buyers just aren't interested in your book. And boom: Amazon stops recommending it. Your book disappears into the Kindle cellar.

The main idea here is that you confuse Amazon's algorithms when you get a ton of sales that have no clear data pattern behind them. And when Amazon doesn't know who to recommend the book to, its automated marketing efforts will be substandard.

All this means in practical terms is simple: **prioritize highly targeted sources of traffic that hit your key audience over broader ones (even if they result in slightly more sales).**

The real reason you want to target your buyers actually has *nothing* to do with fancy technology and everything to do with commonsense. If you advertise your thriller novel to people who like thrillers, they're more likely to buy. This means your marketing costs are going to be cheaper and more effective.

On the other hand, putting your thriller in front of contemporary romance readers is an uphill battle. You'll need to spend more to achieve less.

Thus, when you're considering your traffic sources, remember:

1. PPC is the gold standard for laser-targeting. Facebook, BookBub, Amazon Ads, and other venues allow you to narrow your target to specific sub-genres and authors.

2. Your fans are the best way to train Amazon's data set, provided you don't genre hop. If you do genre hop, then you need separate lists (i.e., one for your thrillers and another for your wizard books) so that you don't muck up the data set.

3. Highly-targeted, genre-specific promo sites "train" Amazon's recommendation engine better than more generalized ones. Unfortunately, highly-targeted promo sites are rare; thus, you often want to save such sites until your book has a more established sales history and Amazon already knows who to recommend it to. Otherwise, you can confuse the baby AI out of the gate, and it can have a lot of trouble recovering later on.

Okay, but *how* sensitive are Amazon's data systems? This is a question I've gotten a few times, so let's clear up some misconceptions before we continue.

IMPORTANT NOTE: MUCKING WITH THE DATA

Some people are so concerned with misleading Amazon's AI that they don't want to send *any* off-target traffic to their book page, lest the algos get permanently confused.

While Amazon's AI isn't a genius (yet), it also isn't that easily duped. A few sales from your friends/family or a well-meaning associate won't scuttle your chances of getting some recommendation love. In fact, even a bunch of untargeted sales won't skew the data set, provided a large chunk of the sales is coming from the heart of your target audience.

How much? I'd aim for **75%+ targeted sales as a rough rule of thumb**. But that leaves substantial room for people outside your core target audience to pick up and enjoy your book without the algos getting confused.

So you can stop worrying about leading Amazon's AI down the wrong path when Grandma Beatrice buys your latest opus. Your book's data set will be just fine.

HOW DO I KNOW IF MY DATA SAMPLE IS OFF?

If you think you might have shotgunned your book out to everyone with a pulse (instead of your target audience), how can you tell if you've confused Amazon's algorithms? To be clear, there's no surefire way of determining this, outside of going under the hood of Amazon's algorithms. Since the chances of them allowing us to do that are less than zero, however, we have to rely on a simple rule of thumb.

We look at our book's also boughts.

Basically, your book's also boughts should match your book's genre. If you have a bunch of cookbooks in your thriller's also boughts, you've confused Amazon's targeting. This can happen when you use more general promo sites, or if you market your book to a more general audience without targeting any genre-specific readers. It can also temporarily shift after, say, a BookBub Featured Deal, since your book will often be "linked" to the other books in that day's newsletter since readers will pick up multiple titles in different genres at once. The shift in also boughts following a BookBub tends to sort itself out after a month or two; in any event, BookBub Featured Deals are the best promotional tool in the business, so it's worth enduring any temporary and minor confusion of the Amazon algos (should it occur).

This is what it looks like when your targeting is correct and you've trained the data monster well (this is for a dystopian/post-apocalyptic book):

And this is what it looks when the targeting is a bit off for an urban fantasy book (though not completely in this case):

Most of the also boughts are also urban fantasy books, but you can see at #4 we have a self-help title. This occasionally happens when you use a lot of promo sites (which I have for this book). In this case, I wouldn't be worried; the other books are supernatural/urban fantasy related, which suggests Amazon has a pretty good idea of who to recommend my book to.

Note that you're also more likely to see a bit more disparate also boughts for backlist titles (that book was over two years old at the time of the screenshot). This is because Amazon refreshes the also boughts for each title. If your book isn't moving a ton of copies, that can mean that some random sales and downloads during that timeframe can slightly skew the sample. This isn't cause for concern when it comes to backlist; it happens naturally, and your older, unadvertised books typically aren't getting a whole lot of organic recommendations from Amazon, anyway.

And what about *fixing* the targeting if it's gone awry? Simple: run some targeted promotions to the page. This could be your newsletter (i.e., run a deal and send an email to your list) or using pay-per-click ads targeted to your specific audience (say, urban fantasy readers in this case). Or you could select some highly targeted, genre-specific newsletters that serve only specific sub-genres (i.e., a sci-fi/fantasy focused newsletter with an urban fantasy or supernatural suspense sub-genre segment). It can take a dose of a few hundred sales to recalibrate Amazon's algorithms to get your book recommended to the right people again. So it's generally better to get this right from the beginning.

NOT A SILVER BULLET

All this talk about algorithms may be conjuring up visions in your mind's eye of riding Amazon's recommendations straight to El Dorado on a cyborg thoroughbred fueled by NOS.

Sadly, I'm here to temper expectations a bit. Yes, leveraging the algorithms to your advantage is critical to maxing out your marketing efforts. But the gains are mostly modest. Remember, this bookselling game is one of compounding and brick-by-brick increases. This is merely a piece of your marketing toolkit.

Effective? Yes.

But still just a piece. Relying solely on the algorithms to lead you to the promised land of sales is not recommended.

It's much harder to get sticky in 2020 than it was even two or three years ago. As mentioned earlier, Amazon's algorithms like *new* content (primarily because people like new content—again, remember that their core focus is customer satisfaction). As such, their algorithms reward new books with visibility boosts. Colloquially, these are referred to as the 30/60/90 day cliffs. A lot of your book's new release mojo wears off after 30 days (when it's no longer eligible for the Hot New Release lists, among other on-site placements). This dips a bit further after 60 days, before the rest vanishes after 90 days.

Practically speaking, this makes it harder for an even four or five month old book to keep riding high in the charts. Amazon's algos just don't shower these "older" books with the same love as new titles.

Indeed, most promo runs see books rocket up the charts, only to crash back into the ranking cellar like they've got lead strapped to their ankles— even when you design them with Amazon's algos in mind. Thus, if you're building your marketing strategy around perpetual organic sales, that has unfortunately become much less viable. I have easily dropped a healthy five-figures in ill-advised marketing spend in pursuit of this white whale.

This comes back to strategy. Promotion is a critical part of your marketing mix. But you must consider how every promotion brings you closer to your **core objective**.

I searched for a silver bullet for years. I found a couple bronze ones, but they never had the firepower I truly sought. That's because the key ingredient to igniting the algos is a **rabid group of fans** (i.e., your newsletter and other loyal readers). No ad spend or marketing blitz can compete with the power of word of mouth and a few hundred (or thousand) dedicated readers who will buy your book during launch week.

While it does you no harm to optimize your marketing efforts for Amazon's algorithms, and I *certainly* recommend you do so, this is *not* a replacement for the difficult business of finding your fans. **Your core marketing focus should always be building your own fan base**. This is a pain in the ass, because it demands *years* of patience. The alternative—an instant vault up the charts, and subsequent full-time authordom—is alluring. But chasing rank or burning massive piles of cash as a loss-leader to prod the algos is often a fool's errand.

I'M WIDE—WHAT ABOUT OTHER RETAILERS?

We touched on this in the beginning: Amazon has essentially staked their business on developing automated merchandising technology that recommends readers *exactly* the kind of books they like. This has been wildly successful for them by any measure. Other retailers, however, work on a much more old-school model: retailer-curated merchandising.

If you enter a brick and mortar bookstore like Barnes & Noble, you'll find books on the front table, on end cap displays (the little racks at the start/end of aisles), and in other prominent locations. A handful of these will be top-selling books, but the majority will be either hand-picked by the staff *or*, more likely, paid to be placed there by the publisher. The front table is valuable real estate—every customer who enters the store must pass by it. As such, publishers pay good money for their hottest books to be stocked in prominent locations.

Similarly, certain merchandising placements on retailers (even Amazon) are purchased by large publishers.

However, there is hope for smaller indies. Other retailers have teams that curate hand-picked selections featured prominently on their site: promotions like First in Free, exclusives to that retailer (for example, making a pre-order exclusive to that retailer), and other manually organized offerings. If you have a rep at one of the other retailers, you can petition them directly to be included in these merchandising opportunities. But the rep-less among us (like myself) aren't out in the cold. If you submit via Draft-

2Digital, you can email D2D's team and ask them if there are any merchandising opportunities available. They can sometimes get you included in these various promotions.

And if you're direct to these sites, you can just cold email the support staff. Yes, they might say no. And yes, as an introvert myself, I understand that the thought of doing so might be on par with swallowing a handful of pine cones. But make them an appealing offer, and you can get an actual human to take notice. It only takes a minute or two, and there's no downside (or cost) to you. And the rewards can be *substantial,* keeping you selling for weeks or months after the promotions are over.

APPLICATION: PROMO STACKING

We've talked about sales rank and training Amazon's data monster. But, if you've been following along, you probably have a question: how do I get enough sales to rank high and trigger Amazon's automatic recommendations? If you've looked at the Top 20 or Top 50 of most sub-genres, you need at least 50 – 100 sales in a single day to crack that visibility threshold. That can be a tough mountain to climb, even for a mid-list author.

Subsequently, one of the most powerful tools in your marketing arsenal is **promo stacking**.

This term originally applied to using multiple promo sites to create a large boost in sales. Here, however, I'll use it to describe combining many separate traffic sources—whether they be promo sites or PPC ads—to push your book higher up the charts. This "stack" is spread over multiple days. Normally, 1 + 1 = 2; but with a promo stack, 1 + 1 = 11.

Or it can, with a little luck and some planning.

We know from our discussion of the algorithms that they reward sales volume and velocity. They also reward consistency. But there's a balance that must be struck between these factors, for a series of sales that looks like this:

8 - 7 - 3 - 10 - 5 - 4 - 3 - 8 - 5 - 2 - 9

will be less effective than:

15 - 16 - 19 - 22

The first scenario might be relatively consistent, but won't get you near any charts if your sub-genre is competitive. And it probably won't trip Amazon's automated recommendations, either.

To maximize your chances of getting the algorithms behind your book, you must hit **critical mass** with sales. No one knows what the exact tipping point is for Amazon to send out merchandising emails and start pushing your book to buyers. But we do know they reward books that are already selling—and their recommendation mechanisms favor books that are selling *big*.

Despite its intricate nature, Amazon's AI is still a baby mammoth that, while sophisticated, responds best to brute force. It likes sales. And it likes a lot of them in a short period of time (3 – 10 days; again, as mentioned before, I prefer 5 – 7 days for launches and promos).

But *getting* a lot of sales in a short period is difficult for authors. Hence the promo stack:

1. Day 1: promo site 1 + promo site 2 + promo site 3 + promo site 4
2. Day 2: first part of personal newsletter + $10 PPC campaign
3. Day 3: second, larger part of personal newsletter + $20 PPC campaign
4. Day 4: $40 PPC campaign + five additional newsletter sites

5. Day 5: $80 PPC campaign + six additional newsletter sites + last chance email to your newsletter.

This is not a prescribed order—your traffic sources and stack will differ. It is merely an illustration of how you can combine and spread out multiple traffic sources to harness the power of Amazon's algorithms. Whereas each individual source by itself might have only generated ten or fifteen sales, in tandem, they form a powerful push.

Of course, like fishing for bass, there's no guarantee the AI will bite. But the tastier the bait, the higher your chances.

And sales are the tastiest bait of all.

Done correctly, each element of the stack adds up to more than the sum of its parts due to tripping Amazon's charts + automated recommendations. So you might get 50 sales from the 4 promos on Day 1—but this turns into 65, because you hit the Top 20 of your genre and got additional organic traffic for free.

Simple, but super effective.

KEY TAKEAWAYS

- Amazon's algorithms are the most powerful bookselling force on the planet.
- Amazon, unlike other retailers, primarily uses automated merchandising based on customer data.
- These automated recommendations appear all over the site in places like the also-boughts, bestseller lists, and pop lists, as well as in emails.

- Understanding how the algorithms fuel these recommendations can massively amplify the rest of your marketing efforts.
- Despite the algos' power, they aren't a magic bullet. Building a career is primarily about building your reader base brick-by-brick.
- The algos are also unpredictable, even if you understand the principles and follow them perfectly.
- The recommendations focus on three primary factors: sales volume & velocity (most important), sales consistency, and a tight sample of people purchasing your book.
- They also look at newness and the book's sales history.
- When scheduling your promos, you want to hit critical sales volume mass.
- Always backload your strongest traffic sources to end promos strong and set your marketing efforts up to generate a gradually increasing sales curve.
- Target people who read your genre/sub-genre to get Amazon to promote your book to readers who match a similar profile in its customer base
- You can recalibrate Amazon's targeting if you accidentally corrupt the data sample by getting a few hundred sales from readers in your sub-genre.
- Having a day where your numbers don't move up isn't a death knell when you're trying to get sticky. General upward trend is the idea, not perfection.
- You can promo stack your various traffic sources (newsletter, social media, promo sites, PPC, etc.) together to produce the necessary sales volume and consistency to trigger the algorithms. By combining your traffic in this way, $1 + 1 = 2$; instead, $1 + 1 = 11$.

ACTION EXERCISE

1. Design a promo stack that properly leverages the organic visibility from Amazon's charts + recommendation engine.

SIX

TRAFFIC

It's time to dive deep into how you can start sending all the readers you could possibly want to your book page.

That's right. It's finally time to talk about generating traffic.

First, a little refresher on our Ultimate Book Marketing Formula, which forms the backbone of the guide:

MARKET RESEARCH + 3 TRAFFIC SOURCES + PRO COVERS + GREAT BLURBS + NEWSLETTER + 4-6 NOVELS PER YEAR

CONSISTENTLY FOR 3-5 YEARS

FULL-TIME AUTHOR

Traffic is the first thing that most people think of when the word *marketing* flashes through their mind.

Visibility.

Eyeballs.

Promotion.

Advertising.

Call it whatever you want; getting potential readers *to* your book page kicks off our traffic-conversion-profit analysis marketing cycle. Remember, **there are only three components to book marketing**: traffic, conversion, and determining whether you made a profit. Traffic is about getting people to the book page; conversion is about convincing these people to buy (and, later, converting them into fans by getting them to join your email list); turn a profit doing this and you can continue reinvesting in your business. Many authors falter in the traffic-generation phase, wondering how they'll ever get potential readers to their book page. Fear not: this is far simpler than it first appears. We'll cover a number of ways to generate traffic, from free methods to paid advertising. By the end, you'll have more traffic sources than you could ever need (or want, perhaps).

In fact, that's where we'll begin: by explaining why effectively marketing your books requires *limiting* your traffic sources.

TRAFFIC: WHY ONLY THREE SOURCES?

This guide's core principle is the 80/20 rule. Always keep in mind that a few key factors drive the majority of the results. Most of what we do doesn't move the needle. Worse, some tasks are outright moving us in the *wrong* direction. By cutting these detrimental activities out of our workday entirely, our results will dramatically improve, even if we do nothing with that newfound time except watch Netflix.

The counterintuitive truth of trying to do *everything* is that we often end up with less than nothing. In a world of endless noise and distraction, narrowing your focus produces massive dividends. This is largely because marketing is a latticework of skills and subskills that demand time to master. The number of areas in which one can truly excel are limited by time. The odds of producing excess value in 10 or 15 disparate marketing areas is zero. But the odds of producing *negative* value by dabbling in many of these areas is high, simply because marketing is competitive. In an ecosystem like Facebook, your ads compete against other people's. If your ads suck, they cost more.

Diverting resources away from your strengths into areas that are liabilities is a losing proposition. Framed as an old proverb: **chase two rabbits, catch none.**

The idea here is *not* to strictly adhere to the concept of "three." You might have four or five traffic sources—or two (relying on one puts you in a precarious position, and is not recommended). Limiting it to three merely encourages careful reflection and analysis. The underlying principle here is to identify what *actually* works, then invest more of your resources there.

TRAFFIC SOURCES

Here's a basic overview of traffic sources, in no particular order. We'll analyze these options in a moment. But right off the bat you can see that your main concern is *picking* what will work, rather than generating ideas.

And for those who might dispute the classifications, I'm just trying to keep things organized; some sources don't slot neatly into a single category.

For now, just get a feel for **all the available options**:

- **Organic**: retailer SEO (e.g., Amazon keywords and categories), retailers' recommendation algorithms, word of mouth
- **Paid newsletter promotion**: BookBub, Robin Reads, etc.
- **Pay-per-click (PPC) ads**: Amazon Ads, Facebook Ads, BookBub Ads, Google Ads, Twitter Ads, YouTube, Goodreads, Pinterest
- **Merchandising**: retailer "first in free" or "series starter" promotions—used on Apple Books, Kobo, and Nook
- **Networking**: cross-author promos, newsletter swaps, multi-author boxed sets, cover reveals
- **Content marketing**: SEO, blogging, guest posting, podcasting
- **Traditional publishing**: publishing stories in industry mags (i.e., *Analog*), trad-pub contracts
- **PR & media coverage**: newspapers, print features, on-air interviews
- **In-person events**: book fairs, industry events, fan conventions, book signings
- **Social Media**: Facebook (e.g., Facebook author pages, groups, takeovers, launch parties), Twitter, Instagram, Pinterest, Goodreads, BookBub, forums
- **Your newsletter**

Overwhelmed yet? See why we're **paring this list down to three traffic sources and your newsletter?** As a simple math exercise, let's say you dedicated 10 minutes daily to each. Just for the overarching categories alone that would be **100+ minutes a day, likely well beyond the time you currently allocate to mar-**

keting. But let's go further: 10 min/ea.; I'll even cut the crappier options, like Goodreads PPC ads.

That's 240+ minutes a day (four *hours*). And, at ten minutes each, you're *barely* getting your toe wet.

I consider each of these broad categories one source. Thus, if I employed PPC, promo sites, and social media, I'd have my three sources. Then, within each broad category, I'd have to be extremely selective about what I chose to do. It's not possible to use Twitter, Facebook, Pinterest, and Instagram all effectively and still write books and manage your other sources. Nor is it possible to manage PPC ads well on nine different platforms at once. Anyone claiming otherwise is kidding themselves.

So if we ever want to develop actual competence—and generate real visibility—we need to start cutting options. Fast.

But before we start chopping, we need to figure out what works for us.

FINDING WHICH TRAFFIC SOURCES WORK FOR YOU

If you're already overwhelmed by marketing, you skimmed that list and probably had a brain aneurysm. What's best? How much does it cost? Will it work for my book? But it didn't work for this other book...can I risk it?

Slow down.

At the beginning, you need to try things before you can cull the list. **The main way to know what works for you is to test.**

You can read tons of guides, take a half dozen courses, ask every author you can think of...but ultimately, you'll have to take the plunge and start trying things on your own books.

This is an approach I call shotgun, then narrow: **go broad before you focus things down**. That means, at least at the start, you'll have more than three traffic sources. **To be clear, this does not mean trying three hundred things at once.** Nor does it mean throwing cash around willy-nilly. We must still delve deep enough to tell whether something works, which inevitably demands time.

Remember: There are many places to find readers. **More sources, in fact, than you could hope to master in a lifetime.** Unlike most other guides, however, we're not looking for just *anything* that can generate traffic.

We're searching for the best sources of readers possible. This idea seems obvious, but it's radical enough to make some people pause and say, *but wait a second. I've been struggling for months, maybe years. I don't deserve the best. I can't ask for the best. I'll just settle for anything. And what if I miss finding those three readers I could've reached on another platform?*

If this is you, cut the shit. We're here to make money. Whatever your hang-ups about narrowing your focus, address them. If you've read the previous sections, you should have a general understanding of your target audience and where you might be able to find them. If not, then performing that market research will help. Once you have an idea of who your audience might be, start experimenting with 5 – 10 promising sources.

After you have sufficient data, narrow your traffic list via the following method:

1. **Analyze your records.** How many sales did you get when you messaged your Twitter peeps? Posted on that ancient weapon forum? Sent out your newsletter? **Double down on what's driving the bulk of your sales.**

2. **Test more things.** What happens when I remove a promo site? What happens when I stop messaging my Twitter peeps/doing a cover reveal/only post on Facebook once a day? Does the world implode? What happens if I only advertise during launches and do minimal marketing otherwise? What happens if I double my Facebook spend? What happens if I email my list every week instead of every month? These are just sample ideas to get you thinking, *not* suggestions. You should develop ones that are relevant to your business.

3. **Different books have different responses to different traffic sources.** Fairly obvious, but Facebook Ads might be a total dud for Series A, whereas they might generate thousands of dollars in profit for Series B. Yes, this happens even if both series are by the same author, in the same subgenre. Don't be afraid to experiment.

You can narrow your focus immediately **by following my Top 5 Traffic Sources for Fiction Writers.** Even if you want to do your own rigorous analysis (which I wholeheartedly recommend) later, these are a good starting point.

TOP 5 TRAFFIC SOURCES FOR FICTION WRITERS

(1 + 2) **Your organic newsletter and Amazon's recommendation engine**. If you have absolutely no time for marketing, focus on these two items and you *will* see results. They're *that* powerful; **harnessing them effectively is critical to your overall success**. For those who are "wide" (have their books on all retailers), you'll

also need to understand **merchandising**; that's a big part of how retailers like Apple Books push titles.

Properly leveraging Amazon's algos doesn't demand additional time once you understand how they work, and building your mailing list is a separate beast that gets its own section in this guide. They are separate from our three core traffic sources.

(3) **Pay-per-click (PPC) Ads:** the big three you'll be using are Facebook Ads, Amazon Ads, and BookBub Ads. PPC ads can be a *huge* money pit, and they aren't effective unless you have $250+/mo that you're willing to learn with over a few months (i.e., lose). PPC requires trial and error and constant monitoring, as winning ads eventually fatigue and turn into losers. However, PPC offers unlimited traffic potential and upside, since you can spend $5/day or $5,000. Perhaps most importantly, PPC ads are **highly targeted.** Recall from our discussion regarding the algorithms in the previous section that we don't just want three sources of traffic; we want **three *targeted* sources of traffic.**

For the right books at the right point in your career, PPC ads can push you to the next level. But for most authors, spending a lot of money here will not produce big returns. These ads are often portrayed as a magic bullet (both in the book industry and for other internet products). The truth is, these platforms are highly competitive, have sharp learning curves, and often don't produce a profit. You need a sizable backlist (5 books minimum, 10 – 20 being preferable), a series (or two) with solid sellthrough, excellent branding (blurbs/covers), and enough available cash on hand to not worry about losing it.

(4) **Paid newsletter promotions**: easy to use, and solid ROI when used for the right series in the right way. A BookBub Featured Deal in particular can be very lucrative. Check out my free curated list of current top sites (**nicholaserik.com/promo-sites**).

(5) **Your choice from the remaining options.**

Why do I prefer paid traffic? Simple: it's controllable, available on demand, and quickly scalable. Facebook will always accept your dollars. Even if you have a great relationship with another author, they might not mention your new book to their fans. And there's no way of forcing them to do so. Let me repeat: Facebook will always take your dollars—even if you're starting out and don't know a soul in this game. With a $100/day budget, you can reach *thousands* of highly targeted potential readers a day. Relationships, by contrast, take months, if not years to build.

If you can't invest a few hundred dollars a month in your business right now, replace the PPC ads and paid newsletter promotions with free alternatives or scale back to what you *can* afford.

To fill out that third slot—and for alternatives to PPC and promo sites, should those prove not to be a fit for your books— here's a more in-depth rundown of the other options from our traffic sources list.

Note that if you're already a part-time or full-time author and have a good grasp on where to find traffic, you may already know most of this information. Feel free to skip ahead to the next section on promotional strategies if you find these overviews too basic.

PROMO SITES

The idea behind promotional sites is simple: the site gathers reader emails (or social media fans) from people interested in hearing about discounted eBooks. You pay the site to advertise your book to their list of readers in your genre (say, mystery or fantasy). Running an ad with a promo site requires your book to be discounted to $0.99 or free (some sites offer the option to advertise at $1.99/$2.99, but this isn't recommended; the readers who sign up for these newsletters do so to receive deals on deeply discounted books).

Examples include BookBub, Robin Reads, and Booksends. There are dozens of promo sites. Most of them aren't worth your time to submit to, let alone the fee. A curated, consistently updated list of recommended sites is available on my site (**nicholaserik.com/promo-sites**).

As mentioned, promo sites have a remarkably simple learning curve: just fill out a form, pay the fee, and your book will be sent out to thousands (or even hundreds of thousands) of readers in your selected genre. But this comes with caveats: top performing promo sites are competitive. BookBub Featured Deals, while insanely powerful, are so competitive that they accept less than 20% of submissions (according to their official word on the matter; I'd say it's more likely to be less than 10%). Some of the other top promo sites, while nowhere near as powerful as BookBub, are booked weeks or a couple months in advance. And, since indies have demonstrated extreme willingness to spend advertising dollars, a number of totally ineffective promo sites have cropped up that charge a ton of money and produce few sales in return.

Three things to keep in mind when evaluating promo sites:

- The total # of newsletter subscribers means very little. An unengaged list of 100,000 will sell far fewer books than an ultra-engaged, tight genre list of 20,000.
- Social media #s are useless. Most of these likes/followers are unengaged.

- Few sites outside of BookBub will net you a positive return on the advertised book alone. This is because it's hard to sell enough copies at $0.99 (which only makes you $0.35 in royalties) to cover the ad cost. And, if you're giving a book away for free, obviously you need additional titles in that series to make things profitable. Thus, you'll need a series with strong sellthrough (readers purchasing Books 2, 3, 4, etc. after picking up Book 1) to generate positive revenue from most promo sites. If you don't have a series (i.e., you write standalones), or your series has poor sell-through, you're better off not spending a bunch of money on advertising

One final, critical note: **don't use a promo site more than once every six months on a given title**. The more frequently you promote a book via promo sites, the lower bang for your promo dollar—using a promo site again has severely diminishing returns (this applies to everything besides BookBub, where the results are often steady or drop only modestly for a second run). For most promo sites, a second run with a service will often net 50% or fewer sales/downloads versus the first use. This also means that you want to be strategic about when you use that first promo blast on a title, since it'll be the most powerful.

PAY-PER-CLICK (PPC)

Pay-per-click is a vast, complicated topic that's difficult to cover with text alone, given the complexity of the various platforms. Further, each platform changes frequently that hot tips and tricks will be useless tomorrow. PPC platforms function like a competitive marketplace, a la the stock market. Pricing inefficiencies and edges are smoothed out of the market as more participants become aware of them.

Currently, these are the big three PPC platforms that you'll use:

1. Facebook Ads
2. Amazon Ads
3. BookBub PPC (note: these ads are different than their famous "Featured Deals"; these ads appear at the bottom of the daily BookBub emails and on the BookBub.com site)

A sampling of the other platforms available:

- Instagram (you actually advertise to Instagram via Facebook)
- Pinterest
- Reddit
- Google Ads

I'd focus on the big three (adding Instagram is a simple matter of checking a box on Facebook if you'd like to throw it into the mix). Goodreads also offers PPC advertising, but the general consensus is that it's totally worthless.

Turning a profit with PPC ads is hard; they are *not* a magic bullet. These platforms are still insanely useful, but you must be careful. Start with small amounts of money that you can afford to lose.

Four general principles that apply to all platforms:

- **Test a lot**. This is the "secret" to PPC: constantly test different ad objectives, different images, different ad copy, different audiences, different regions, and so forth. When you're testing, expect a maximum of 1 in 10 or 1 in 20 ads to be winners. Many will be terrible. With practice, you may be able to get this up to 1 in 5 (i.e., a 20% hit rate—the 80/20 rule in real-life action).

- **This is about profit**. Not rank. Not CPC. *Money in your pocket*. Thus, you want to focus on *conversion*—the number of sales the ads are producing. Reads are important, too, but it's very hard to nail down whether Ad A is producing 10 reads or 2,000 per day. The simplest method is to focus on your daily or weekly profit numbers (royalties – ad expenses).

- **When you find a winner, ride it for all its worth**. The key to success is quickly eliminating your losers, so they don't suck up a bunch of cash.

- **Move fast**. This applies to everything in marketing and publishing. The faster you make ads, test them, analyze the results, and then make the necessary adjustments, the faster you can improve. Too many authors get bogged down in analysis paralysis, endlessly deliberating about whether an ad, book concept, blurb, price, etc. is the right choice. You need to get actual *data* by testing, then make changes. Get things to 90% quality. I call this A- level. Sometimes you get an A; other times you get a B+. But quality never suffers dramatically, and your time investment to get to 90% is probably 10x – 100x faster than what it takes to try to reach perfection. Which doesn't exist in the real-world, anyway.

And again, to reiterate: **test, test, test**. Most of your ads and audiences will *not* be successful. This isn't an indication that you suck at PPC. It's to be expected. Keep testing.

Since you'll need to test constantly, which does cost money, I recommend that you only start with PPC if you have $250/mo you're willing to spend as an educational endeavor. And, in the beginning, you won't get that back—this is tuition, so make sure it's money you can lose without any concern (*not* money you're charging to your credit card or borrowing). However, I think this "risk" is worth it, since PPC offers you a nearly unlimited number of customers, and control over your own marketing destiny if you crack the code.

But *don't* feel that you need to leap into the deep end right from the jump. If you want to experiment, start with $5 – $10 a day rather than hundreds. When you're ready to take the next step, I offer a comprehensive course on Facebook, Amazon, and BookBub Ads at **nicholaserik.com/ads** that covers everything from the fundamentals to advanced tactics.

MERCHANDISING, NETWORKING, CONTENT MARKETING, AND SOCIAL MEDIA

These all fall under a similar banner for two reasons: they're free, and they all rely on relationships with other people. This means that they're less within your direct control and often slower to grow than other avenues of promotion. **This does not mean they cannot be effective**. If you like interacting with people more than you like tweaking Facebook Ads, then these can be far more fruitful promotional avenues for you.

MERCHANDISING

Merchandising is controlled by the retailers. Those hardcovers face out on the front table at the local Barnes & Noble? A prime example of merchandising: publishers pay a premium for that space. While prominent print placement is a pipe dream for indies, you can acquire similar front-of-the-store, highly visible merchandising space on retailers' websites for your eBooks.

Amazon's imprint books (e.g., 47 North, Thomas and Mercer, and Montlake Romance) often receive prominent merchandising. The most obvious example is their First Reads program, which allows Prime subscribers to borrow one of six books on offer that month. This almost always vaults all six of the books included into the Top 100 of the entire store (with some titles hitting the Top 10, and even #1). Almost all of Amazon's best merchandising opportunities are reserved for their imprint authors (or Big 6 books). However, indies with Kindle reps can be offered various merchandising opportunities. How do you get a rep? Sell well.

Getting merchandising opportunities on non-Amazon retailers is mostly about selling well enough to attract a rep's attention on that specific retailer. If you've been exclusive to Amazon and have an impressive sales record, you can also approach a retailer to request a rep—and see what perks they'll offer for bringing your books wide.

Even if you don't have a history of strong sales (on Amazon or any other platform) you can still reach out to see if you're eligible for any special promotions. It's free to ask, and the worst thing that can happen is they say no.

For Kobo specifically, if you go direct (i.e. not through an aggregator), you'll have access to their promotions tab. Here, you can apply for various upcoming (paid) promotions on the

Kobo site. These can help get your books moving on Kobo and I recommend that you apply regularly for these (when it makes sense to do so based on your marketing strategy).

If you're publishing to these retailers via the aggregator Draft-2Digital (**draft2digital.com**) you can still be considered for merchandising. Simply email Draft2Digital support and ask if your titles are eligible for any current merchandising opportunities. If you have a permafree and a series of books, you can usually get placement in a first in free promotion. One such promo on Apple Books pushed about 1,000 free copies of a title with a **much higher sellthrough rate** than a typical promotion site.

How to: ask D2D what genres they're currently looking to promote via merchandising. Outline your sales record, the books in your series, and what offers you might be open to. For example, Apple Books sometimes offers indies merchandising placement in exchange for an exclusive pre-order period.

NETWORKING

Networking with your fellow authors is not only a good way to make like-minded friends who can commiserate about arcane concepts like fluctuating Kindle Unlimited payouts, but also offers a way to pool your resources for enhanced firepower. Examples include:

1. **Multi-author boxed sets**: a group of authors (usually 10 – 20) each contribute a full-length novel to a themed, limited time offer boxed set available for a discounted price. E.g., 10 urban fantasy novels or 10 contemporary romance novels with spice. Usually sold at $0.99 or free as a lead-in to

the participating authors' work. Another riff on this is an anthology of new, exclusive stories/novellas, where each author contributes a story set in the world of their existing series.

2. **Co-authoring**: a number of popular authors team up with co-authors to write new series volumes, spinoffs, or entirely new IP. This can increase your production speed and expand your backlist considerably. Typically only works once you have an existing fan base (a great trad pub example is the immortal Clive Cussler); successful indie examples include Michael Anderle and Shayne Silvers.

3. **Collaborative series**: a single pen name/series, with each book written by different authors. An example is the Veil Nights series by Rowan Casey.

4. **Newsletter/social media swaps**: you and another author agree to promote your new releases to each other's readers on certain dates. Only works for authors in the same genre/sub-genre. Be sure you've set expectations with your newsletter subscribers beforehand about what type of emails you'll send, otherwise this could be viewed as spam. Additionally, if you're constantly sending your readers uncurated recommendations, this is a good way of burning out your organic list.

5. **Cross author promos**: a bunch of authors come together, each offering a free or $0.99 book; everyone then shares with their mailing list to generate sales or mailing list signups. These can build your list rapidly, but they can also burn out your organic list by sharing them with dozens of other authors, so proceed with caution. Many of these are shared in private groups; for public lists, visit BookFunnel and StoryOrigin's lists of current promotional opportunities.

6. **Cover reveals and blog tours**: often done together, but can also be used separately. Can be coupled with an author interview, a swag giveaway (bookmarks, tote bags, post cards, signed paperbacks, etc.), or an Amazon Gift Card/ Kindle. Leveraging relationships you've formed with other authors helps maximize the reach. Primarily used in romance, but cover reveals and blog tours are occasionally seen in other genres. You can pay an established company to organize a blog tour, or you can contact blog owners/ fellow authors to organize one yourself.

7. **Making friends**. Being a real human being and interacting with other authors in your genre can be hugely beneficial to your career. One single email blast from a top author in your genre (i.e., an "influencer") can put your book on the map and change your life. However, trying to make friends solely for the purpose of exploiting their platform is sociopathic and ill-advised, as this behavior tends to be irritatingly transparent. Be helpful, do favors, read their books (if you're a fan), and be a positive force in the community. Don't expect anything in return, because you often won't get it—and if you do, the dividends probably won't be seen for many years.

CONTENT MARKETING AND SEO

Content marketing is effective for building a non-fiction readership. In fact, it takes over #4 on the Top 5 list for non-fiction peeps, knocking off promo sites. I've built most of my non-fiction readership through content marketing, with minimal paid advertising. **However, it's important to mention that this audience**

does not cross over to my fiction. For fiction authors, activities like blogging, guest posting, and podcasting (either your own, or appearing as a guest) are ineffective ways to reach new readers. These endeavors might be fun, but they're also time consuming; your podcast that gets 50 downloads a month isn't helping you unless you're using it as a networking vehicle to make friends with folks in your sub-genre.

Technically **website SEO** (search engine optimization) is its own beast, but it's so tightly knit with content marketing (in many cases) that I've placed it under the same umbrella. Website SEO is a waste of your precious time as a fiction author. Your website is an important hub for your brand, but organic search traffic is not the objective here. The chance of appearing on the first page of Google for, say, "thriller novels," is abysmally low.

SOCIAL MEDIA

We're saving the best for last in **social media.**

To put it bluntly, I know little about social media, and use it rarely. I'm not going to regale you with a rewarmed summary of a crappy blog post imploring that you **act like a real person** and **make it about readers.** I have no idea if those things are true, but they sound true-ish. Of course, I only mention them to make a point: 99% of social media tips are pulled out of someone's ass, rather than fact tested.

What I will say is this.

Most authors use social media so poorly that simply abstaining would *massively* increase their ROI. Many are fooled by the "free" price tag, failing to recognize that their time has value. If you have the choice of spending one hour on social media and one hour writing, the new words are going to win every time.

But I would be remiss if I claimed social media can't be used effectively. It can. Despite this most authors would probably be better served dropping it almost entirely, save for the occasional post to their Facebook Page about their latest release. I'd also consider checking out BookBub; they're building out their social platform into something that resembles a modernized Goodreads. You can recommend books to your followers extremely easily. This is a good way of connecting with your core audience (readers) without it becoming a huge time sink.

Finally, a monthly newsletter is great for building engagement with your core fans. This takes all of fifteen to thirty minutes, but is far more powerful than a few stale memes occasionally tossed up on your Facebook page.

Assorted social media observations:

- **Master one instead of being everywhere**. There's an obsession with signing up for every social media site in existence, then using none of them...or using them all poorly. Focus on one; Facebook is probably the best bet for most authors, because it's gigantic, it's not going away, and your readers are likely here. If you don't like Facebook, then consider your other options; there are plenty to choose from.
- **Each platform has its own flavor and rules**. Blasting the same message out to fifteen different platforms seems like a time saver, but it's dumb. Not only does receiving an identical message with no customization on three platforms have a decidedly spammy feel for those following you everywhere, it's simply ineffective. Each platform has different unwritten rules of audience engagement, as well as different

ways of generating visibility (hashtags etc.). **What's important to Instagram junkies is not necessarily of interest to Twitter addicts**. By crafting a generic message, you fail to leverage the unique features that will make you stand out amidst a maelstrom of content.

- **A note on reach (and in general)**. Visibility rules change frequently. Facebook has systematically nerfed the organic reach of pages; now you must pay to "boost" posts if you'd like for more than a handful of your followers to see them. This speaks to a larger problem: Since you don't run social media, you don't make the rules. They can revoke your privileges or change the contract at any time. Their land, their rules. Further, the land in this analogy can be seized by creditors and disappear entirely. Remember Myspace? It's now a desert filled with tumbleweeds. Or, as deserts are called in internet parlance: a portal site.

- Estimates vary, **but a mailing list subscriber is worth anywhere from 20x to 50x as much as a like or follow**. As such, I prefer to spend my limited energy building my newsletter. It's more effective, and I completely control it.

TRADITIONAL PUBLISHING

This guide's focus is on indie publishing, but many indies are also traditionally published (known as "hybrids") or actively submitting to such outlets.

In the interest of full disclosure, I should mention that I've never submitted a manuscript to either a trad publisher or an industry magazine, so this information is based on other sources. I *have* worked with an author whose book was picked up by an

Amazon imprint, so I have first-hand knowledge of the general process.

These can be a source of traffic as well; if you get a traditional deal, then your book publisher will throw some marketing weight behind the release.

Right? Kind of. Let's break it down.

Publishing Stories in Industry Magazines

Single page spreads in short story genre magazines like *Analog* cost hundreds, if not thousands of dollars. Getting your multi-page short story published, then, is like receiving thousands in free advertising—plus, *you* get paid. If the story ties into a series of yours, even better. Of course, the relative "sellthrough" will be low, as readers have to jump from your story to a computer to find more of your work. But if you're targeting a specific genre (sci-fi, fantasy, etc.), then short story magazines offer a nice revenue stream and a way to attract new, relevant readers into the fold.

Keep in mind that quality publications like *Analog* are highly competitive, so it might take many submissions before you get accepted. This demands a lot of time for (likely) modest returns.

Publishing via Amazon's Imprints

Amazon generally picks up indie authors already selling well, so this is kind of a chicken-egg situation. You can also submit directly to their imprints, but you need an agent. But having one of your titles republished by their imprints—or working on a new series for them—is a potentially career changing opportunity. Not only do Amazon's imprints offer competitive contracts and royalty rates, they also can tap into Amazon's best merchandising capabilities. Stuff like $2 Kindle Deals, prominent banners for new releases and First Reads—most of the really premium merchandising space is reserved for Amazon imprint titles (or trad pubs). Of course, 99% of the Amazon published books don't get the supernova merchandising, so temper your expectations. Plenty of APub titles dwell in the Amazon ranking cellar; landing a publishing contract with one of their imprints is nowhere close to a magic bullet. Still, if they come knocking, any offer is worth serious consideration, as it has major potential upside.

PUBLISHING VIA A TRADITIONAL PUBLISHER

A common misconception is that Big 5 publishers do a lot of marketing for you. This is true—if you're fortunate enough to get a big advance. The stories from midlist or first time authors are much more sobering, however. For these folks, the publisher generally throws the book out there, does a couple of vaguely marketing-related things, and expects the author to perform the bulk of the heavy lifting. This varies from publisher to publisher and author to author, so there's no telling exactly *what* experience you'll have. But expecting a traditionally published book to raise your indie boat is wishful thinking, unless the publisher wants to make your book a tentpole of its publishing schedule.

While this is a complex subject, the general idea is this: **if you're pursuing a hybrid publishing route, you should still expect to do the bulk of your own marketing**. Unless you get struck by lightning (a Kindle First Reads selection, for example), the spillover from your trad pub books to your indie backlist will likely be modest.

MEDIA COVERAGE

I've never been featured in traditional media, so I can't tell you how to accomplish this particular feat, nor what to expect. Consider this information sourced from others, then. That being said, for an indie fiction author, this type of press often has limited direct value for selling books, even if you get featured in a popular and well-respected venue like the *New York Times*.

Building up your media credentials, however, can have other perks. It can open doors if you're a non-fiction author, and works great as social proof on your site (you've surely seen "as featured in..." logos around the web). Such credentials are important in non-fiction, where a credit in, say, the *Wall Street Journal* can "verify" to potential readers/clients that you're an authority in your field. However, these opportunities usually only come about when you have done something of note. It is far easier to receive media coverage once you're selling well or have an interesting story to tell (e.g., Mark Dawson, Russell Blake, or Hugh Howey) than if you're just starting out. The *NYT* is not looking for a story on the upstart indie writer who is struggling to sell their book.

Further, it seems that the increase in sales one receives from traditional media coverage is relatively modest (perhaps even nonexistent). This is unsurprising, since someone has to *read* an article, go to their computer, remember your name, and then finally click purchase. Or, if they hear you on the radio, they need to remember your name for the rest of their commute and then still be inclined to purchase your work upon finally rolling into the driveway.

Thus, I think it's best to put accumulating media credits in the same bin as getting your "letters" (i.e., being a *New York Times* Bestseller) or getting a favorable review from, say, *Publisher's Weekly*. Nice things to have in your back pocket, sure, but hiring a PR specialist or doing loads of gruntwork for years under the incorrect assumption that a high visibility media appearance will make your fiction career is a fantasy. Having hit the *USA Today Bestseller* list, I can attest that the returns have been vanishingly small (if they've produced any effect at all).

Indeed, 99.9% of the bestselling indie authors have zero traditional media credits, letters, or professional reviews of any kind. And those indies who have been featured did not *build* their platforms upon these appearances; these interviews came as a *result* of their wild success. It's worth noting that traditional media tends to be somewhat condescending or dismissive of indie authors. This sentiment is shifting, but many journalists and their publications still remain stuck in a traditional publishing paradigm, where writing not validated by the gatekeepers is considered suspect. This makes sense, given that these outlets are gatekeepers *themselves*, and thus have a vested interest in protecting their turf. So even when you *do* score an appearance, you and your work might not be presented in a favorable light.

For all these reasons, I don't recommend actively pursuing such coverage unless there's a specific reason you need a media credit.

IN-PERSON EVENTS

I haven't been to a book signing or convention, so I can't tell you what to expect. However, if you're hoping for people to cross over and buy your eBook, remember that there are *significant* barriers to them doing so:

1. They need to remember your name.
2. They need to go to the Amazon website.
3. They still need to be interested enough to do #1 and 2 three hours later, when they're tired from walking around and have met 60 other authors.

Hand-selling paperbacks is limited by the number of copies you can bring with you—and how many you're willing to print in advance.

If you're a friendly person, these events can be a fun opportunity to meet like-minded fans and authors. If you're seeking a trad-pub deal, or want to network with authors in your genre, relevant conferences can help you connect with these folks. But unless you're a big-name author getting paid to make a speech or appear on a panel, it's unlikely that fairs, conventions, conferences, and so forth are going to directly move many books.

Other than taking up a substantial chunk of time—perhaps an entire weekend—you'll likely have to pay booth or attendance fees, in addition to travel and lodging expenses. Given printing costs (and transportation), it's going to take a lot of hand-sold paperbacks to make that back.

Thus, for 99.9% of indie authors, in-person events should be considered "vacations" rather than an effective source of promotion.

WRAPPING UP

That about covers the traffic sources available to indie authors. In the interest of not making this guide a million words long—or overwhelming you with information—the points above trended toward the brief. If you pursue any of these avenues, you should expect to do additional research beyond the scope of this more general guide.

Even the lengthier traffic list at the beginning of this guide does not encompass **everything you could possibly do**. Swag (bookmarks, beach towels, postcards, tote bags, stickers), signed paperbacks, banner ads, King Sumo giveaways...you get the picture. Promotion is an endless topic.

It bears repeating: more is not better. It's easy to succumb to shiny object syndrome by chasing each flavor of the month strategy that comes along.

Choosing is difficult for two reasons:

1. **It demands reflection and careful thought**. In a world full of constant distraction, I understand this is a big—and perhaps uncomfortable—ask. But it's necessary and, ultimately, beneficial for sales and your overall sanity.

2. **Gurus claim you have to be everywhere, taking "massive action."** Not multitasking somehow feels "lazy." I assure you that focusing is the exact opposite: it is cognitively demanding and much more intense. You will get far more work done in a lesser amount of time, but it will be *challenging*. However, it will also be satisfying—not least of all because you will see results.

But while humans crave choice, too much also results in massive unhappiness. We are always concerned about missing out—and whether we made the *best* choice.

The panacea is narrowing your focus, and pretending that everything else doesn't exist. Twitter, anthologies, conventions, and trad-pubs are invisible to me. I give them zero minutes of my precious time. They are simply not even on my radar.

You do not want to prematurely narrow your focus before you understand what works for your books, however. **Trial and error** is essential to success. Test things, discard what doesn't work, then **iterate and optimize** what does to hone your skills in that area to a razor's edge. This all takes time; you can't force things into a 90 day challenge or a one year plan. The process takes as long as it takes.

I'm going to keep stressing this, since it's counterintuitive: **take things as slowly as necessary.** If you only have five minutes—or can only concentrate on PPC ads for five minutes before wanting to scream—that's fine. Start small and build up your focus/skills. **By going slow, we actually go fast**.

It's okay to take two months to get something under your belt; **after that, you'll own the skill forever**. It took me over a *year* to understand how to create profitable Facebook Ads. This may seem like too long. But if you plan to write for the next ten or twenty years, this is a drop in the bucket. And competence is empowering—far more so than dabbling amidst a dozen options you don't understand and can't use effectively.

KEY TAKEAWAYS

- There's an almost unlimited number of ways to generate traffic (visibility) as an author.
- Use **trial and error** to narrow your traffic options to **three effective sources** that mesh with your time, personality, and capital constraints. Then **iterate and optimize** to hone your skills.
- **Paid promotional newsletters** like BookBub Featured Deals and Robin Reads and **pay-per-click (PPC) ads** like Facebook and Amazon Ads are both excellent sources of traffic since they're directly controllable and available on demand. **I recommend that 99% of authors use both**, thus taking up the first two traffic slots. The third is up to you. A list of curated promo sites, with links, is available on my site (**nicholaserik.com/promo-sites**).
- **PPC** also has the benefits of being **scalable** (you can spend $5 or $500/day) and **highly targeted** (you can target authors in your specific sub-genre).
- **PPC** is best used when you have a large backlist (5+ books), a series or two with decent sellthrough, and available cash that you can lose without worry. It is not a magic bullet, but for the right books at the right point in your career, it can be exceptionally powerful.
- Certain books and genres will be better fits for different options; shotgun, then narrow according to your results.
- Tracking results is vital to knowing which traffic sources are moving the needle and which are expendable.

ACTION EXERCISE

1. **Choose your three traffic sources and write them down**. Be realistic about your time and budget constraints as well as your personal preferences. If you're never going to post regularly on Facebook, don't lie to yourself. Just pretend that Facebook doesn't exist, rather than wondering what could have been.

7 PROMOTIONAL STRATEGIES

After you know how to get people to your book page, the next step is to structure that traffic into a cohesive strategy. You'll find that you can use your three primary traffic sources (e.g., stuff like promo sites, PPC ads, and so forth) in a variety of ways. Unfortunately, this flexibility is a double-edged sword: it can be a frustrating exercise in trial and error determining which approaches work, and what situations to use them in. And simply flinging dollars around and hoping for the best rarely turns out well.

My aim here is to cut through the massive number of possibilities and present the methods that I've found most effective. To that end, this guide isn't an exhaustive list of everything you can possibly do; much like the rest of the *Ultimate Guide to Book Marketing*, this section uses the 80/20 rule as its North Star. Thus, consider these strategies building blocks that you can combine, tweak, and adapt to create entirely new ones.

The more creativity you bring to the marketing table, the better chance you have of forging a career. After all, it's hard to stand out when you're doing the same exact things as everyone else.

The seven strategies we'll cover are:

1. PPC Ads on Backlist
2. The Netflix Strategy
3. Permafree
4. BookBub Featured Deal
5. Kindle Countdown Deals
6. Free Run
7. $0.99 Kindle Unlimited box set launch

These are *not* ranked by effectiveness or quality. Instead, I've organized them according to applicability: we'll begin with strategies that work for both wide and Amazon exclusive books, before moving into more retailer-specific approaches.

Before we hop into the guide, I'd be remiss if I didn't mention launching, which is the most powerful promotional strategy of all. Since launching has its own rules, however, it receives a dedicated part unto itself. Keep in mind, however, that many of these strategies are effective when used in conjunction with a new release.

Finally, it's also important to mention that these strategies, while useful, are not an antidote for slow or nonexistent releases. You must be releasing new books at a consistent clip. While you can survive with minimal marketing in certain genres should you release at a fast pace, the opposite is not true; with no new books, your earnings are destined to dwindle, even if you employ an arsenal of effective promotional strategies.

Before we get into the details of said strategies, however, let's talk about **blocking out the noise**. Specifically, a common refrain: *that no longer works.*

THE NOISE

There is a *ton* of BS out there when it comes to marketing books, none more so than in the promo arena. Although it's an indie truism that book marketing experiences an axis shift every six months or year, I have not found this to be the case. Many of these strategies have worked for years.

Nonetheless, "that doesn't work any more" has been shouted for as long as I've been an indie author. You'll no doubt have seen a half dozen or more authors claim that each strategy listed within this guide is no longer effective. I've even seen some say that releasing more books is no longer an effective strategy because there are people/content mills that can produce content weekly (or even faster).

This is lunacy. Releasing a new, high-quality book is the best tool in an author's marketing playbook. To suggest otherwise is ridiculous.

The reason for the discrepancy in opinions is simple: strategies have multiple moving parts that require varied skillsets. Those expecting marketing to be a fully plug and play endeavor will be met with disappointment. And, inevitably, folks seeking immediate success are disproportionately likely to share their experiences with others.

If you listen to enough of this chatter, you'll be frozen in a state of analysis paralysis. The key, then, is to assess the available information, filter out the noise, then take action. It takes experience (and failure) to fine-tune these strategies to your own books. You will never have a 100% hit rate. Promotions and launches will flop. As with anything, your mileage may vary depending on genre, quality of your writing, phases of the moon, and a host of other factors that can't be anticipated. Those seeking guarantees are in the wrong business. A major reason entrepreneurs receive sizable rewards when they succeed is because they're willing to assume risks others are not. This does not mean being rash; rather, when the probabilities are favorable, it means you make strategic bets and let the chips fall where they may.

Ultimately, you should base your business decisions upon your own data and books. Because, as the old saying goes, everything else is just noise.

FULL PRICE, DISCOUNTS, OR FREE: WHAT'S BEST?

While we'll discuss the mechanics of finding your optimal standard price later, *discounting* is a key ingredient in running successful promotions. While a lower price doesn't automatically generate traffic to your page, it has two benefits:

1. **Lowers objections (and thus raises the conversion).** A $4.99 price might be "wait and see," whereas $0.99 draws in impulse buyers. More sales volume = a higher rank, which generates organic traffic from Amazon's recommendations.
2. **Opens up promotional opportunities.** For example, promotional sites really only work with $0.99 or free books.

It's important to note that while lowering the price *usually* increases sales volume, this is *not* always the case. Pricing in the real world does not work in accordance to the neat theories you might find in an economic textbook. You may find that *raising* your price increases sales volume. Make sure that you base your decisions on *your* data.

Downsides of lower prices include:

1. **Lower royalties.** It's hard to make a living on $0.99 or free books. You need a funnel in place (a fancy marketing word for a series) to make money. Your free/$0.99 Book 1 or box set is a loss leader; the real money is made on Books 2 – infinity.

2. **Lower review scores.** Studies have shown that people rate cheaper or free items more harshly. At free or $0.99, you'll get more people seeking to subconsciously confirm their suspicions: that this book is cheap because it's crappy. This is a quirk of human psychology. You'll also get people outside your target audience picking up the book merely because it's cheap. These effects are most pronounced with free books.

3. **Less refined targeting.** Readers tend to pick up cheap books in bulk, which means that they might purchase ten or fifteen titles at once that have little relationship with each other (not even genre). This can confuse Amazon's baby algorithmic AI, and cause your also-boughts and other recommendations to become screwy. More of a problem with free books, where there's literally no downside to picking up forty or fifty titles at once.

4. **Lower organic visibility (permafrees).** Permafree books don't appear in the also-boughts at all, which is one of the

major sources of organic visibility. Books made free via
a KDP run remain visible in the also-boughts while free.

For the strategies in this section, I'll explain which pricing structures typically work best. **It's important to reiterate that your price does not generate visibility on its own.** You still need to bring the traffic yourself. It's just easier to find this traffic and convert it into sales at a lower price.

BRIEF REFRESHER: THE ALGOS

Since we've covered a lot of ground in the first six parts of *The Ultimate Guide to Book Marketing*, a little refresher on the algorithms is in order before continuing. Getting the algorithms working in your favor is critical for the Kindle Unlimited centric strategies outlined below. If your KU book isn't being recommended to Amazon's Kindle Unlimited customer database, your book is often DOA. When you're wide, having a grasp on how Amazon's algos behave can still enhance your promo efforts, but it's far less critical. Not all promotional strategies require activating the algorithms; there are plenty of other ways to sell books, which we'll go over.

Three things matter more than anything else for tripping the algo wires:

1. **Sales volume & velocity** (this is the main factor) (key for pop lists/bestseller charts)
2. **Sales consistency** (key for pop lists/bestseller charts)

3. **The sample of people who buy your book** (key for Amazon's automated emails, also-boughts and on-site merchandising)

The algo also factors in:

- **Newness**: promotes new content more readily than old backlist
- **Sales history**: if a book has a consistent history of poor sales, it's harder to revive it than one that has a steady history of solid sales. Don't worry; if your book is in the cellar, you can market it. Just understand that a book with steady sales is going to be easier to revive/boost up than one camping in the telephone number ranks.

Note that the most important factor here is **sales volume & velocity**, which means that you need to hit **critical mass**. If you nudge an elephant with a stick, it might not even wake up. But blow an airhorn in its ear and you have a stampede.

Same thing with Amazon's algorithms: if you don't push enough sales during your promotion, you won't get the visibility necessary for Amazon's algorithms to sit up and take notice. The elephant will remain asleep, and you will have wasted your time and money. A big part of hitting critical mass is **stacking**: combining multiple different traffic sources (promo sites, newsletter, various ad platforms) on the same day to push as many sales as possible.

As a basic illustration of critical mass, if you have the option between two $500 promos and one $900 promo, the latter gives you a better shot at triggering the algorithms. There is a point, of course, where it makes more sense to split the money between multiple promos. Why? Because it's easier to spend $5,000 apiece on two series than it is to efficiently spend $10,000 on a single title or series. In the latter scenario, you'll be contending with rising ad costs and diminishing returns. Such higher dollar campaigns thus require more skill (with Facebook, BookBub, and Amazon Ads in particular) to run properly.

With budgets of up to $5,000, you want to focus on a single series. At dollar amounts above $5,000, assess your own skillset and genre—if you can efficiently spend that additional money on a single series, go for it. Otherwise, consider putting additional funds beyond $5,000 toward a different series (so long as it's profitable to advertise).

This is merely a general guideline, as are the budget recommendations that accompany each strategy. You'll get a feel for the lower and upper limits of what you should spend as you promote more.

PAGE READS: A BRIEF PRIMER

The Kindle Unlimited promotional strategies **are primarily centered around generating page reads**. This is where the real money is in Kindle Unlimited for many authors, particularly in genres like romance, where page reads can account for 70%+ or more of an author's income. This, combined with the fact that each borrow counts the same as a sale in Amazon's ranking algorithm, can lead to explosive results from promotional efforts.

Given that Kindle Unlimited is an Amazon product, it's unsurprising that the majority of reads are driven by Amazon's own algorithms and ecosystem. Mechanisms like promo sites and pay-per-click ads don't often generate tons of page reads directly;

instead, you'll use these tools to push your book high enough for Amazon to recommend it to its expansive KU audience.

There are five primary ways to generate page reads:

1. Releasing a new book in an existing series.
2. Releasing a highly successful new book in a new series in the same genre as the rest of your backlist.
3. Discounting your backlist—e.g., a KCD on Books 1/2/3 in a series, a box set at, 99c etc.—so that you can get the ranks up (and hence visibility) enough to get Amazon recommending the books to KU readers
4. Amazon Ads
5. Facebook and BookBub Ads (both hit or miss)

Methods 1, 2, and 3 are all based around generating Amazon visibility, which in turn produces page reads. This makes them somewhat indirect methods of producing page reads. New releases provide visibility, which in turn triggers Amazon's recommendations to people who have borrowed/bought the series in the past. If your new release is popular enough, you'll also be recommended to new readers.

If your backlist is all in the same sub-genre (i.e., you write urban fantasy exclusively), then a single hit produces significant spillover to your previous books. This is for two reasons: Amazon will start recommending these titles to people who enjoyed your breakout hit (since they're in the same sub-genre). And people who enjoyed your recent book will naturally go and look for similar stuff you've written in the past. If they're Kindle Unlimited readers, they'll often borrow these books as well, since it's free for them to do so.

Without the benefit of a new release providing significant visibility, however, you must get that backlist visible enough for Amazon's algorithms to take notice. Advertising a full price book directly can work, but it's often difficult and expensive. You'll find that each book typically has an equilibrium point where it likes to stabilize at full price. Breaking beyond that can incinerate money at an alarming rate.

Thus, instead of storming the gates directly, you can break through that ceiling by discounting the book and heavily promoting during a brief window. With a concerted ad spend, it's possible to get a backlist title into the Top 1,000 or Top 500—which will trigger Amazon's recommendations and a page read tail. You can then work in concert with Amazon's algos, lengthening the tail by advertising the book when it goes back to full price. You'll often find it's more receptive to ads, and settles in at a far higher equilibrium point than it did previously.

It's critical to emphasize that there's a delay in page reads. The reason for this is two-fold: one, people must actually read the book, then have their reading device sync with the cloud. This takes time. Two, the recommendation system driving reads is delayed. Expect reads to peak somewhere between four days to two weeks following your promo.

Amazon Ads (Method #4) are not based around generating visibility. They're the main *direct* method of producing page reads, in that you can turn on ads, and see your page read graph go up if the ads are converting. Facebook and BookBub Ads, depending on genre, can do this as well, but they're much more hit or miss. If you're trying to produce reads with these platforms, make sure you're referencing Kindle Unlimited in the ad. You can (and should, if you have a lot of titles in Kindle Unlimited) advertise on Amazon Ads to keep the page reads flowing when you're not running a launch or special promotion.

But what if you're wide and don't have any page reads to worry about? Don't worry. I have you covered with some general tactics.

WIDE: GENERAL TACTICS

The number one thing you need to keep in mind when promoting wide books: **it's a slow burn**. You'll read stories of people hitting it out of the park with their first KU book or series (although to be clear, such situations are still rare). Barring a lightning strike, that's just not gonna happen when you're wide. As such, chasing rank (or focusing on it at all) is a waste of time. Your sales ranks will be terrible because you're not getting borrows. Resist the temptation to advertise with the sole intent to boost the rank. Plenty of wide authors, despite their ranks, are making far more than high-ranking Kindle Unlimited authors, because they're consistently selling books at full price.

Remember that, when you're wide, you have very little algorithmic assistance. Amazon heavily favors Kindle Unlimited titles, and the other retailers' recommendations are largely based around editorial curation and merchandising, rather than data. That means *you* **have to bring the traffic** when you're wide. And you'll have to wring every last ounce out of the options at your disposal.

To start, **make sure you have links to all retailers on your website**. Fairly obvious, but many wide authors only link to Amazon. By the way, if you *don't* have an author website, you need one when you're wide.

The same principle applies to your autoresponder and broad-cast emails: include buy links to all retailers. If you sell well in specific regional stores, include direct links to those as well.

If going wide is a central part of your publishing strategy, **go direct to each retailer**, when possible, to take advantage of site-specific promo opportunities and to maximize your royalties. You're not completely left out in the cold on the merchandising front if you're using Draft2Digital, however; just contact their support to inquire about upcoming opportunities. There might be nothing available, but all it costs you is an occasional email.

In your back matter, **use a direct link to your website to push the next book in the series** instead of a universal link a la Books-2Read. I use a page on my website where I display the entire series + all the retailer links (example: **dnerikson.com/ruby**). Getting readers to my site allows them to explore my backlist and also subscribe to my newsletter. In theory, uploading retailer-specific editions with a link straight to that retailer will probably produce higher sellthrough versus sending them to a landing page. Linking directly is worth doing if you can spare the hour or two it takes to create and upload the retailer-specific versions. But it's also a pain in the ass that I personally skip, as you have to repeat this misery any time you update a backlist title.

A few assorted notes:

- **WIDE:** other retailers have a stronger foothold in inter-national markets, so make sure your prices are properly set (i.e., not auto-converted) for regions like Canada and Australia
- **WIDE:** readers tend to be less price sensitive, especially in non-US countries

- **KOBO and APPLE**: you can price higher than $9.99 and still get 70% royalties. This allows you to sell "Complete Series" sets exclusive to these two platforms for higher prices while still offering readers a compelling discount.
- **KOBO**: The Kobo Writing Life team is receptive to providing merchandising placements for these Complete Series sets, so reach out to them for consideration.
- **KOBO**: has promotions that you can apply for when you're direct
- **KOBO**: when using pay-per-click ads, you can strip out the country codes from URLs to auto-redirect readers to the correct regional store.

None of this stuff is going to make you rich. But remember our goal: brick-by-brick. Each of these is a tiny cobblestone. But over time, with each promotion, they compound into something much, much bigger.

FUNDAMENTAL GROUNDWORK

To maximize the effectiveness of the strategies below, we need to lay some groundwork. Some of this is a review of what we've already discussed, but it's important to put that information into context.

The first order of business is establishing **the real goal of promotion**. Reasons such as "promoting because someone told me it's necessary" or "running ads just to run ads" are common, but not valid. There are real dollars at stake here, and while it's not the end of the world when a promotion bombs, you want to stack the deck in your favor. That requires keeping a keen eye on your advertising dollars and using them judiciously.

Turning a profit is part of the goal, but it's not the complete picture. Many people making good money five years ago are no longer in business. Why? Because they didn't consider how each new book and promotion built their career.

So that's the number one goal of promoting: laying another brick (or five, or ten) in your author career. You don't build a house in one day, and you don't build a thirty-year author career with a single massive launch. Instead, each new book and promotion compounds slowly until you hit an inflection point.

People will call this overnight success or say that this was their "breakout" book. But this is really just the cumulative effect of making sure each promotion and launch are focused on moving you forward. Even if it's only an inch.

This mindset helps us avoid short-term home run thinking. Don't get me wrong; money today is great. More money today is even better. But chasing dollars too early often just results in poor decisions and wasted effort. Because marketing and writing are complex skills that demand experience to master.

That's why I recommend focusing on (and hopefully mastering) three traffic sources. Being *amazing* at Facebook Ads is far more useful than being mediocre at two dozen different things. At first, when you don't know what will work, you'll go much wider than three, then cull things to the absolute essentials. This is an approach I call **shotgun and narrow**. Take the time to figure out what works for your books and your genre, then work hard to hone those marketing skills to a fine point over the ensuing months and years. You needn't do this before embarking on your first promo; indeed, you build your marketing chops through the fires of launching and promoting. There will be successes and failures. But through them, you will learn.

How do you analyze what works? You **track your numbers**. At the very least you want to do this weekly, monthly, and annually, but for certain scenarios outlined below where you're spending quite a bit of money (particularly on PPC ads) you'll want to track things daily.

With your traffic sources and tracking systems in place, you'll need to set a **promotion budget**. Promotions can be stressful, and authors often retreat at the first sign of trouble. Knowing your numbers is one half of avoiding making emotional decisions in the heat of the moment; the other half is setting a budget beforehand. Make sure this is money that you can afford to lose. Your goal, naturally, is to turn a profit, but even the best laid marketing plans can be scuttled by any number of factors. Knowing you won't be out on the street if your promo is a flop removes a tremendous amount of stress off your shoulders and frees your mental resources to focus on executing your strategy.

You can set a budget for each specific launch or promotion, or on a monthly basis. I do a combination: if I have a promotion or launch scheduled for the month, I'll earmark a set budget for it. In a non-promo or launch month, I'll set aside a specific amount to use for backlist marketing, then divide that daily. If my monthly budget is $1,500, for example, then I know I can spend $50/day on ads. This, too, relieves stress: I don't have to wonder if I'm spending beyond what I can afford. As long as I'm adhering to my monthly budget, I'm golden.

As for how often to promote, I have a simple rule of thumb: **launch a new book or run a big promotion on a backlist series *every* month**. If you have six series and release six books a year, you can advertise something new every month, rotating through.

By consistently having a promotional iron in the fire, you ensure that your royalties don't precipitously drop from month-to-month. It also helps keep your ads and audiences fresh; continually running the same ads to the same series each month can result in ad fatigue.

If your backlist, budget, or time constraints don't allow this level of marketing (or you just hate it), **aim for a launch or a big promo every *other* month**. Your royalty valleys will be deeper, but this should still be often enough to keep your earnings steady and books visible.

Note that if you're good at using PPC ads, you can run ads continually to sell books and keep your earnings relatively steady, as an alternative to frequent large launches or promotions. While this sounds easier, it's generally a harder path to sled, however.

By the way, that word series? It's critical. **The larger your backlist, the more fruitful your promotional efforts will generally be**. A sizable backlist ensures that each new reader who buys one of your books has a lot of additional products they can potentially purchase. If you have thirty books to sell a reader, and they read ten of them, you can spend way more on advertising than someone who needs to make their money back on a single book. This tenet is hardly exclusive to book marketing; in business, **if you can pay more to acquire a customer, you generally win**. That's just reality. Many authors struggle because they're trying to push their obscure translation of short stories or a standalone with no follow-up. You want to make it easier to win, instead of rigging the game against yourself.

Naturally, our objective isn't to brute force this by outspending everyone. You want to make sure you're leveraging each ad dollar to its maximum potential. But it's always nice to have a war chest to fall back on when all else fails.

To reiterate:

1. Each promotion (or launch) is a building block in your career
2. Master your three traffic sources
3. Track your numbers
4. Set a promotion budget
5. Launch a new book or run a big promotion on a backlist series every month (or every other month)
6. Series are critical for turning a profit and allow you to spend more acquiring each reader
7. Use your war chest and resources to your advantage, but also leverage clever/low-competition ways to maximize your ad dollars.

Finally, make sure your books and website are optimized for sellthrough and subscribers, which directly relates to item #1: always be building your platform. For more on that, check out the section on optimization.

I HAVE NO MONEY—WHAT CAN I DO?

Things will be more difficult. There's no reason to sugarcoat it.

But you're also not screwed. If you're willing to grind, you can build up your business one step at a time. It's just going to take longer, because advertising is like having a book of matches: if you have the right pieces in place, you can quickly get a fire burning. Sans matches, you can craft a bow drill from sticks you found in the surrounding woodlands, but it's a hell of a lot more time consuming to even produce a spark.

First, you'll want to make sure you have a professional cover/ formatting and a proofread book. People will try to skimp here, but these are mandatory in 2020. If you don't put out a professional-level product, your book will be buried among the millions of other titles available. You can barter for these services or find low cost providers. There are cover designers who do solid custom work for around $100 and folks who will format your book in Vellum for $15 – $30 (you can also format your book for free in Word).

1. Write in the hottest Kindle Unlimited genre that fits your writing style and release a full-length novel every month. The more tropes and expectations you hit, the easier it is to gain momentum. Kindle Unlimited readers tend to have specific tastes. Traveling too far outside their tropes and expectations makes it difficult to get traction.

2. Implement the tips within the optimization section later in the guide so your back/front matter and website are set up to boost sellthrough and newsletter subscribers.

3. Build your newsletter via cross promotions.

4. Use some of the low cost or free traffic sources outlined in the Traffic section to generate inexpensive visibility for your books.

5. Rinse and repeat. Build up your subscriber base and war chest over the next 12 – 24 months, reinvesting some of your royalties into paid advertising.

To answer the inevitable follow-up question: **what if I can't write a book a month?**

Answer: write one every two months. Or every three.

If you can't do that, then your third option is to have excellent craft chops. If your titles are *noticeably* a cut above the competition, then you can survive with only producing a couple books a year.

The fourth is to seek a trad pub deal.

This quality gap is not about lyrical writing, but rather about storytelling: pacing, characters, plot, and so forth.

And the other question perhaps on your mind: what if I hate all the tropes?

Well, things will go slower if you adopt this strategy. Your trope-less books will likely not do very well in KU, which is heavily weighted toward very specific tropes and expectations. And Kindle Unlimited tends to be the quickest (though not necessarily the best, nor the most stable long term) path to generating money with your books.

In any business, you need a **competitive advantage**. Remember our indie trifecta of success: productivity, craft, and marketing. If you publish slowly, write mediocre books, and have no money, success is unrealistic. There is a lot of competition. No one is owed success. It's best to be at least decent in all three areas, but if one is average or below average, the other two must be that much stronger to pick up the slack.

So if you can't throw some dollars at marketing, you need to release faster *or* your books need to be *really* good.

1: PPC ON BACKLIST

- **BUDGET:** $200+ a month
- **KU or WIDE:** Both

- **TIMEFRAME**: indefinite.
- **THE STRATEGY**: run ads on Facebook, BookBub, or Amazon to first-in-series books (or box sets) that have strong sellthrough to a long series.
- **THE GOAL**: sell your books profitably via pay-per-click ads.
- **ALTERNATIVE GOAL**: maintaining rank/visibility after a big promotion or launch.
- **OTHER**: Works best with a long series (i.e., 5+ books) that has solid sellthrough (30 – 40% from full price Book 1 > Book 2; 50 – 60% for KU readthrough from Book 1 > Book 2), as you'll often lose money to generate a sale of the first book/box.

This is the hardest strategy on the list. It's also what most authors gravitate toward, because PPC is often presented as a career changing magic bullet. It sounds easier than writing new words: just throw a few ads up on Facebook and watch the dollars roll in.

It isn't. Competition is fierce on these advertising platforms, and learning how to employ ads effectively requires a significant investment of time and money. It also demands strategy: short-term sales are nice, but the goal (as the refrain in this guide goes) is to build a long-term fanbase. And if your blurb and cover are not on point, any problems will be quickly exposed with this type of advertising (in the form of high CPCs and low conversion).

That being said, if you *can* hone your advertising chops, the buzz is true: ads can change the trajectory of your career. They can be accessed on-demand, at any time, at tremendous scale. Nowhere else can you spend hundreds or even thousands of dollars a day *instantly*. But you have to build your chops before those dollars have any hopes of generating a positive return. And most authors give up long before they see rewards. That's not surprising; most available information is incorrect or poorly explained. The main reason, however, for failure is one of strategy: authors almost inevitably gravitate toward advertising their *worst* performing series.

I understand the urge. It also makes no sense: series that performed poorly upon release or when marketed on other platforms will likely produce poor results when advertised via PPC. Nonetheless, authors persist in pushing boulders up hill, forever doomed in a Sisyphean loop until they inevitably throw in the towel in frustration.

Thus, you want to focus on running PPC ads to your most profitable series. These are the easiest candidates to run profitable ads to. Ads are usually directed toward the first book in the series (usually either free or priced at $0.99 or $2.99) or a box set of the first three books, unless you're pushing a new book or using them for one of the strategies outlined below.

By focusing your money on your best performing series, you not only maximize your profitability on the ads, but also lift your underperforming series much higher, too.

How can this be?

Well, let's say you get 30 sales a day via PPC ads when you advertise only your best performing series. About a quarter or half of these readers might go on to finish the entire series. Then, a handful of these will go on to read your *other* books and sign up for your newsletter (where you can push your backlist—see the Netflix Strategy coming up next for more information).

So you may end up with 30 sales of the advertised book, but 50 or 60 additional sales and 1 or 2 organic subscribers when all is said and done.

Depending on your genre (size and click costs) and the series length, you can often scale to higher spends. There's no limit here, other than when the ads become unprofitable (or your cash reserves are exhausted).

If you instead split your spend between your best performer and mediocre ones, that same number of ad dollars might produce 17 sales (15 of the best series and two for Book 1 of the mediocre one). This then has a direct effect on the sellthrough to that series and the rest of your backlist—less volume means fewer overall sales, fewer organic subscribers, less profit to then reinvest in scaling, and *massively* worse overall results.

Focus your spend on the best performers (and just-launched books). These will lift the rest of your backlist.

It's important to reiterate that advertising your backlist via PPC is very difficult, and most series will not be profitable. Don't push if the results aren't there. You can lose a ton of money.

If you're ready to take the leap into paid advertising, I have a course covering Facebook, Amazon, and BookBub Ads, from the fundamentals to advanced tactics. Learn more at **nichola-serik.com/ads**.

2: THE NETFLIX STRATEGY

- **BUDGET**: $0
- **KU or WIDE**: Both
- **TIMEFRAME**: indefinite.
- **THE STRATEGY**: set up an autoresponder that sends out an email every Friday (or other day of the week) introducing a new backlist series to your readers.

- **THE GOAL**: introduce people already interested in your work to *more* of your books.

Services like Netflix, Hulu, or HBO have vast content libraries that can be overwhelming to navigate. To keep you engaged (and subscribed), these companies periodically highlight shows or movies that you might enjoy via curated emails. This happens more frequently than you might expect. Don't believe me? Do a quick search for their name in your inbox. You'll be shocked at the number of emails you receive.

Netflix sends me an email about new or backlist content every few days.

We can adapt this same idea to our own backlist by **sending subscribers an automated email every week introducing a new series to them.** All you have to do is schedule an autoresponder email every Friday (or a different day of the week) with a subject line like "looking for your next weekend read?" Want to do Wednesday instead? Try something like "Work sucks. This book doesn't." Obviously, you want to be on-brand: that irreverent tone might work for urban fantasy, but won't fly for sweet romance. Calibrate things to *your* readers.

As for the content? It takes about five to fifteen minutes to write the email itself. All you have to do is have a one to two paragraph backstory on something related to the book: the writing process, the research you did, what inspired it, etc.

Then have a one or two sentence teaser (or the blurb) to introduce the book. And end with the purchase link(s).

That's it. You don't even have to do this all at once; the beauty of the autoresponder is that you can add to this over time. Released a new series? Drop it into the autoresponder when you're ready.

Send an email every week until you run out of series.

You can adapt this idea to standalones as well.

If you have a *huge* backlist with tons of series and standalones, you might not want to inundate readers with all of them to perpetuity. I'd keep the autoresponder to your five or ten best performing series/standalones.

And don't lump all the series in a single email. This can be tempting, but it's overwhelming and counterproductive. I've tried this to "streamline" the process, but it's ineffective. **Introduce one series or standalone per email**.

This strategy is an excellent, passive way to sell books without active promotion. Never assume your fans are familiar with all of your books—this won't be the case, especially if you're prolific.

You may be worried this will irritate your subscribers. The reason I had you do that quick inbox search was simple: you don't even realize how many of these emails you're getting. Why? Because they're *relevant*. Even when you don't watch the content, Netflix's recommendations are solid. That's because they have a massive amount of data on your viewing habits.

Luckily, we don't need a multi-million-dollar analytics department to determine what our readers like. Because they've already told us they like our books by signing up. Thus, our other books will be relevant and interesting to them. They might not buy them right away. They may *never* buy certain titles. But they also won't be annoyed to learn more about them. That's why they signed up in the first place: to find more books like the one that encouraged them to subscribe. You're doing them a favor by introducing them to new books they might like.

A related method of promoting backlist titles is to mention a specific book in your broadcast emails in a PS. This will often drive a surprising number of clicks, especially if the book is discounted or free.

3: PERMAFREE

- **BUDGET**: $0+
- **KU or WIDE:** Wide
- **TIMEFRAME:** indefinite.
- **THE STRATEGY**: indefinitely make your first-in-series book (or box set) wide.
- **THE GOAL**: enjoy a trickle of free organic traffic to your Book 1, which, if people enjoy, will in turn produce sales of the latter books.
- **OTHER**
- There are high-sellthrough exceptions (i.e., romance duets where Book 1 ends on a cliffhanger), but you generally need at least 3+ books in a series for this to be viable.
- Can mix a permafree Book 1 + the rest of the series in Kindle Unlimited, but this isn't recommended because of how Amazon's algorithms work.

Permafree (a portmanteau of "permanently" and "free") is an old standby. For those concerned about the "permanent" part, it's more indefinitely free; you can raise your price back to whatever level you choose at any time. The strategy is simple: set your book to free on non-Amazon retailers, then get Amazon to price match it (since they don't let you directly set the price to indefinitely free from their dashboard). Amazon rarely does this automatically, so it's best to directly *email* KDP Support with the relevant retailer links and request that they price match the book in question on all Amazon Stores. Occasionally they'll reject your request or won't put it through properly; if this happens, just contact support again. A different rep will make the change.

While permafree isn't as powerful as its 2013/2014 peak (at least in terms of being a "set and forget" strategy), rumors of its demise have been greatly exaggerated. Hooking customers with a free sample is a tried and true marketing method across almost every industry, and books are hardly exempt. If you have a quality product that readers actually enjoy, a certain percentage will pick up later volumes at full price.

Three misconceptions make authors shy away from permafree:

1. They expect much higher sellthrough from the free title to paid ones. While higher rates are occasionally possible (usually in romance), 2 – 5% sellthrough to Book 2 is more typical.

2. They expect it to be completely passive. More competition means that you must bring visibility to your permafree book. It also means that the free product must be of higher quality than in previous years, since readers have significantly more choice (Kindle Unlimited subscribers essentially have a "permafree" library of 500,000+ titles available to them at any time).

3. They don't have a series behind their permafree book. Making your only book permafree is pointless. **You must have a series/backlist for people to buy after they read your free book.**

To maximize the effectiveness of your permafree book, you need to get your book in as many hands as possible. If you have 1,000 copies of Book 1 out there, you might expect to sell 20 – 50 copies of Book 2. If you only have 100, that number drops to 2 – 5.

In addition to having your permafree book available on all retailers, you'll want to put it up on Story Origin and Book-

Funnel too. Depending on the platform, you'll generate some additional passive downloads. But you can also enter cross promotions with your permafree to extend its reach and get it out to more readers (while generating email subscribers, to boot).

Adding a PS to standard newsletter broadcast emails with a link to the permafree could produce in ~25 – 100 downloads each time you send it to your list (assuming you have a few thousand subscribers). A permafree book also makes for an effective addition to the weekly autoresponder strategy outlined previously.

You can also advertise your permafree book. While huge blitz campaigns are generally not recommended, you can run occasional newsletter promos or even daily PPC ads to your permafree book. While paying to advertise a free book might seem foolish, with strong sellthrough and a lengthy series, it can actually be extremely profitable.

With a long series, you can get even more aggressive with this strategy. Instead of making a single book free, you can make a box set of the first three books permafree.

An alternative to permafree is "perma" $0.99, where you keep Book 1 (or a box set) at $0.99 indefinitely as a loss leader. It's worth experimenting with your backlist, but generally speaking, the higher volume of free downloads will make it more profitable than the nominal royalties, but much lower download volume, you produce at $0.99.

HOW TO MAKE YOUR BOOK PERMAFREE

The process for making your book permafree is simple. Some resources will suggest that you click the little "report lower price" link on your book's page. This is ineffective. Instead:

1. **Publish your book on all retailers**: Barnes & Noble, Apple Books, Kobo and, Google Play. Apple Books and Google Play are the most important for getting Amazon to do the free price match. Make sure the price is $0.00 everywhere.

2. **Email Amazon.** Go to your KDP Account, click "Help" at the top right, and then scroll down to the yellow "Contact Us" button located at the bottom left corner of the screen. Click Pricing > Price Matching.

3. **Use this template**:

"Hi, my book [title] (ASIN: XXXXX) is currently available for free on [other retailers]. I am emailing to notify you of the lower price and request a price match.

Retailer link 1:

Retailer link 2:

Thanks for your help!

[Name]

If support gives you boilerplate nonsense about not price-matching, just try again a few days later. And that's it: soon enough your book will be indefinitely free, until you decide otherwise.

4: BOOKBUB FEATURED DEAL

- **BUDGET**: $200+
- **KU or WIDE**: Both, although it's much easier to get a Featured Deal on a wide title.

- **TIMEFRAME**: indefinite.
- **THE STRATEGY**: submit regularly to BookBub and hope they accept your book or box set.
- **THE GOAL**: get the most powerful book marketing service on the planet to advertise your book to millions of voracious readers and then sit back to collect your money.

BookBub Featured Deals have long been the Holy Grail of indie book marketing. While their career-making power has always been a bit overblown, they're the most effective marketing tool, dollar-for-dollar, in our arsenal. Naturally, authors are more apt to share mind-blowing results rather than run-of-the-mill ones, which is why, perhaps, there have been recent rumblings about BookBub declining in effectiveness. Unrealistic expectations, rather than a sudden shift in their efficacy, are the likely culprit behind these rumors. It can seem that BookBub has become a shadow of its former self when the majority of stories you hear are about five-figure returns, and yours triples its investment for "only" a low or mid four-figure haul. The latter scenario, however, has always been far more common.

Tales of truly *massive* windfalls are indeed far rarer these days, so there is some truth that the *ceiling* for a BookBub Featured Deal has been lowered. The reason for this, I believe, is that Amazon has refined and tweaked their algorithms to mitigate the impact of BookBub on the bestseller charts. That greatly reduces the chances of a book sticking indefinitely at a high sales rank following a Featured Deal. But 99% of authors never experienced this perpetual stickiness anyway (I haven't in the 30+ deals I've gotten). Thus, for all intents and purposes, BookBub functions the same as it always did for most.

Getting back to the main thread: BookBub Featured Deals are worth taking whenever you can get them, which won't be often. But they're lucrative when you do, often earning out their cost on the same day of the ad. The only downside, as anyone who has ever tried to get one of these deals knows, is their elusiveness: BookBub rejects the vast majority of applicants. Their website claims that less than 20% of books are accepted, but I'd imagine the actual number (based on my own acceptance stats) is below 10%, perhaps nudging toward 5%.

But I'm not here to tell you what you already know: Book-Bubs are awesome and hard to get. Having bagged over thirty of these across a variety of genres, allow me to share five tried and true tricks for increasing your chances of getting a BookBub Featured Deal:

1. **Perseverance.** Oh, you thought I had some stunning secret? The number one reason most people never get a BookBub is because they stop submitting. Seriously. You want to know the main reason I've gotten 30+ BookBubs? I've submitted over 230 times. Here's the trick: when you get rejected, you mark the calendar, then you submit on the first date you're eligible. And again. And again. Most people stop submitting after a single try; perhaps two. It takes less than 30 seconds to submit a book. Just keep doing it.

2. **Submit for free immediately after you get rejected at 99 cents.** You can do this the moment after you're rejected; you don't have to wait 28 days to resubmit. While you may be hesitant to offer your prized work up for free, it's worth noting that the free BookBubs are cheaper than their 99 cent counterparts—and often more powerful, to boot.

3. **Subscribe to the email.** Make sure you're subscribed to the genre(s) you write in. Look for trends: do they only accept

wide books? Box sets? Only trad pubs? This will clue you in to how to maximize your shot at a deal.

4. **Go wide.** They're more likely to accept wide books.

5. **Submit a box set at 99 cents.** BookBub loves box sets because their readers love deals. A set of three quality books for $0.99 is the epitome of a tremendous deal. If you're having trouble getting them to run your single novels—a tall order in certain genres—consider boxing up at least the first three titles and submitting it.

Finally, if you're offered an International Deal, you may have heard mixed reports on their efficacy and thus be reticent to accept. The rumors are somewhat true: the international deals are far less powerful than their US-brethren (although if your book has significant international appeal, these can be very effective). Nonetheless, in my endeavors, I've broken even; and with a series for readers to snap up after the advertised books, these usually end up being solidly profitable. And it's worth noting that BookBub's editors seem to use the International Deals as a sort of proving ground: should your book perform admirably here, your chances of receiving a US deal are enhanced.

Like all things in publishing, of course, a BookBub Featured Deal is not guaranteed to make money. But in a business filled with uncertainty, it's about as close to a sure thing as you'll find.

5: KINDLE COUNTDOWN DEAL

- **BUDGET:** $1000+
- **KU or WIDE:** KU

- **TIMEFRAME:** 5 – 7 days (full 7 if only doing KCDs, 5 if they coincide with a free run). Absolute minimum of 4 days.
- **THE STRATEGY:** use a combo of PPC, promo sites, and your platform (newsletter/social media/promo swaps) to push the first three books (or more) in a series via Kindle Countdown Deal.
- **THE GOAL:** get Book 1 into the Top 2k – 3k (preferably Top 1k) and generate a page read tail that peaks 4 days to 2 weeks after the promo.
- **OTHER**
  - The more books in the series, the better, since this offers substantial opportunity for profit if people go on to pick up later volumes at full price (or read them in KU).
  - It significantly helps if the advertised series is in a popular Kindle Unlimited sub-genre, since a lot of your revenue will come from the page read tail generated by the promotion.

For the uninitiated, Kindle Countdown Deals (henceforth referred to as KCDs) are one of the benefits of Amazon exclusivity. At first glance, KCDs seem like a throw-in perk, paling in utility to free runs or getting page reads. But they have two major benefits:

1. When you discount a book to $0.99 (or $1.99) via KCD, you get a 70% royalty rate instead of 35%.
2. There's a timer ticking down on the page, which introduces urgency and also establishes that the discount in question is actually limited. This improves conversion.

The upside of these two factors is not immediately obvious, however. You might have run one or two, been relatively uninspired by the results, then promptly forgotten about their existence. That was certainly my approach until I discovered the foundations of this strategy in David Gaughran's book *Amazon Decoded*. Following that revelation, I've spent the better part of a year-and-a-half fine-tuning and testing various permutations. It can be used in conjunction with a variety of the other strategies outlined in this guide: by itself, with a BookBub Featured Deal, or as part of a launch.

The reason for their efficacy is simple when you dig beneath the surface: the 70% royalty rate makes a massive difference in profitability. It's often enough to turn a mediocre promo into a good one, and can transform a well-designed promo into a smash hit, as you net 70% on your promotional sales and set your series up for a huge boost in page reads after the promo ends. Coupled with the increased conversion thanks to the ticking timer, you can blast your Book 1 into the Top 1,000 or higher.

You can even run a KCD on a just launched book. Set a pre-order for at least 30 days and tick the enroll in Kindle Unlimited box. You'll then be able to run a KCD on the new book when it comes out. Give it at least a three-day buffer (i.e., if your book comes out the 15th, don't schedule promos until the 18th), since you can't actually schedule the KCD until your book is live.

We'll be aiming to get Book 1 into the Top 1k (Top 2k - 3k at minimum) via the steps outlined below. This strategy is all about hitting **critical mass**—pushing the books as high as possible in the store—and has three components:

1.   Choosing a price structure.

2.   Structuring your traffic sources to maximize your rank on the last day of the KCD, and directing these sources to the series page.

3.   Maintaining the tail by running PPC ads after the promo ads to "pin" Book 1's rank between 5k – 10k in the store.

A final, but important administrative note: whenever you change your price, you're locked out of using a KCD on that book for 30 days. So if you're planning a promotion, keep your prices static.

Here are three price structures you can use (feel free to come up with your own variants; these are starting points).

THE STANDARD KCD

1.   Books 1, 2 & 3 $0.99/ea, rest of series full price
2.   Book 1 free, Books 2 & 3 $0.99/ea

This is tried and true, and works in a variety of scenarios: from launching to promoting backlist. Getting the first three books high in the store gives the series solid visibility on the charts, while also letting you bank sellthrough to later full price volumes.

THE STAGGERED KCD

1.   Book 1 free or $0.99, Book 2 $1.99, Book 3 $2.99, rest full price

This is a little more conservative; you won't sell as many copies of Books 2 and 3, which limits their respective visibility. Many authors gravitate toward this, but in my experience, this is the worst price structure. The goal of the KCD is to push enough books to get massive visibility. Anything that cuts down on that visibility is a huge negative and dramatically impacts the page read tail.

THE AGGRESSIVE KCD

1. First book free, rest of series $0.99/ea
2. All books $0.99/ea

Aggressive discounting on the entire series make more sense if you have a completed series that's been languishing in the ranks. The instant sellthrough gives the entire series a shot in the arm as people purchase all the books at one time, thus massively boosting the series' visibility in the store. This limits your opportunity for sellthrough, of course (unless you have a spin-off series), but it has the highest upside (in terms of a page read tail) if Amazon starts pushing the entire series to Kindle Unlimited readers after the KCD concludes. Plus, with a fairly long series (5, 7, 9 books), that ~$0.70 you get from each sale adds up to good money.

If you don't get the latter books high enough, however, the page read tail won't make up for the lost sellthrough that you would've generated at full price. So while this option is better than the staggered, I usually go with the standard 1/2/3 approach.

After you've chosen your price structure, you heavily advertise the deal via the following avenues:

1. Promo sites on Book 1. These generally produce a lower cost per sale than PPC ads, unless you're extremely skilled at running ads. Use my curated list of promo sites for current best options (**nicholaserik.com/promo-sites**).

2. Your newsletter/social media. Set up some cross promotions and newsletter swaps with authors in your genre if you're feeling ambitious. Be sure to direct your readers to the series page.

3. If you have a larger marketing budget and have booked all the effective promo sites, use Facebook/Bookbub PPC ads. BookBub Ads are the most useful, by far, since their conversion is the highest of the three platforms when pushing heavily discounted books. Amazon Ads are less useful because the ads don't kick in or show impressions reliably, and conversion doesn't dramatically increase when you discount a book to $0.99. Direct readers to the series page.

Sending readers to the Amazon series page instead of a specific book's page has two primary benefits:

1. Readers can buy the entire series with 1-click at a discounted price on the series page instead of clicking through to the individual pages. They are especially likely to 1-click the series if all the books are $0.99, since the insane deal falls into impulse buy territory.

2. There are currently a limited number of ads on the series pages - far less than the rest of the Amazon site, so your conversion is better sending readers to these pages versus a book page that's overwhelmed by ads.

You do sacrifice the Countdown Timer (which only appears on individual book pages), but these benefits are worth it.

When structuring these promotions, you're trying to trigger Amazon's algorithms, meaning you need to consider the following:

1.   If my budget is smaller, I run the KCD for 5 days, and use a free run on Book 1. Visibility is cheaper to generate for free books, and it's easier sales for 5 days versus the maximum 7 days you can run a KCD for. With larger budgets, however, I'll use the full 7 days to my advantage.

2.   Heavily backload the promo sites and ad spend for the last two days. I generally use the first few days to test ads. Then I'll spend 50% – 75% of my budget on the final two days, making sure I end the final day with a bang. My goal is to end the promo at peak rank. Backloading everything also increases conversion: when people see the promo is ending soon, they're more inclined to buy. And Amazon's algorithms respond best to a sales curve that trends upward over the promo

One vital point to reiterate: there's a lag when it comes to the page reads kicking in. Peak reads won't arrive until anywhere from 4 – 14 days following the promo. If your reads are anemic during the actual promotional period or the day after, fear not: provided you got the books' ranks high enough, the page reads should hopefully be forthcoming. That being said, poking Amazon's algos is an inexact art at best, so *never* risk money you can't afford to lose (and *never* charge massive promotions, or anything else in this business, to a credit card to pay off later).

This waiting period can be stressful, particularly when you're spending money at a loss to promote the book. But knowing what to expect can help you prevent making decisions that can chop your promo off at the knees.

Finally, you can increase the tail and prolong the effects of the promo for weeks or even months by running PPC ads to the book in question.

By working in conjunction with Amazon's algorithms, you can often keep Book 1 in the top 10k at full price with about $50/day in ad spend. Thus you want to keep some money in reserve to taper off when it goes to full price. This is a *critical* part of the strategy and cannot be overlooked. If you spend a huge amount of money during the KCD then promptly drop your ad spend to zero, your book often plummets into oblivion. You greatly increase your chances of generating a solid tail if you leave some money in reserve to advertise things after.

PUTTING YOUR **KCD** TOGETHER (AN EXAMPLE):

This is for a hypothetical 7 day KCD with the first three books at $0.99/ea and a budget of $1,500.

- Day 1: newsletter/social media, Facebook or BookBub testing ($25)
- Day 2: Facebook or BookBub testing ($50)
- Day 3: Facebook or BookBub testing ($75)
- Day 4: Facebook or BookBub testing ($100)
- Day 5: start scaling Facebook and/or BookBub ($150+)
- Day 6: promo sites ($100+), Facebook ($100+), BookBub ($200+)

- Day 7: promo sites ($200+), Facebook ($150+), BookBub ($300)+, thank you newsletter
- Day 8 and beyond: run FB ads to Book 1 at $50 a day (can be more or less, but $50 is often the equilibrium point where you maximize profitability on a series).
- Monitor the book's rank and sales to make sure that these ads are converting. You should hopefully see Book 1 settle in somewhere in the top 10k over the week following the promo. You want to continue the ad spend if things are working, but be prepared to cut down if performance isn't where you want it.

Note that if you aren't good at BookBub ads, you don't want to run this level of budget to them. Bad BookBub ads will torch money at an alarming pace. However, if you have good ads, I've found that few things produce higher conversion on deals like this. Facebook can be a substitute if you find that BookBub doesn't work for you.

Additionally, if you've promoted a book multiple times via promo sites, then you'll probably experience significantly diminishing returns. In that case, it might make sense to go light on the promo spend (i.e., only the very best sites) and use that money toward PPC.

Don't sleep on Kindle Countdown Deals; they're one of the most flexible and useful strategies available to Amazon exclusive authors. I've used them to effectively promote both launches and backlist. If you've never run one and have the budget (remember, we're aiming to get Book 1 into the Top 1k, then pin it in the Top 10k), consider experimenting with them. You might be pleasantly surprised.

6: FREE RUNS

- **BUDGET**: $0 – $500+
- **KU or WIDE:** KU
- **TIMEFRAME:** 5 days.
- **THE STRATEGY**: run a KDP free promo on Book 1 (or any book in the series if they can be read out of order) for 5 days.
- **THE GOAL**: Give away a lot of copies to generate sell-through to other books.
- **OTHER**
  - The more books in the series, the better, since this offers substantial profit upside if readers buy later volumes at full price (or read them in KU).
  - It significantly helps if the advertised series is in a sub-genre popular with Kindle Unlimited readers, since a chunk of your revenue will come from page reads after the promotion.

The goal here is *volume*. You want to generate as many down-loads as possible of the free book with the hope that some of these readers will go on to purchase later books in the series at full price. Sellthrough from a free book to a paid book tends to be fairly low (2 – 5%). Thus, we need a lot of downloads to produce results.

This is a simple strategy. We have two structure options when it comes to organizing our traffic sources:

Structure 1:

- Day 1: pretty much everything
- Days 2 – 5: coast

This maximizes download volume. While free downloads do have an algorithmic impact, it's relatively minor. You're mostly doing free runs to generate *sellthrough*, which is why having a series and pushing a lot of free copies are both so critical to your success.

People who open the promo site emails and other traffic sources on Days 2 – 5 can still download a copy. You can also hit the Top 100 on Day 1, then coast from some of that visibility for the rest of the promotion.

Structure 2 keeps the algorithms in mind, but sacrifices some download volume since the book flips back to paid after the big push on Day 5. Thus anyone who opens the promo site email or sees the deal later is out of luck:

- Day 1: promo site/newsletter/cross promo
- Day 2: 1 – 3 promo sites
- Day 3: 1 – 3 promo sites
- Day 4: 2 – 4 promo sites
- Day 5: 3 – 6 promo sites

One benefit here is actually that on Day 6 (when the book returns to full price), some people who find it in newsletters or other places for free may decide to buy it anyway. So you can get a paid sales pop from this.

While free runs are simple, there are a couple wrinkles on this strategy that I'll discuss below. Note that these alternatives are not better than simply giving away a book for free. They are merely additional things to have in your marketing toolbox.

This is simple. All that you do is give away one of the books in your series away for free (Book 1 if they must be read in order).

Then, in the back matter of that book, typically you will have a link to Book 2 (or the next individual book in the series) to encourage sellthrough to the rest of the series. Here, instead of that link to Book 2, you have a link to the box set. You can include both a link to the individual next book *and* the box set. But by including *only* the box set, you ensure that you funnel significantly more readers to that specific product.

You can send readers to Books 1, 2 & 3 box set, but it typically works best with longer sets—say 1 – 5, or a complete series.

Why?

Because sending them to the box set ensures that they pick up multiple books at once. This is good in Kindle Unlimited, because they will be able to seamlessly go from Book 2 to Book 3 to Book 4 and so forth without returning and then borrowing each title individually. This extra step inevitably leads to some people dropping off between books.

By making it so they have multiple or all the books in a single volume (and thus don't have to reborrow), you mitigate this drop off. You end up ahead in Kindle Unlimited, since you get paid the same regardless of whether or not they read the books individually or as part of a set.

Note that it doesn't make sense to box up very long complete series, or make box sets while the individual books are selling well. You don't want to cannibalize significant *sales* revenue while chasing Kindle Unlimited revenue, since the max you can price in the Kindle Store is $9.99 (if you want to get 70%). And if you have five or seven novels that sell well at $4.99 each, you're giving up a lot of money at $9.99.

But if your primary revenue stream is Kindle Unlimited or the individual novels have tapered off in popularity, this is a great way to push

Free Book to $0.99

This is an alternative to a more involved blitz like the Kindle Countdown Deal strategy we just covered. It's both cheaper and easier to run.

It involves three steps:

1. Set Book 1's price to $0.99.
2. Run a KDP Free promotion on Book 1 for the full five days. Stack promo sites to get the book into the Top 100 Free, structuring them so the bulk of your firepower is on the last two days.
3. Run low budget PPC ads to Book 1 when it returns to paid. Or simply let the tail run its course.

The basic structure looks like this:

- Day 1: promo site/newsletter/cross promo
- Day 2: 1 – 3 promo sites
- Day 3: 1 – 3 promo sites
- Day 4: 2 – 4 promo sites
- Day 5: 3 – 6 promo sites

This is just an example; you could kick things off with nothing at all, then essentially coast with a few cheap promo sites or a couple newsletter swaps until the last couple days. Or you could replace the bulk of your promo sites with cross promotion or your author platform, if those have enough firepower to push hundreds of downloads. You don't have to mention the free run to your newsletter or on social media at all, of course. The only thing you *must* do is you load up your heavy hitters on the final day so you're hitting the Top 100 overall on the free list.

The reason this works? Free runs produce visibility in the Paid Store. How? When you're a Kindle Unlimited subscriber, the button on the book pages default to "Read for Free in Kindle Unlimited," even when the book itself is available for free download. Thus, a decent number of KU subscribers who see your free book will actually borrow it in Kindle Unlimited. This not only generates page reads, but since each borrow counts toward your sales rank, should you hit the Top 100 Free chart, you can return to paid with a rank below 15k.

The $0.99 price point ensures that you'll sustain this visibility longer than if your book is available at full price. You'll often get 20 – 30 sales on the day immediately following the promo from people finding the deal in promo newsletters, clicking on it, then deciding to pick it up at $0.99, which is still an impulse buy. These sales, combined with the visibility from the borrows during the free run, can keep your book at a decent rank for a week or two, thus generating page reads and sellthrough to later volumes.

If you run ads to Book 1 at $0.99, this can be a less pricey alternative to "pinning" Book 1 in the Top 10k than the KCD outlined above. You won't experience the potentially explosive burst of reads on the discounted books associated with the KCD, but you can keep Book 1 selling for a while at $0.99.

7: 99 CENT BOX SET LAUNCH IN KINDLE UNLIMITED

- **BUDGET:** $1500+
- **KU or WIDE:** KU
- **TIMEFRAME:** 5 - 7 days for the launch push. PPC ads on the set for the first 30 days.
- **THE STRATEGY:** release a box set of at least three books (minimum 1,000 KENP, preferably 2,000+) at $0.99 and get it into the Top 500.
- **THE GOAL:** make readers the proverbial "offer they can't refuse" by offering them a no-brainer buy at $0.99. This blasts the book up Amazon ranks, and gets it recommended to Kindle Unlimited readers, which can be insanely lucrative, given the huge KENP count.
- **OTHER**
  - Most commonly used in voracious Kindle Unlimited genres like certain sub-genres of sci-fi, fantasy, and romance.
  - Can be significantly more profitable if you have a corresponding audio set, since Audible members can pick this up for a single credit.

This is a simple strategy, but it's also one with a high degree of difficulty. Basically, you're trying to push a deeply discounted box set into the Top 500 and hold it there until Amazon starts recommending it to Kindle Unlimited subscribers. Since the box set is a gigantic number of KENP, this can produce a correspondingly massive number of reads (50k – 100k+ a day) and even things like All Star Bonuses.

However.

If Amazon doesn't grant you this visibility, because most of the ads and promotion you'll be running will be producing sales at $0.99, your royalties will be anemic if the reads don't kick in. And this can be both nerve-wracking and completely out of your control.

Thus, this is a high upside, medium risk strategy. You can hit low to mid five figures during the ensuing tail. And while it's unlikely that it completely bombs (unless you spend $5k+ on promo), it's possible you could lose a few hundred to a thousand bucks if things don't break your way. More likely, if things don't break in your favor, you'll break even. It'll just take 3 - 4 months to recoup your ad spend.

If you want to give it a go, the principles are much the same as we've already discussed: spend the first few days testing ads, then backload most of the spend for the final two days. Follow this up with a consistent ad spend to hopefully get the set within the Top 1,000 (Top 500 if possible).

In fact, you can use the same structure outlined for the KCD:

- Day 1: newsletter/social media, Facebook or BookBub testing ($25)
- Day 2: Facebook or BookBub testing ($50)
- Day 3: Facebook or BookBub testing ($75)
- Day 4: Facebook or BookBub testing ($100)
- Day 5: start scaling Facebook and/or BookBub ($150+)

- Day 6: promo sites ($100+), Facebook ($100+), BookBub ($200+)
- Day 7: promo sites ($200+), Facebook ($150+), BookBub ($300)+, thank you newsletter
- Day 8 and beyond: run FB/BB ads to the box at $50 – $100 a day (can be more or less, but this is generally the equilibrium point).
- Monitor the box's rank and sales to make sure that these ads are converting. You want the box to settle in the Top 3k (optimally Top 1k) over the week following the promo. It may not be possible to keep the set in the Top 1k; this does *not* mean disaster. It's more likely you can stick higher if you're in a popular KU genre. And sometimes it's more profitable to slash ad spend, even if it means seeing your rank drop from, say, 800 to 2,000.

Generally speaking, the more money you have to push the box set, the better your chances of hitting a home run. Naturally, this increases the risk, because if you only get a bunch of $0.99 sales, that won't be enough to cover your ad expenses. 5,000 sales sounds like a lot, but at $0.35 a pop, you're looking at a meager $1,750 in royalties. And you're probably looking at a cost-per-sale of $1 each, minimum. The math here goes south very fast.

If you have an audio set that you can link to the eBook set, this can turn the numbers *dramatically* in your favor. Why? Because Audible members can pick up the set for a single credit, getting 15 – 20+ hours of audio for the same cost as a single book. This is our only real way of discounting audio. And the massive visibility on the eBook set will generate huge spillover visibility to the audiobook set, which audio listeners can often Whispersync for $7.49 after they pick up the eBook version.

I'd only recommend the 99c box set strategy if you have money you can afford to lose. This applies to any strategy involving paid advertising, of course, but it's especially important to note here: this strategy is not one to roll out if you *need* something to work. Because Amazon's algorithms are fickle. And while this has massive upside, they could leave you out in the cold.

KEY TAKEAWAYS

- Block out the **noise** about things not working and rely on your own experience and data to make the best decisions for your catalog.
- Make sure you understand Amazon's algorithms, particularly if you're advertising a KU book.
- If you have no money to advertise...
- Write in the hottest Kindle Unlimited genre that fits your writing style and release a full-length novel every month.
- Optimize your back/front matter and website to boost sell-through and newsletter subscribers.
- Build your newsletter via cross promotions.
- Use some low cost or free traffic sources to generate inexpensive visibility for your books.
- Rinse and repeat. Build up your subscriber base and war chest over the next 12 – 24 months, reinvesting some of your royalties into paid advertising.

Seven fundamental keys to keep in mind when using any strategy:

1. Each promotion (or launch) is a building block in your career
2. Master your three traffic sources
3. Track your numbers
4. Set a promotion budget
5. Launch a new book or run a big promotion on a backlist series every month (or every other month)
6. Series are critical for turning a profit and allow you to spend more acquiring each reader
7. Use your war chest and resources to your advantage, but also leverage clever/low-competition ways to maximize your ad dollars.

The seven strategies you can use to promote your books are:

1. PPC Ads on Backlist
2. The Netflix Strategy
3. Permafree
4. BookBub Featured Deal
5. Kindle Countdown Deals
6. Free Runs
7. $0.99 KU box set launch

ACTION EXERCISE

1. Choose one strategy, adapt it for your series, and execute it.
2. If you don't currently have money to advertise, either design and execute a low cost (or free) option, or outline a hypothetical strategy with a budget of $3,000.

EIGHT:

BRANDING (BLURBS, COVERS, AND MORE)

I t's time to dive deep into book covers, blurbs, pricing, and other key aspects of your branding and packaging.

Let's revisit the Ultimate Book Marketing Formula for a moment:

MARKET RESEARCH + 3 TRAFFIC SOURCES + PRO COVERS + GREAT BLURBS + NEWSLETTER + 4-6 NOVELS PER YEAR

CONSISTENTLY FOR 3-5 YEARS

FULL-TIME AUTHOR

We've spent the last three parts of this guide covering traffic in granular detail, from the importance of Amazon's algorithms to the places to get it and strategies to use. After you generate that traffic, however, comes conversion: getting people to buy. **This is where the real money is made.** Recall the Internet Marketing Formula, which states that there are only three essential steps in the marketing and sales process:

1. **Traffic**: directing the right potential readers to your book page via paid ads, your mailing list, social media, Amazon's algorithms, and so forth.

2. **Conversion**: convincing readers to buy your book via a stellar blurb and cover, competitive price, hook-filled first few pages, and so forth.

3. **Profit**: did you make money? Track your numbers, so you know if your traffic and conversion efforts have been effective. After analyzing the numbers, you have two options:

- If you made money, you repeat the process or, if you have additional marketing funds, slowly scale up your spend to grow your business.
- Ultimately, this can be summed up with the following rule: **double down on whatever makes you money and immediately stop or fix what doesn't.**

This process usually breaks down (i.e., becomes unprofitable) at the conversion step. It is fairly straightforward to get traffic to your book's page. Getting people to buy, however, is a tricky beast indeed. In short, you have control over the following elements on Amazon:

- Section 1: Covers (and titles)
- Section 2: Blurbs
- Section 3: Pricing

- Section 4: Categories & Keywords
- Section 5: Reviews
- Section 6: Front & Back Matter

If you want to skip to a specific section just jump straight to it. But before we hop in, we'll start with a reminder of why market research is so important.

BRANDING STARTS WITH MARKET RESEARCH

The main reason most books don't sell is simple: they were written for a market of one (i.e., the author). Attempting to create a market or demand for a product is a common mistake marketers in *all* disciplines make, but it's especially common in writing, where people often write the book of their heart with little regard for what *readers* want.

This is totally fine, of course. Not everything is about money. But if your goal *is* to make money (or find an audience), then **market research** is essential to effective branding. Contrary to popular belief, it is very hard to generate demand for a product that people do not want. Thus, if you write a book with no market, even the slickest cover and best blurb will be hard-pressed to sell it. On the other hand, if you write a book in a market with a voracious readership, even mediocre writing and packaging often can't stop it from succeeding.

Of course, if you can couple a story that has significant market demand *with* professional packaging that grabs the attention of those voracious readers, then *that* is when you have the potential for real marketing magic.

Market research doesn't stop with the writing process, though. It'll be critical throughout the branding process, because you'll be basing your own decisions when it comes to covers, blurbs, pricing, and more on the market at large. If you need a refresher on the subject, head back and read the section on Market Research. Otherwise, let's get started with a quick and dirty definition of branding and packaging.

BRANDING AND PACKAGING: WHAT ARE THEY?

I use the terms **branding** and **packaging** somewhat interchangeably. But just for clarity's sake, here's what each means:

1. **A brand is a promise of a consistent customer experience**. The heart of your brand is your **unique selling proposition (USP)**. Getting to the heart of your brand is as simple (and difficult) as answering this question: **what makes your books distinct?**
2. **Packaging** is the brand's visual presentation. Starbucks' cups and logo, for example, echo the premium experience and drive home the brand.

Don't get too hung up on granular definitions. The takeaway here is simple: your book's packaging *will* make or break its chances of success. So you need to master how they work.

The reason these terms are semi-interchangeable for our purposes is simple: blurbs and covers (your packaging) are the most prominent outward-facing pieces of your brand. These two elements are the 20% that drives 80% of the conversion results—or, in this case, more like 99%. Once you have your genre and USP established, the blurbs and covers will be responsible for broadcasting these to the correct target audience. So, for all intents and purposes, the blurb and cover *will* be your brand, since that's what readers will see.

In many ways, the points discussed herein are simply the price of entry. If your cover is off-genre, your book is DOA. If your blurb is boring, your book is toast. Put it in the wrong categories and you're going to reach the wrong buyers—and so forth. Nailing these elements is critical, but most authors **completely and utterly fail**. I thought I was doing it right for the first three years. I wasn't. This was both expensive and frustrating. But you can be the beneficiary of my mistakes.

WHAT MATTERS MOST

For those with perfectionist tendencies convinced you can do everything correctly, I implore you to reconsider. This is particularly important for authors with limited time, but it's a lesson we can all benefit from: focus your energy on what matters most. An 80% cover + 80% keywords is perhaps 1% as effective than a 99% cover and 5% keywords.

The hierarchy of what matters, from most to least:

1. Your book (genre/craft)
2. Cover
3. Blurb
4. Price
5. Reviews
6. Categories/keywords

1: COVERS & TITLES

Let's get one thing straight right away: your cover is not a piece of art, but a piece of packaging. If the reader cannot immediately identify your book's genre and tone from the cover, it has failed and needs to be replaced. Aside from market research, the cover is the most important part of book marketing. Getting it right is paramount.

Before we discuss cover design, however, we need an appropriate title.

TITLES

Perhaps you have a beautiful title that you just can't let go of—a song lyric, or a passage from your favorite book. You envision the story behind the title receiving its own sub-section on your book's Wikipedia page.

If this sounds remotely like what you're doing, **stop immediately.**

There are many questionable recommendations regarding the elements of a good title. Most of the advice on the topic tends to be fuzzy: "make it sing," "metaphors are the best option," or "follow your heart." All such information is egregiously incorrect for genre fiction—I have some awful selling books to prove it—so I recommend this instead: as with the cover, **the title should clearly signal to the reader** what the book is about.

There are innumerable exceptions to this rule: *Divergent, The Hunger Games, Red Rising, The Sound and the Fury, Infinite Jest,* and *The Sun Also Rises* are but a few of the titles that tell you little about the book prior to reading. To which I say: yes, you're right. But we don't have a big publisher who will put our book on the front table of Barnes & Noble and spring for a nice spread in *Publisher's Weekly*. We will not be reviewed in the *NYT*. We must create our own little marketing storm.

Overly clever and artistic titles tend to confuse or mislead the reader. Remember, you have seconds (milliseconds, even), to grab their attention. Make it count, and don't make them do more work than necessary. As one book out of thousands on Amazon, you haven't earned the benefit of their doubt yet.

This doesn't mean you title your latest romance *Two People Who Fall in Love and Bang at the End*.

Consider the book *Killing Floor*. If you didn't recognize the title, you surely won't be surprised to learn that it's the first book in the Jack Reacher series. It captures the genre and subject matter perfectly, without being overtly cliché or obvious.

Titling your book correctly isn't a magical fix—I released a book in 2016 called *Ashes of the Fall*, and it sold 148 copies in its first 30 days (and 260 during the entire year). But with zero additional information, you know that it's a dystopian/disaster/post-apocalyptic book. If you're interested in that genre, there's a good chance you'll consider clicking the cover thumbnail and giving it a closer look.

COVERS

Now that we have our title nailed down, we need a fantastic on-genre cover. This process entails three key things:

1. Research what's already selling.

2. Get a professional **cover artist**—don't design it yourself.

3. Don't let your own terrible ideas to get in the way.

While spending a few bucks on a pro cover doesn't guarantee sales, it makes your book dramatically more competitive in a crowded landscape. That being said, as we've mentioned already, the most important element of your cover is not the beauty of the design, but its effectiveness at conveying the genre at a one-second glance.

I've commissioned plenty of well-designed covers that didn't match my sub-genre. My main concern was being unique. I suspect most other authors have similar approaches.

If your cover is super-unique in genre fiction, you are missing the point.

Case in point: my original covers for a post-apocalyptic survival novel set on an island resort. These demonstrate that competent, professional covers are *not* enough to sell books. The designer was not at fault here; he followed my briefs and reference covers exactly. The failure and idiocy were mine alone. The end result is a professional cover (and title) that had no chance of selling a disaster book:

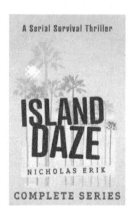 

The new title and cover were right on the money. As an aside, here are the free download numbers before vs. after I changed the cover:

	Dates	DLs (Amazon)	DLs (Wide)	DLs per Day
Island Daze	1/1 - 3/31	147	159	3.4
Paradise	4/1 - 4/30	336	128	15.5

Adjusting the cover and title to something genre-appropriate increased the number of downloads by almost 5x.

One final note: a good cover and title can't save a book that readers don't like. While the packaging for *Paradise* was on point after the rebrand, it still never translated to sales of my other books. It was my second novel, which is about all we need to say about that.

How to Commission a Kick Ass Cover

To avoid purchasing a beautiful piece of art that will not sell any books, here's a repeatable process for commissioning an appropriate genre cover:

1. **Find 3 – 5 covers that you like on your sub-genre's Amazon Top 100 bestseller list.** Identify a mix of traditionally published books and indie titles. Readers have voted with their dollars that they prefer these covers in this genre. Maybe you're getting sick of me mentioning the bestseller charts; too bad. These charts are like the ultimate

focus group that definitively answers the question "what do readers want?" totally free.

2. **Find a cover artist with a portfolio matching your desired style and book genre.** Visit my resources (**nicholaserik. com/resources**) if you're stuck. I only list designers that I've personally worked with and recommend.

3. **Send your 3 – 5 sample covers to the designer and tell them to MAKE IT LOOK SIMILAR TO THE EXAMPLES.** It is crucial to provide your designer with clear visual expectations, as text can be easily misinterpreted. Be specific regarding the design elements you do or do not want. The more clearly you communicate expectations, the better your final cover will be.

4. **Ensure that the typography is consistent in terms of font/ placement across your series.** This is critical for branding and to signal that books are in the same series.

This has been repeated almost ad nauseum, but you are *not* commissioning a piece of artwork. Unfortunately, this is *exactly* what I see many authors doing. Your cover art is your book's product packaging. Its only purpose is to signal what's inside. Do not package a Snickers bar in a Starburst wrapper. This will only attract the wrong customers and make them very angry.

You will *eventually* get to the point in your author career where you'll want to stand out from the crowd and really signal your author brand. This is smart, but you need a firm foundational understanding of why your readership responds to certain cover tropes/elements *before* "zagging" off on your own. Even slight deviations from the sub-genre formula tend to spell disaster for less experienced authors, as their "minor" deviation removes a key trope without replacing it with another more subtle element that triggers the same underlying psychological "feel."

Understand what the glowy hands on urban fantasy covers (or the naked man torso on steamy romances) *signals* before you reinvent the branding wheel. Once you have the basics down, feel free to subvert, lampshade, and omit cover tropes—just as you would in your novels. But the freedom to improvise is *earned* through a deep mastery of the fundamentals.

COVERS IN PRACTICE: COVERS FROM A

USA TODAY BESTSELLING SERIES

Using text to explain these principles is all well and good, but as the old saying goes about pictures and words (to view these in hi-res, visit **dnerikson.com/ruby**):

I want to highlight two things here: first, **consistent typography is one of the most critical factors for tying books together at a glance.** If you take a closer look at this series, the prequel novella (on the left) and the box set cover (on the right) are visually different from the others. The former is a close-up of a woman's face; the latter is hand-illustrated. Yet they *feel* like they're part of the same series. Why?

The fonts are all the same. There's also a little "badge" on each one (shaped like a shield) that ties the books together. Finally, the typography *placement* itself is consistent, taking up the bottom third of the cover (save for the box set, where the author name couldn't fit).

Two, other subtle touches maintain the branding. The close-up model on the left? Same one as featured on the three individual books. The shotgun makes an appearance on all five covers. Even though the hand-illustrated cover doesn't use the model as a reference, the broad strokes of the character's appearance remain the same. At a thumbnail, they fit in cohesively.

2: BLURBS

Your cover is the most important tool in your marketing arsenal. A truly great one can sell a book on its own with minimal advertising. A crappy one *will* scuttle your book's conversion.

But your book description—usually referred to as the "blurb" (or "jacket copy" in traditional publishing)—shouldn't be given short shrift. Covers have steadily risen in quality over the past few years, making it much harder to close the sale with shiny packaging alone. An excellent blurb is crucial to convert browsers into buyers. That's because the general evaluation process goes something like this:

1. Click on book because of cool, relevant cover.
2. Scroll down and read the tagline/first few words of the blurb.

3.   Leave, click buy, read sample, or read a few reviews.

In other words, a strong cover and blurb can sell your book without the reader scrolling any further. This is key: we want our presentation to be so good that the reader *must* click buy. Unfortunately, authors have an uncanny ability to perform reverse alchemy, penning blurbs that transform fascinating books into ones that sound unreadable, boring, and terrible.

Authors often note that writing the blurb is more difficult than writing the actual novel. That's not a surprise, since the blurb is a piece of sales copy demanding a different set of writing skills: *copywriting*.

What follows are the common elements underpinning effective book descriptions. Actually writing an effective blurb of your own is a matter of practice and repeated revision—unfortunately, there are no shortcuts.

But don't worry: we'll cover how to improve, too.

Writing Your Blurb: Guidelines

The blurb's job is to grab your reader's attention and pique their curiosity in a condensed space. For a $5 eBook, the only question/objection you must answer is simple: **as a fan of genre x, will this book satisfy my expectations and entertain me?** This does not require that much text, just the *right* text.

Some guidelines to help you make that happen:

1.   **TONE:** this should reflect the tone of the book/reading experience.

2. **STYLE:** short sentences. Fragments are okay and can help the rhythm.

3. **FORMATTING:** a splash of bold (particularly for the tagline) can give a professional flair. Don't be afraid of the return key—white space is your friend, since most people will skim.

4. **READABILITY:** write the blurb at a reasonable reading level. I aim for fifth to seventh grade.

5. **CONFLICT AND TENSION:** these are the heartbeat of fiction, so you want to make sure your blurb overflows with these. If your blurb is boring, usually it doesn't have enough conflict.

6. **CURIOSITY:** "what happens next?" is the most powerful question in fiction. You can use techniques like cliffhangers to pique the reader's curiosity.

7. **CHARACTER/PLOT:** characters drive most books, although some genres (thriller/mysteries) are more plot driven. Show what makes your story/characters strong + unique. Note that is *not* about the fancy names you came up with for your fictional fantasy realm. It's about the *feeling* and emotional *experience* you're going to provide. Don't be overly general. Be clear about the stakes.

8. **SETTING:** try to seamlessly incorporate it within the first or second sentence, especially in genres (e.g. fantasy/sci-fi) heavily reliant on setting. Also holds true where region is of interest to readers (e.g. New York, London, etc.).

9. **PROPER NAMES/NOUNS:** avoid unfamiliar ones. Only mention the protagonist and antagonist—or the male/female leads in a romance.

10. **LENGTH:** typically no longer than 200 - 250 words.

11. **AUDIENCE (GENRE):** you can select the audience by using nouns common to the genre (e.g. mentioning wizards and vampires for an urban fantasy book). You can be more explicit by mentioning the genre, or similar authors—this can be done via a statement like "a magic-fueled urban fantasy romp for fans of Jim Butcher." This type of mention is usually used as the tagline/hook at the top of the blurb or at the close.

The General Structure

1. **Hook/tagline**: the most important part of your blurb. Must pique serious curiosity in a very brief time frame. A hook is a high-concept idea that can be summed up in 15 words or less. Most books don't have them. Thus, you'll often rely on a snappy tagline (**Only a demon can save the world from burning**) that hits precisely the right genre notes. Or a statement opening (**A new snarky, magic-fueled urban fantasy thrill-ride for fans of Jim Butcher and Ilona Andrews**). Not all good blurbs have taglines, but it's worth coming up with a few anyway.

2. **80 - 90 word lead:** the lead is the first few sentences of your blurb. A pithy lead combined with a strong tagline or hook can sell the book on its own. The area "above the fold" (before readers have to click read more) on Amazon totals less than 90 words (30 on mobile). Most readers will only see this, so make it engaging. Browse your genre's best-seller lists to find effective examples. You'll see how good taglines and leads not only make you want to read the book,

but also quickly communicate the underlying flavor, tone, style, and experience a reader can expect.

3.   **Body:** this is where you establish the book's core conflict. Focus on *one* thread, rather than a myriad of subplots that distract or confuse the potential reader.

4.   **Snapper/cliffhanger:** end with a "snapper" —a rhythmic, pithy line that establishes the stakes, hooks the reader's attention, and forces them to either purchase or check out a sample. Alternative is a simple cliffhanger, which works the same way as it does within the book. Please don't write "scroll up and grab a copy." This is a direct-response hard-sell call-to-action (CTA) that is out of place in fiction.

That's it: tagline, lead, body, snapper. Four parts.

It's helpful to consider that a blurb is just a fractal story. A fractal is a part that resembles the whole: a puddle has the same characteristics of a lake, just on a smaller scale. The same idea applies here: a blurb is, in effect, a miniature story with a beginning, middle, and end. If you can use your storytelling chops, then you can write an effective blurb.

Standard Blurb Formula

Here's a standard formula adaptable to most genres. I maintain an updated, downloadable blurb cheat sheet with additional formulas on my site (**nicholaserik.com/blurb-cs**) (note: this link goes straight to the PDF download). The formula below should cover *most* books.

1. Start with a hook/tagline (e.g. "The world's burning. And only a demon can save it.") or a hooky review quote/bestseller accolade etc. (note that using excerpts from Amazon reviews is not allowed in the TOS).

2. Then introduce the main character/plot hook (e.g. he's a demon with a conscience). This should be powerful enough to sell the book on its own—one sentence, or maybe two short ones. It must be above the fold.

3. Follow that up with the stakes/main story question. This will introduce the antagonist or threat to the world.

4. End with a "snapper" or a cliffhanger a la what you would have at the end of a chapter. A "snapper" is hard to define, but it's a sentence with a certain rhythmic finality to it that firmly establishes the stakes. The reader should be so interested that they have no choice but to buy the book to find out the answer.

5. (optional) End with a hard sell (e.g. "for fans of Sookie Stackhouse and Anita Blake" or "a pulse-pounding international thriller, *Spies & Lies* will keep you on the edge of your seat").

6. Sprinkle in the tropes/themes to flesh out the details. The optional hard sell is a great place to clearly state the genre, or allude to it, if you're having trouble working it in elsewhere ("full of bloodthirsty vampires and brooding alpha werewolves").

EXAMPLE 1 (STANDARD)

Groundhog Day meets The Dresden Files in this time-looping twist on urban fantasy.

Supernatural bounty hunter Ruby Callaway has survived for over two centuries by following a single rule: shoot first, ask questions never. Which may explain why she spent the last twenty years in jail.

But now the FBI has an offer she can't refuse: kill a necromancer, she gets her freedom.

Only two problems.

This necromancer is unlike any creature Ruby has ever hunted.

And the FBI will never let the world's most notorious bounty hunter roam free without serious strings…

EXAMPLE 2 (FIRST PERSON)

This style is popular in urban fantasy and romance—note that this example is pretty long, and could probably be tightened up, although it does convert well.

I'm Kalos Aeon. I've been around for longer than you could know—and most people don't want to know me, being half-demon, and all—but right now I've got a big f'in problem. A woman just came into my office, and I gotta say, from the photo she slipped me, someone's got a serious issue with the supernatural.

Life expectancy is looking kinda low if I don't figure out who's kidnapping magical creatures, selling their blood and trying to reveal magic's existence to the mortal world. Last time that happened it didn't end well. I'm not optimistic about this time, either.

Joke's on me, anyway, for setting up a magical salvage and retrieval business. 50% of an item's magical essence and a per diem can't cover the damages this job is gonna inflict.

Money and magic aren't of much use to a dead man. And If I didn't have a code (yes, I'm a demon with a code), then I would jet out of Texas faster than a vamp at a sorority party (you don't want to know).

But I agreed to the gig, she paid the cash, so I gotta see it through.

Did I mention the super-powerful witch - who I used to have, ahem, relations with - just returned from a long hiatus in a place worse than hell? And she's still obsessed with finding a certain god's spear that I may or may not have.

Seriously. This situation is code red. I'm almost willing to accept help from wizards. On second thought, no wizards. I hate you guys. I'd rather die.

So um, if I don't make it through the next three days, anyone want a talking dog that's read too much for his own good? Because the way things are going, Argos is gonna need a new home after the spells stop flying...*

*His only request is that you suck less than Odysseus. Apparently the epic poems got that all wrong, and that guy was a major asshole. Or my dog might just be bitter. Tends to rub off when you live with a demon.

HOW TO PRACTICE

Okay, so it's great to have basic principles, a formula, and examples.

But how does one actually apply all this info to get better?

Here's how to practice your copywriting chops, step-by-step.

1. **Find 5 blurbs in your sub-genre's top 20 lists that make you want to read the actual book**. Make sure they're not discounted $0.99 books enjoying a temporary promo surge. Try to find indie books priced above $2.99. Read + copy them over to a document. This is known in copywriting as a "swipe file."

2. **Find 5 more blurbs—not necessarily in your genre—from NYT Bestsellers**. These are usually written by pro copy-writers. Read them and copy them to your swipe file.

3. **Find 5 more blurbs that have been in the top 50 in your sub-genre for months or years**. These books are likely there because of consistent advertising. The only way to advertise long-term? Have it be profitable. That means those blurbs are converting well.

4. **Skim the reviews of popular books in your genre**. What did readers consistently hate/like the most? Does the blurb reference these elements? These are the tropes readers will expect to see mentioned in your blurb (and in your book).

5. For professionally written (and split-tested) copy, subscribe to BookBub's newsletter in your genre(s) of choice. Add good ones to your swipe file.

Then, each day for the next 30 days, set a timer for 15 minutes and:

1. **Hand copy one blurb word-for-word**. This is a classic copywriting technique and works wonders to get the feeling in your bones. Analyze what tropes the author is using, how the language flows, what encourages people to buy.

Why did the writer use a certain word? Why did they leave another detail out?

2. **Then write your own blurb**. Don't focus on making things good, just write it and put it in a document on your computer.

3. **Read it out loud**. It should flow well. You can do this the next day, or as a last check to iron out any rough spots before you either test the blurb on FB or put it up on Amazon.

4. **Bonus**: test your blurbs/taglines on Facebook to get direct feedback on what's working with your target audience (and what isn't). Judge the quality based on CPC (lowest CPC wins).

You can either split your time each day between the hand copying and writing (i.e., 7.5 minutes each), or alternate days—one day hand copying, the next writing.

This may seem too basic to work. I have personally done a lot of hand copying and can attest to its efficacy. It is the *best* way to improve your blurbs and ad copy, bar none. If you do this exercise consistently for thirty days, you'll massively improve your blurbs. And you can apply the same concept to ad copy, creating a swipe file of Facebook, Amazon, and BookBub Ads that catch your eye, then breaking them down to understand the key principles.

3: PRICING

There is one key question to answer when pricing: **what price maximizes my long-term profit**? This, however, can be broken down further into two sub-questions:

1. Is my *current* primary goal profit or long-term visibility/ fanbase building?

   - **Based on this goal, what is the optimal price for my specific book/series?**
   - **General rule of thumb:** lower price = more visibility/ more volume/less revenue; higher price = less visibility/ less volume/more revenue. Sometimes this is thrown out of whack, i.e., where a book sells more volume at a higher price.

2. Look at the indie bestsellers in your genre—what do readers expect to pay?

A good baseline if you have no idea what to charge: price your book around **what indie authors in the Top 100 of your subgenre are successfully charging.** In romance, there's generally a cap of around $4.99; in other genres, it might be higher or lower. And if you have a name brand or a big fanbase, you can generally command more dollars.

FINDING AN OPTIMAL PRICE POINT

Nailing down the exact optimal price point for a specific book requires testing.

There are two ways of doing this—without ads and with ads.

(1) **Without ads.** Start with the "baseline" genre price above, and track sales for two to four weeks. Once you have that data (or if you already have it), adjust to a new price, **changing no other elements.** Track sales for the same amount of time, then compare the average sales per day.

This type of testing typically requires that you're running PPC ads or have a book that is selling well on its own, since you need a steady amount of traffic to ensure a large enough sample size.

Here's what happened when I price-tested an adventure book (in KU) with revenue as the goal:

Price	Days	Sales/Day	$/Day
$ 0.99	14	6.2	$ 7.05
$ 3.99	19	2.3	$ 12.25
$ 4.99	48	3.4	$ 15.77

You should try to make the length of the comparison periods identical. Additionally, you want to maintain the same advertising/marketing during each period. But this back of the envelope type of analysis easily tells me that $4.99 is the best price for my goal. Interestingly, the book also sold slightly better at $4.99 versus $3.99, thus increasing the visibility, as well. This is not an unusual occurrence, because some readers use price as a signal for quality and ignore lower priced books. If you're in a genre that expects premium prices, pricing your books low might reduce revenue *and* visibility.

I decided not to test $5.99, as most of the indie books in the adventure genre cap out at around $3.99 – $4.99. Page reads also increased with the price increase—readers are more likely to buy a book at $0.99 and borrow it when the price is higher.

(2) **With ads**. This method is a lot quicker and much easier, taking about 3 – 7 days for each price, depending on how much money you're spending on ads. You can rapidly test multiple prices, thus settling on your optimal price point with 2 – 3 weeks, rather than months.

This is simple: start by running ads (I recommend Facebook, since you have the most control over how much you spend) to the book at the current price.

Then calculate the conversion rate, which is **sales / clicks**.

Then change the price to the new one, making sure you're running the *exact* same ads (different ads and ad platforms will have different conversion rates) and calculate the conversion rate.

A final wrinkle that applies to both methods: if you have a series (the numbers above are for only one book), you should look at the total money generated by the *series*. The increased sales volume on Book 1 at $0.99 might produce less immediate revenue, but you might sell more copies of Books 2, 3, 4, and so forth, thus generating more *total* revenue in the long run.

To do this, we need to compare our series revenue at the tested price points over equal periods. Since it takes time for readers to get through a series, I'd recommend a minimum of two weeks (but preferably a month) to get an accurate snapshot of which price point produces the most series revenue.

4: CATEGORIES & KEYWORDS

Ah, keywords.

How much time you've wasted me.

I've tried most of the techniques suggested in books and courses, and used most of the popular keyword tools—Publisher Rocket, Merchant Words, Keyword Inspector, Kindle Spy, Kindle Samurai, as well as the basic "enter the first letter in the Amazon search box" technique.

My conclusion: Keywords on Amazon do very little, unless they're in the title or subtitle. If you have a specific term you want to show up high in Amazon's search results for, it needs to be in the title or subtitle. People have abused this to the point where it's basically useless in fiction (the subtitle will be something like "A Supernatural Suspense Novel of the Paranormal Witches Wizards Fantasy Thriller"). But if you're publishing non-fiction, consider using a title that incorporates a popular keyword phrase or two.

By the way, to bust a myth you might have seen floating around: Amazon book descriptions aren't searchable, so don't try to pad your blurb with a bunch of additional keywords and categories. I added the nonsense word "dgrzprseamp" to one of my descriptions, then searched for it over a six-week period. My book didn't show up.

But let's say you don't believe me and want to enter keywords anyway. I'll show you how to perform that research so you can generate more than you'll ever need.

FINDING KEYWORDS

While generating keywords isn't useful for Amazon KDP, it is useful for their ads platform. Thus, the techniques below have value, albeit not for boosting your position in organic search results.

A few technical notes for entering keywords on Amazon KDP:

- Amazon gives you seven keyword boxes; each box has a 50 character limit.
- Repeating keywords is unnecessary. E.g., vampire love story and vampire paranormal romance. You can just have "vampire love story paranormal romance" and Amazon will spit out your book when someone searches for either term.
- Use the full 50 characters. Don't repeat the same word twice (e.g. paranormal romance vampire romance - second romance not necessary). Plurals don't seem to matter—e.g., the search engine treats "books" and "book" the same way.
- Don't use words like "free," "best-selling," other authors' names, or Kindle Unlimited unless you want Amazon to get angry with you.

After you've gathered your organic keywords, enter them until you max out each 50 character string. Simple, although it's also time-consuming.

KEYWORD TOOLS:

- **OneLook** (onelook.com) is actually the most useful tool I've found for generating keyword ideas. It's basically a super-thesaurus that will return all terms related to a word. So if you put in "island," you'll get stuff like "archipelago" along with six degrees type stuff a la "cove," "plantation," and "reef."

- **Google Keyword Planner tool**. Just type in a phrase like "science fiction" or "aliens" and write down all the relevant phrases that have decent search volume. Alternatively, plug in a competitor's book page into the "landing page" box and get keywords from there.

- **Keywordtool.io** (keywordtool.io) generates suggested keywords from a number of different search engines—including Google and Amazon.

Amazon Ads only:

You can't use author and book names for the keywords you enter on the KDP Dashboard; it's against the TOS. But they're usable—and quite useful— for Amazon Ads. Here are the best sources:

- The also boughts and sponsored products for popular books and authors in your genre.
- The Top 100 charts in your sub-genre.
- Find book titles at bookseriesinorder.com, which is exactly what the name suggests.

Special Google Play Note

Keywords are critical on Google Play, since your book's blurb is indexed. There's no specific place to add keywords—so insert them at the end of the description.

Results (Jan 1 – March 31 data is with *no* keywords; April data is *with* keywords at the bottom of the description):

DOWNLOADS PER DAY			
Book	No KWs (1/1 - 3/31)	KWs (4/1 - 4/30)	Other changes in April 2016
Shadow Memories	0.3	1.4	*new blurb/categories
The Emerald Elephant	0.3	1.1	*new blurb/categories
Paradise	0.1	2.4	*new blurb/categories/cover/title

Not a massive boost, but we'll take what we can get.

Categories

On Amazon, the main (small) benefit of using keywords at all is to get into specific sub-categories. There are "secret" keywords not on Amazon lists that also place your book in additional categories.

Speaking of categories: you can have up to 10. It's worth putting your book in as many relevant categories as possible, as this maximizes your visibility across the store—as an example, one of my urban fantasy series is set in the future and has sci-fi elements. Thus, I put it into both sci-fi and fantasy related categories.

When it's riding high on the charts, it'll show up on both bestseller lists and be recommended to both genre readers. This expands my footprint on the store and increases my overall visibility.

My basic recommendation for dealing with categories and keywords:

1. Place your book in the correct categories on the KDP dashboard (i.e., if it's an urban fantasy book, place it in that category)

2. Enter any *relevant* keywords from Amazon's official list (**nicholaserik.com/keywords**) to get into a few additional sub-categories.

3. Fill out the remaining keywords with relevant generic terms (e.g. "urban fantasy").

4. Call it a day.

While you'll find some of the sub-category keyword on Amazon's official list, others that are unlisted. You can randomly try keywords to gain access to these sub-categories, or just email KDP support and request that your book be added.

The sub-category names are located right below the book's sales rank:

Lending: Enabled
Screen Reader: Supported ⌄
Enhanced Typesetting: Enabled ⌄
Amazon Best Sellers Rank: #88,621 Paid in Kindle Store (See Top 100 Paid in Kindle Store)
     #1186 in Dark Fantasy Horror
     #1416 in Dark Fantasy
     #4365 in Paranormal & Urban Fantasy (Kindle Store)

Requesting additional categories is refreshingly easy: just email KDP and ask. Here's a basic template:

Please place my book [TITLE] (ASIN: XX) into the following categories:
Dark Fantasy Horror
[category 2]
Thanks!

This isn't some sort of magic. I had a book ranked 19k in the free store that was in four categories. But it takes five minutes and can help maximize your visibility, particularly after a promo when you hit high enough on various genre lists.

Some authors will be tempted to abuse this—hell, some already are—and cram their book into as many categories as possible. This is a poor practice, as it annoys readers and doesn't get your work in front of the *right* eyeballs. Category stuffing doesn't gen-erate any visibility boosts for books already languishing in the ranks.

Note the repetition of the word *relevant* when it comes to cat-egories. You don't want to shotgun into as many categories as possible; you want to be in the *right* ones. If that's three catego-ries, don't add more for the heck of it. That will screw with the algorithm's recommendation targeting. Which, as we've covered earlier in the guide, would be bad.

5: REVIEWS

New authors tend to focus far too much on reviews. When you're not selling, they can seem like the skeleton key to success. They are far less important than you think; reviews are not a driver of sales, but a byproduct of them. Popular books have sold more copies, ergo they have far more readers who can potentially leave you a review.

That being said, some promo sites have review requirements, and social proof is a factor in getting people to buy. A book with *no* reviews or an assortment of poor ones might receive a wary eyebrow from a prospective buyer. Especially if they can find a similar-looking book that has far better reviews.

Thus, a few guidelines for generating quality reviews:

- Don't get them from friends/family. This is against the Amazon TOS. Don't freak out if your mom leaves you a review, however; this won't get you banned. Amazon is just likely to remove it.

- You can ask for reviews in the back matter of your book. This is generally not advised when you have more than ten (see the next section on front and back matter for why). But when you have no reviews, this can get the ball rolling— particularly in conjunction with a free run. If you promote your free book with the link in the back matter and generate a few thousand downloads, you can expect a few reviews to come in.

- Start your own ARC (advance review copy) team. These people receive an early review copy of the book. They often will then review it for you come launch day. Note that you can't demand or force them to leave a review (or a positive one, either). But they tend to be willing if you remind them on launch day. You can include a message in your newsletter autoresponder inviting people to the ARC team, or simply send out a regular newsletter announcing that you're looking for ARC readers for your next release. You should get at least a few takers if you have 500+ people on your mailing list.

For more on getting reviews, check out my Mini Guide to Getting Reviews (**nicholaserik.com/reviews**).

6: FRONT & BACK MATTER

The front and back matter are both invaluable marketing real estate. Too many authors waste them—either by not putting *anything* there at all, or polluting each with hundreds of links. A substantial portion of your income will come from your **backlist**. Effective front and back matter helps sell your other books (and also get people on your mailing list, so they buy your upcoming *and* previous releases).

It's critical to understand a few basic principles of **conversion** before we go ahead. First and foremost, the more actions or choices you offer a person, the less likely they are to take *any* action. This is why you want to cut down the number of calls-to-action (CTAs) to a minimum. Make sure you're only asking folks to take actions that will move the needle. Once you have someone on your mailing list, for example, you can send them other links: social media, backlist, and so forth. But first you need to actually get them on the list.

Two, you need to make a specific *ask*. The easier and clearer you make this (e.g. by including a link with phrasing like "TAP HERE TO BUY BOOK 2"), the more action readers will take.

In the front matter, you'll want to include a link to your newsletter on its own page. This can increase subscribers by 2x or more. In practice, this looks like:

While the image-based options look appealing, they increase the delivery fees, so I generally go with a one or two sentence text only request.

In the back matter, we want to limit our CTAs to two (newsletter and an upsell to Book 2):

The back matter on the left was already optimized—it had three links. A CTA asks the reader to do something specific. In this instance, the CTAs were a link to my mailing list, a review request, and a link to buy the next book.

I recommended this back matter for years.

It produced 3.4% sellthrough to Book 2.

The one on the right stripped all the other CTAs away other than the link to Book 2.

It produced 4.8% sellthrough to Book 2—an almost 1.5x increase. That's *massive* when you compound out over months and years.

This is especially aggressive in that it only has *one* CTA.

Just remember the principle: limit your CTAs. I'd include no more than two—a newsletter link and a link to the next book.

And don't phone in the CTA text! As writers, we often forget that words matter when it comes to things like blurbs or CTAs. A little copywriting goes a long way.

The specific words you use (i.e., "free," "download," and "get" are all effective CTA components) influence how many people will bother to click on the offer link. *Telling* people specifically what to do helps a surprising amount (e.g. a link with the text "tap here to get the next book now" is better than a link that just says "get the next book").

Finally, a note on excerpts: they don't seem to increase sellthrough for books within the same series (i.e., from Book 1 > Book 2) in Kindle Unlimited. But they do help when you're wide.

And they *can* increase sellthrough to unconnected books (e.g., one standalone > another standalone in the same genre, or Book 5 of Series A > Book 1 of Series B) regardless if you're exclusive or wide. As such, including an unrelated excerpt can be a clever way to introduce readers to a new series—or plug a standalone that's not getting much sales love.

A CLOSING THOUGHT

For many, my assertions that your book, title, cover, and blurb are critical won't exactly be a revelation. However, I hope that even if you're well-versed in branding this guide has at least provided some concrete evidence that, in fact, these are the right paths to focus on. Too often we get attracted to new and shiny things, while declaring the fundamentals old hat.

So before you tweak your book until you're seeing keywords in your alphabet soup, know this: Most of the time, the answer to "why is my book not selling?" is because *you've written an unsellable book.*

This isn't meant to be discouraging. Instead, it should be liberating: I see too many authors obsess over the Sisyphean task of propping their poorly selling books up with continued revision, promo, and never-ending tweaks. After a certain point, it's better to marshal your resources to other ends—like studying what readers want, and then delivering a book that satisfies their expectations.

If you have a pro cover and blurb, have your price dialed in, and get some traffic on the book, and it *still* doesn't sell, don't despair. But don't force the issue.

But before you write off a poor seller, see if there's anything you can do to improve its chances of success. You probably won't vault up the best-seller lists, but if you have an extensive backlist, you can generate a comfortable bump in revenue by getting the branding on point.

KEY TAKEAWAYS

COVERS

- Cover = packaging, not artwork.
- Make sure your title clearly signals the genre. Don't go for metaphors or esoteric imagery.
- You want a cover that is professional, clean, readable, and instantly signals the genre/expectations at a small size.
- Browse Amazon's top 100 bestseller list in your sub-genre. Note the trends in terms of titles, covers, and other elements (e.g., is the typography usually distressed? Is it a sans-serif or a serif?).
- Find a designer with a portfolio that indicates they can pull your genre off well.
- Send your 3 – 5 examples to your designer with very clear instructions.

BLURBS

- Answers this reader question: as a fan of genre x, will this book satisfy my expectations and entertain me?
- A blurb has just four parts: tagline, lead, body, snapper.
- Practice blurbs by hand-copying one blurb and writing another each day.
- Read your blurb out loud when it's done.

PRICING

- Determine your price by answering two key questions:
- Is my main goal revenue or visibility?
- **What is the optimal price for my goal (either revenue/ visibility) given my specific book/series?**
- **General rule of thumb:** lower price = more visibility/less revenue; higher price = less visibility/more revenue.
- Sometimes this is thrown out of whack, i.e. where a book sells better at a higher price.
- Look at the indie bestsellers in your genre—what do readers expect to pay?

KEYWORDS

- Keywords aren't useful on Amazon unless they're already part of the pre-existing title and subtitle.
- Keywords can be used to access special Amazon subcategories.
- Keywords are *very* useful on Google Play.

CATEGORIES

- Plug in keywords to get into the categories you want.
- Alternatively, email KDP support and ask them nicely to put your book in other categories.

Reviews

- Start your own ARC team to get reviews on release day.
- Run your book for free and have a request in the back matter (with a link directly to the review form) to get reviews.

Front and Back Matter

- Include a link to your newsletter on its own page in the front matter.
- Limit the number of CTAs on the same page as THE END to two: newsletter and an upsell to the next book.

ACTION EXERCISES

Cover: Action Step

1. **Find 3 – 5 covers that you like on your sub-genre's Amazon Top 100 bestseller list.** Identify a mix of traditionally published books and indie titles. Readers have voted with their dollars that they prefer these covers in this genre. Maybe you're getting sick of me mentioning the bestseller charts; too bad. These charts are like the ultimate focus group that definitively answers the question "what do readers want?" totally free.

2. **Find a cover artist with a portfolio matching your desired style and book genre.** Visit my resources (**nicholaserik.**

com/resources) if you're stuck. I only list designers that I've personally worked with and recommend.

3. **Send your 3 – 5 sample covers to the designer and tell them to MAKE IT LOOK SIMILAR TO THE EXAMPLES.** It is crucial to provide your designer with clear visual expectations, as text can be easily misinterpreted. Be specific regarding the design elements you do or do not want. The more clearly you communicate expectations, the better your final cover will be.

4. **Ensure that the typography is consistent in terms of font/ placement across your series.** This is critical for branding and to signal that books are in the same series.

Blurb: Action Step

1. Write a new blurb based on the principles and the formula that best fits your book.

Back Matter: Action Step

1. Reduce the number of CTAs on same page as THE END to two: a mailing list link and a link to your next book.

NINE:

NEWSLETTER BUILDING

In this section, we'll cover a step-by-step process for how you can build your email list to 1,000 subscribers (and beyond, if you've already hit that milestone).

First, let's take a look at our Ultimate Book Marketing Formula:

MARKET RESEARCH + 3 TRAFFIC SOURCES + PRO COVERS + GREAT BLURBS + NEWSLETTER + 4-6 NOVELS PER YEAR

CONSISTENTLY FOR 3-5 YEARS

FULL-TIME AUTHOR

At this point, we've covered everything in the book marketing formula except for one critical piece.

Your newsletter.

As it so happens, we've saved the most important part for last. Your email list is a direct line of communication with your biggest fans. It's the cornerstone of your platform and your second most valuable business asset (the first, of course, being the actual books). A solid email list can drive hundreds of full price sales on launch day.

But it's no secret that most authors struggle to build one. Which begs the question: *how do you get those elusive subscribers on your list in the first place?*

I know how frustrating it can be to build your list as well as anyone: at the start of 2016, I had four subscribers on my author list, despite having had one for over *three* years. Organic subscribers came in a rate of one or two a month, since I wasn't selling many books. Big promotions rarely produced any new subscribers. I never contacted my list, because I was too tentative. I built my list up to around a hundred names two, maybe three times, but never contacted them. Each time I'd delete the subscribers and dutifully start again.

Meanwhile, I'd tweak my autoresponder and book formatting constantly, trying to test and optimize when I had no traffic.

The struggle was real.

Finally, I'd had enough. Come hell or high water, I was going to contact my list regularly—even when it was twenty people. And then I was gonna build it up to 1,000 subscribers by the end of the year.

I did it—and then some.

By April 2017, I had 3,000+ subscribers across my lists.

Fast forward to February 2018. I had 16,000+ subscribers.

And now, as of February 2020? About 6,900.

Wait, what? Don't worry: this time, I didn't reboot and start over. Nor did everyone up and unsubscribe. Removing nearly 10,000 subscribers was a deliberate decision to *increase* the effectiveness of my various lists.

We'll cover why (and how) you might remove a large block of subscribers in the next section (on newsletter engagement). Before we can engage people, though, we need to actually get them on the list. So what follows is a step-by-step system for cost-effectively adding **1,000 quality email subscribers to your list in a month**—whether you're starting from scratch and don't even know what a newsletter is, or have 20,000 already.

Before we hop into the newsletter building, though, let's revisit our old friend the Internet Marketing Formula.

INTERNET MARKETING FORMULA, REVISITED

It's been a little while since we discussed one of our cornerstone formulas, so it's time for a quick refresher. This is how you sell anything online, from shoes to books. We've discussed how it applies to books, but here's how it can help you build an email list, too:

1. **Traffic**: subscribers. You get people to sign up for your list. Covered in this guide.

2. **Conversion**: engagement. You convert these subscribers into readers by crafting engaging emails, an autoresponder, and writing books they like to read. Covered in Newsletter Engagement.

3. **Assessing ROI (return on investment)**: sales. Are your newsletter building efforts generating sales?

4. If yes, continue with the same subscriber building and engagement strategies. Try to scale them up, if possible.

5. If subscribers aren't purchasing your books, or are lukewarm in terms of engagement, you need to reassess their source, the quality/frequency of your emails (and free book, if you offered one to get them on the list), and the effectiveness of your autoresponder.

Simple: generate subscribers, convert them into sales by writing good emails/books, and then assess whether your efforts were successful sales-wise, tweaking as needed.

But not easy, as you probably already know.

Which is why I'll begin by explaining *why* you should go to the trouble of building a list at all.

BENEFITS OF A MAILING LIST

Simply put, your mailing list is the most powerful book marketing tool in existence. A quality list can jumpstart Amazon's algos like a nuclear fuel rod, sell more books in a day than you might've sold this year, and skyrocket you into the full-time author ranks. And it's an asset that you can use for years— today or two decades from now. Suffice to say, reports of email being replaced by social media or other "disruptive" technologies are wildly overblown.

The terms "email list" or "newsletter" are *really* synonyms for **platform**. You need a direct communication conduit to readers— be that your newsletter, social media (Facebook/Twitter), a forum, or some other place where you can tell fans about your books. Otherwise your career is on borrowed time.

Here are the five main benefits:

1. **You own it**. The reason the newsletter beats *all* the available alternatives is simple: it is 100% under your control and ownership. Visibility on other platforms can be taken away or change on a dime. Facebook, Twitter, even your Amazon account—these are all third-party platforms. Yes, if you abide by the TOS of these sites, you're not going to get booted. But the landscape of these third-party platforms shifts with little warning. Facebook has massively reduced the organic reach of Pages, for instance, which means you now have to pay to reach most of the people who like your page. Everyone who built their platform on Facebook woke up one day to suddenly find it was a whole lot pricier to reach their hard-won fans.

2. **Your personal customer list is better than anyone else's**. Yes, you can, and should, market your books via PPC ads, promo sites, and other mechanisms. But these cold readers, even if they love the genre, will never respond as well to your books as a well-maintained mailing list. And engagement rates are higher for email than Facebook or other social media platforms.

3. **You can push a massive sales volume at full price (i.e., visibility)**. When you have a high-quality, engaged list, you can sell hundreds of copies on launch day at anywhere from $0.99 to full price. This juices Amazon's algorithms and can also bring in thousands of dollars on launch day.

4. **You can get dozens of reviews on launch day by setting up an ARC (Advance Review Copy) team.** No more using review services or giving your book away for free in hopes

of netting a few reviews. And no more launches scuttled by an ill-timed 1-star review arriving on Day 1.

5.   **You can interact directly with readers**. You can send readers surveys. Give 'em signed paperbacks or swag. Or just talk with them about your upcoming books to get feedback—because readers will respond to your emails.

Numbers three and four are the primary benefits: **using your mailing list, you can sell enough books at full price to make a full-time living, even with a modest monthly advertising budget**. And even the ability to get five reviews on launch day solves a myriad of problems, from providing social proof to qualifying for most promo sites.

In short: if you only have time for one marketing endeavor, make sure you're building a list.

WHICH EMAIL SERVICE SHOULD I USE?

There are dozens of email service providers. Comparing and contrasting them can be an exercise in extreme analysis paralysis. I'm here to cut through the noise: each one pretty much does the same basic thing (especially for our purposes as authors), but the interfaces, advanced features, and pricing differ.

After testing a half dozen, here are my two recommendations:

1.   **MailerLite (mailerlite.com)**. Free up to 1,000 subscribers; $10/mo for 1,001 – 2,500 subscribers.

- **Pluses**: intuitive and simple interface. Autoresponders available for free accounts. Continually improving, since they're relatively new.
- **Minuses**: bare bones sign-up forms. Missing a few advanced features for power users. Requires your own email (e.g. name@yourauthorname.com).

1. **ConvertKit (convertkit.com)**. $29/mo for up to 1,000 subscribers.

- **Pluses**: robust and easy-to-use tagging features. Beautiful sign-up forms. Has advanced/premium features usually reserved for more expensive services (i.e., Infusionsoft). Great support that responds quickly. Excellent email deliverability. Continually improving, since they're a relatively new company.
- **Minuses**: expensive. Need a separate account for each pen name (I have separate accounts for my fiction and non-fiction) because you can't have separate lists on a single account—only tags.

Mailchimp is also an option if you have fewer than 2,000 subscribers (it's free until then, although its free plan is limited in comparison to MailerLite's). After that, it gets pricey and its interface is *terrible*. If you're going to pay a premium, I'd highly recommend ConvertKit instead.

For most authors, I'd recommend MailerLite, especially if you just need to set up a basic autoresponder and send out the occasional newsletter. As mentioned, I use ConvertKit (I use MailerLite and Mailchimp, too). I think the enhanced deliverability is worth the heftier price tag.

There is no perfect email provider. Pick one and move on.

On a related note, I'd recommend getting your own email (**name@yourauthorname.com**) as soon as possible. It increases deliverability and helps build your brand recognition in someone's inbox. A custom email address runs about $50/year from Google GSuite (**gsuite.google.com**).

HOW MANY SUBS DO I NEED, THEN?

This sounds like a reasonable question, but it's the wrong one. **Engagement** (click and open rates, plus the number of sales your newsletter generates) is far more critical than the actual size of your subscriber base.

A list of 1,000 organic subscribers can sell 200 copies on launch day.

A list of 10,000 people from giveaways might be lucky to sell 20.

Therefore, you don't want low-quality subscribers; you need each person to earn their place on the list, since you're paying a monthly fee for their presence. **Plenty of six-figure authors have lists totaling less than 1,000 – 2,000 subs**; the key is that each of their subscribers is ultra-engaged, with 30 – 50% of the list purchasing a new book at release (often at full price).

Number of subscribers is largely a **vanity metric**. Don't pay for big numbers; focus on open and click rates, and, most importantly, *sales*.

Much like generating traffic to our books is relatively easy once you understand how, the same is true about building your mailing list. While you might have balked at the claim in the introduction—*a thousand subs in a month? that's so many!*—it's an achievable goal. The difficult part comes in *converting* those subscribers into sales.

LIST BUILDING: ORGANIC V. NON-ORGANIC

List building comes in two flavors: organic and non-organic. We'll start with organic, which comprises primarily of people who sign up via your front and back matter.

Strengths:

- Much higher engagement than non-organic subscribers.
- Requires less effort to convert subscribers into fans of your work, since these are "warm" leads, having already read and enjoyed one of your titles.
- Almost entirely passive—takes ten minutes to set up forms and links, then no ongoing maintenance.

Weaknesses:

- Far slower to accumulate than non-organic subscribers, even when you incentivize people to sign-up (e.g., with a free novel or novella).
- Can produce zero subscribers until you have a steady stream of people buying/downloading your books first.

Methods:

Place your newsletter sign-up link in the following locations:

1. Front matter (have it on its own separate page; having the link in the front matter can double organic subscribers).

2. Back matter (have it on the same page as THE END; the only other CTA on that page should be a link to Book 2).

3. Social media profiles: things like a pinned Tweet or button on your Facebook page. You can also ask your FB likes/ Twitter followers to subscribe.

The first two are mandatory; the third is nice to include if you use social media often. The link simply goes to a page on your website with the sign-up form installed (a la dnerikson.com/bone). Make sure that your website itself is optimized for subscribers. Put a link to your subscribe page in the menu. And make the first thing on the home page a sign-up form.

Organic list building occurs passively: once you put the link in your front/back matter and install the sign-up form on your website, you don't have to do much. Fans trickle into your email list, you send them updates and news and other stuff about your books when you have it—and that's about it.

You can, of course, set up an autoresponder to increase engagement and deliver free books, but this is optional.

NON-ORGANIC/ACTIVE

The biggest advantage you have with these sources is **volume**. On average, overall engagement rates will be lower—but you can find plenty of superfans via these methods.

Strengths:

- The biggest positive is simple: You can get thousands or tens of thousands of subscribers in the time it would take you to crack a hundred organic subscribers.

Weaknesses:

- Easy to accumulate hordes of unengaged subscribers who have no interest in your work.
- Requires more maintenance: autoresponders, reactivation campaigns, joining giveaways/swaps.
- The obvious downside is that all this requires the management of additional moving parts. Not only do you have to schedule outside promotion in the form of a giveaway, newsletter swap, etc., but you'll also need to write a solid email autoresponder sequence to weed out non-buyers and those who aren't interested in becoming fans.

Methods:

1. **Story Origin** and **Book Funnel cross promotions**: each site maintains a list of upcoming swaps that you can join.
2. **Author newsletter swaps and other cross promotions**: some of these cross promo opportunities won't be posted publicly and are only posted in private author groups.
3. **Newsletter building services**: you pay a service to run a giveaway and they send the ensuing subscriber list to you.
4. **Giveaways**: you run the giveaway yourself via a service like KingSumo, Rafflecopter, or Gleam. Basic approach is to give away a Kindle, Amazon gift card, set of books in your genre, etc. that requires people to give you their email address for a chance to win.

5. **Buying a list**: don't do this under any circumstances, unless you want to get your email account suspended.

Non-organic sign-ups will be colder, since they usually won't be familiar with your work. This relative coldness, however, is made up for in volume. Turning this raw volume into actual readers requires sending them through an onboarding sequence known as an autoresponder. To entice non-organic folks to subscribe, it's mandatory to give something of value away, like a free novel or novella.

Remember, our primary objective is to maintain a *responsive* list of readers who buy, review, and like our books. Finding those readers takes a little more effort when we're using non-organic mailing list building methods.

The engagement of non-organic sign-ups is based on three factors:

1. Their source (i.e., subscribers from giveaways offering a free Kindle or iPad tend to be freebie seekers, rather than actual buyers).
2. The quality of your free magnet (so give away something *good*).
3. The quality of your autoresponder welcome sequence.

OTHER

These two don't really fit into non-organic or organic, so I've placed them under their own heading. Generally, these two approaches are more applicable to non-fiction, where you can join a community or podcast related to your specific sub-niche and help solve people's problems.

1. **Manual outreach**: e.g., asking friends/family, going on forums/Reddit/FB groups, etc., becoming a member of fan communities
2. **Guest posting, podcasts,** and **webinars** (for non-fiction)

That about covers everything. Much like with promotions, you likely have a lot more ideas to play with than you first thought.

OKAY, SO WHICH SHOULD I CHOOSE?

Normally, I recommend narrowing your choices to avoid spreading your resources too thin. But since organic subscribers are entirely passive—truly one of the only set and forget things in indie publishing—this means I recommend doing **both** (at first). You can reuse most of your work; if you write a good autoresponder for your organic peeps, then you can use that for the non-organic folks as well.

So if you're coming at this fresh, here's the approach I recommend:

1. Set up the organic sign-ups. I show exactly how below; just copy what I did.
2. Once the organic side is working fine and has been tested, join at least one cross promotion or giveaway per month until you hit 5,000 – 6,000 subscribers.

Why 5,000 to 6,000? Each cross promo site has a limited pool of readers. The same authors will join the same promotions month after month. When you first enter, say, a promo on Story Origin, you'll be reaching entirely new readers. However, over time, you're going to find that you're fishing in the same reader pond. Thus, you start hitting a point of diminishing returns to the point where you'll eventually be *losing* more subscribers than you're actually generating from the cross promotions.

When this happens, either switch to a different source (e.g., a different giveaway company or a different cross promo site) and continue *or* wait three to six months. When you return, there will be new readers to reach.

One very important note: make sure your organic and non-organic lists are segmented. That way, you can target cross promos, giveaways, and similar offers *exclusively* to your non-organic lists. These will be people who are interested in this type of content. You *don't* want to share your organic subscribers with 20+ other authors; and, perhaps more importantly, you don't want to bombard them with offers they're not interested in. These folks signed up to hear about *you*, not a hundred other books they can receive for free.

You will likely get to a point where you shift over to *exclusively* building your list via organic means. This is my current approach with my own pen names. However, it's important to mention that I have 6,000+ subscribers at this point, and am *not* just starting out. I used quite a few cross promos and other methods to help build my list at the beginning.

If you're strapped for time, **just focus on organic subscribers**. Setting this up is mandatory; the other stuff is optional.

THE BASIC NEWSLETTER FUNNEL

Before we get into the mechanics of growing and using our list, we need to talk about the three basic building blocks that will turn casual readers/cold traffic into fans.

1.   **The offer**: what you're giving the prospective subscriber in exchange for an email address. **This is the most important piece of list building**. Give away something of *actual* value: a professional-level novella or novel. You get reader eyeballs on your offer by using the organic/non-organic list-building methods already discussed.

2.   **The landing page**: the website page where you send the reader to actually collect their email address. Can be just a form, or a fancy, custom designed page. **Just go with a form unless you're trying to get subscribers via Facebook (not recommended).** You don't need a website; you can send readers directly, say, to a Mailchimp form. This is *not* recommended, since you'll need to change *every* link in your books if you ever switch to a different service provider. Linking to a page *you* own ensures future flexibility and control.

3.   **The autoresponder**: this will automatically deliver their free book (if you give them one), as well as a series of emails introducing your work to new readers.

We could break this into a million smaller parts, but you just need to focus on these three things.

THE SIX STEP ORGANIC LIST BUILDING PROCESS

You'll want to set up your organic list first, since it runs passively in the background 24/7. These subscribers are also free (and they'll usually be your best ones), so you want to make sure you start collecting them ASAP.

Step 1: Sign Up for Your Email Client

Use MailerLite or ConvertKit.

Step 2: Create a List for Your Fiction Readers

If you have multiple pen names, create a separate list for each name. **Do not use double opt-in**. 25% – 30% of your subscribers will *never* click the confirmation link. Yes, every email service on the planet recommends double opt-in, and regales you with (fictional) stories about how they increase engagement and decrease SPAM reports.

This is all bogus; confirmation emails often never arrive, and waiting for them is a miserable customer experience (I hate them with a vengeance as a subscriber). I've received SPAM complaints on the confirmation email (yes, for real). Unless you're getting a proliferation of fake/bot-driven/spam sign-ups that you have to weed out, or double opt-in is legally required in your jurisdiction, single opt-in is fine.

Step 3: Create a Form and Install It on Your Website

The page you install the form on is called a **landing page**. While you can create extremely complex landing pages, you don't need to overthink this. Just send them to a page with your sign-up form, like so:

Basic breakdown:

- **Layout**: book cover is on the left, so the can see what they're getting (people read from left to right). Form is on the right.
- **Headline**: make this clear and obvious. Here, it's **Get Your Free Copy of Bone Realm**.
- **Text**: explain a little bit about the newsletter/book.
- **Instructions**: give them clear instructions. This is vital. Here, it's **Enter your best email address below to instantly receive the exclusive Ruby Callaway prequel novella Bone Realm**.
- **CTA**: make sure the button contrasts with your site design. There is no one best color for this, and anyone claiming otherwise is full of it. Here, I'm using lime green because it stands out on the page. The CTA text reads **Get My Book Now**. Note that I'm framing the text from the *reader's* point of view, which is why I use "my" instead of "your." The first person tends to convert better.
- **Spam**: tell them you won't spam them and other details.

Depending on the laws and rules in your location, you may want to include other information. Most problems can be avoided, however, by using common sense (re: not being a spammy idiot).

Alternatively, for those who don't have a website yet, here's a nifty tip: take the URL that links to the form and put it into SmartURL (**smarturl.it**). Then use this SmartURL in your front/ back matter.

That way, when you get your own website or if you ever switch to a different mail service, you don't have to update the back/ front matter in every book (a miserable experience if you have more than a few books). All you have to do is update the SmartURL with the new link and boom, you're done in two minutes.

STEP 3B: WHAT ABOUT POP-UPS AND OTHER STUFF?

There's no shortage of software, services, and plugins you can use to build your list. Most of these are designed for bloggers/ non-creative businesses.

Can you use them to build your fiction list?

Yes.

Should you?

Don't bother. Most of the pop-ups, exit intent pop-ups, welcome mats/gates, content locking, and other stuff you encounter on the web are for capturing leads via content marketing (i.e., articles like the ones on my Nicholas Erik site). Collecting emails via these methods is highly dependent on website traffic. As authors, it's unlikely we'll get much more than a trickle of website traffic. The few people visiting our website will not arrive via SEO or Google, but instead because they came after reading our books.

Unless you have 5,000+ people visiting your author site on a monthly basis, I wouldn't bother. If you're a #1 NYT Bestseller or traditionally published author getting print press, then it's possible—even likely—that people have heard your name through an outlet other than your book. Turning these "cold" leads into fans may demand more aggressive marketing tactics.

But for indies? Neither necessary nor beneficial. Save your time.

STEP 4: CREATE A COMPELLING OFFER

Since the offer is the most important part of this whole newsletter building enterprise, it pays to give it a little thought. The text (and image, if you have one) matters, but not nearly as much as the offer itself. If you're having trouble building your list, this is where you should look first.

The offer is commonly called a "lead magnet," "reader magnet," "incentive," or "ethical bribe." Basically, you *give* the reader something of value for free to compel them to sign up.

I've tested a number of approaches. Here are seven basic offers:

1. **An exclusive novella**: i.e., a prequel where you explore some aspect of your main character's back story or an unanswered, burning question from the series. An example can be found at **dnerikson.com/bone. You want this free novella to be as good as any of your paid products—or better**. Spend the extra money for a professional cover and proofreading. It'll be worth it. Novellas in the same series as the book generate a far greater number of sign-ups than unrelated freebies. This also helps with engagement: readers

242 | The Ultimate Guide To Book Marketing

who sign up for a prequel novella will be **actual fans of the series and not freebie seekers**. A novella also has tremendous utility when you expand your mailing list building efforts to non-organic sources (i.e., cross promotions).

2. **Epilogue**: this is common in romance, where it revisits the characters after their HEA (happily ever after). These convert really well, from what I've heard, and they're quick to write (a few thousand words at most). If you're a romance author, definitely explore this option.

3. **Book 2**: get the next book in the series for free. In my experience, this converts the best, even better than an exclusive novella. However, you obviously give up sales on the next title, so it's only valid for longer series, and you can't use it if you're enrolled in Kindle Unlimited because of the exclusivity agreement. As such, I wouldn't recommend doing this.

4. **Starter library**: giving away 2, 3, or 4 titles (or more, I guess, if you want). Generally consists of the lead-ins to your series (i.e., Book 1s), but can be standalone novels, novellas, and so forth.

5. **Worldbuilding stuff**: maps, dossiers, character backstories, concept art, and so forth. Only big fans of the book/series will sign up for items like this.

6. **Discounts**: something like, "**Newsletter subscribers get exclusive discounts on my newest novels during the first 24 hours of release—sign up here to join**." This is a discount offer, with scarcity— they're likely to miss the deal if they don't sign up, since they're unlikely to see the book in its first 24 hours of release otherwise. If you have no story/novel, etc. to give away, this can be effective. The downside is that you're effectively locked into discounting for perpetuity.

7. **Get updates**: while common, this is not a compelling offer. If you have nothing else, you can use it; just understand that unless you're selling a decent number of books, the number of subscribers you get will be extraordinarily low. I'd use this instead of the discount one because I'd prefer not to lock myself into anything.

As an aside, if you're a non-fiction author, you have much more leeway to come up with compelling offers: cheat sheets, checklists, in-depth guides like the one you're reading, free videos… you're basically only limited by your imagination.

Here's some click rate data on the above offers that came from the front/back matter of one of my sci-fi adventure novels. The front matter sign-up produced 2 – 5x more clicks than the back matter.

Offer	Clicks	Free Downloads	Click Rate (%)
Book 2	137	1746	7.85%
Starter Library (3 novels, including Book 2)	69	1211	5.70%
2 Exclusive Novellas	44	1327	3.32%
Nothing (updates)	29	4573	0.63%

While it should be noted that *click* rates aren't *conversion* rates (i.e., the actual subscribers produced), these are still helpful for assessing the relative appeal of each offer. Here, we can see that Book 2 is the most enticing (not surprising). Including Book 2 in a starter library with *two additional* books, however, actually produced fewer clicks.

The novellas produced a lower click rate, even though they were all directly tied in with the book/series.

My recommendation is to offer either an exclusive free novel or novella to maximize subscribers. The full length novel will likely produce more sign-ups; however, you don't want to spend an inordinate amount of time creating a free book at the expense of your paid work. For most authors, a novella will be a nice com-promise: you can write a 12,000 – 25,000 word one in a month, adding a nice piece to your marketing toolkit without spending too much time. Avoid using short stories; these aren't particu-larly exciting. A starter library is overwhelming, and seems to *decrease* the number of sign-ups; if you have multiple free books to give away, make sure you send them in separate autoresponder emails, rather than in one big block.

Finally, if you have *nothing* to offer, "get updates" is a viable fallback offer. It can be enhanced when you have another book coming out by using language like "Want to hear when [charac-ter] returns in [book]? Subscribe to my free author newsletter and be the first to hear when [book] comes out!"

Step 5: Put the Sign-Up Link in Your Book's Front and Back Matter

It's **very important** that you place the sign-up offer in the front matter, on a special page by itself before the book. The bulk of your sign-ups will actually come from the front, not the back. Including this link in the front can increase your subscribers 2x. There are three primary ways to present this:

Generally speaking, while you *do* want a professional cover for your lead magnet, you often want to go with the simple text offer illustrated on the right. Why? Because including images increases your delivery costs (Amazon subtracts these from your royalties). Thus, any image must dramatically increase the number of sign-ups to be worthwhile, since it's costing you a penny or two on each sale. This sounds insignificant, but can add up to actual money over a large backlist.

Thus, I'd go with the simple text version. In this instance, it's laid out as such:

1. **HEADLINE**: clearly states the offer (Get Storm Pale for Free)
2. **TEXT**: tells them what they'll get and ends with a CTA (To instantly receive the free novella *Storm Pale*, featuring Ruby Callaway's ally, the immortal half-demon Kalos Aeon, sign up for D.N.'s free author newsletter at **dnerikson.com/storm**.)

Short, and right to the point.

The other benefit, as you might have surmised, is customization: I can easily tweak the text to the book/series at hand to make the offer more specific and thus, a little bit more enticing.

If you *do* decide to include the cover, you can simply insert it above the text. The argument for including an image is compelling: it stands out if you've got other front matter (copyright, table of contents, also by). For a reader skimming through, an attractive image will catch their eye.

I generally go with the text, however.

In the back matter, I'll include a similarly worded offer on the same page as THE END.

Step 6: Deliver the Book via a Welcome Email

You deliver the book by setting up an automated welcome email. This can be just a single email, or a full-fledged autoresponder (which we'll cover below).

The welcome email's basic purpose is threefold:

1. **It delivers the free book.**
2. **It asks the new subscriber to whitelist your emails**. Do this with the following language: "To ensure you get these emails, please add **nick@nicholaserik.com** to your address book. Or, if you're a Gmail user with inbox tabs enabled, drag this email over to the Primary tab."
3. **It sets expectations in terms of email frequency, content, and tone**. These topics will be covered in the next section, but basically your Welcome email is your first impression. Make sure it sets the table correctly for everything to come.

Use BookFunnel (**bookfunnel.com**) to automagically get your free books on to any reader device. Otherwise you're going to be fielding tons of support questions about not being able to read the books.

This is one of the best services I've ever used. Easily worth the price.

Also fairly self-explanatory, but critical: double-check the download links to make sure they work.

That's it! You now have a system that will produce subscribers forever without further maintenance or input. But let's break down some ways to troubleshoot things if you're not getting many subscribers.

TROUBLESHOOTING

After implementing the steps above, you may find that you're not getting many subscribers. The three most common problems are:

1. **Lack of traffic**. If you're not selling many books, you're not going to generate many organic subscribers.

2. **Unappealing offer**. If you only offer "updates," then you're not going to get many subscribers unless you're selling a ton of books.

3. **Lack of clarity**. When wording your offer, make it super clear. Include a direct link *and* the actual URL (e.g. I type out dnerikson.com/bone) in the front/back matter so people can enter the URL on another device easily. Make your landing page uncluttered, and make sure it's extremely easy to find the subscribe form on your website. Have a clear subject line on the free book delivery/welcome email. Clarity always trumps cleverness.

OKAY, SO WHAT ABOUT NON-ORGANIC LIST BUILDING?

You know all that stuff you just did for the organic list building?

Good news. You have everything in place for building your list via giveaways, cross promos, and so forth.

You only need to do three more things:

1. Set up a separate list or tag, so that anyone who comes into your list via non-organic means is tagged. You want

to be able to send these subscribers different emails than your organic peeps.

2.   Enter a cross promotion (or two) on Story Origin or Book-Funnel. Each maintains a list of upcoming promotions on their sites.

3.   Have a 5+ email autoresponder and delete (or do a reactivation campaign to) anyone who doesn't open any emails by the end.

That's it. And about that autoresponder: let's look at a basic one below.

BUILDING A BASIC AUTORESPONDER

We've covered the first two aspects of the funnel in the offer and landing page, but we still have one piece left: the autoresponder.

Each email service provider has their own terminology. ConvertKit calls autoresponders "sequences"; MailerLite calls them "workflows." Whatever the term, autoresponders can be remarkably complex beasts when you get into tagging, segmentation, and other automated behaviors. We're not going to do that; to be honest, while that stuff looks sophisticated on the outside, most of it is low leverage BS that falls *way* outside the core 20% in the 80/20 rule. Ultra-complex autoresponders or segmentation aren't necessary.

Here's the extent of what you need to do:

1.   If you have a large catalog, segment/tag based on series. (optional)

2. If you write in multiple genres, segment/tag based on genre. You might go a step further and run separate lists, depending on how disparate the genres are. For example, I maintain completely separate lists for my non-fiction, urban fantasy, and sci-fi subscribers.

3. If you have multiple pen names, use a separate list for each one. Don't be lazy and dump all the subs into the same one.

That's all pretty much commonsense.

Next comes the autoresponder. If you're organically building your list and just delivering a single book, or offering updates, all you need is a simple "Welcome" email. You don't have to go beyond that.

Do include this welcome, though. If a subscriber joins your list and receives nothing, this is a confusing user experience. They'll be unsure if their subscription was successful (especially if you're not using double opt-in).

An autoresponder becomes more important when you have more free books to deliver or a bigger backlist to introduce. It's also mandatory if you're doing extensive non-organic list building. You'll need it to weed out the unresponsive subscribers who aren't interested in your books.

With that out of the way, here's a basic five-part autoresponder with template subject lines. This doesn't include the confirmation email for those who still insist on using double opt-in:

1. Immediate (Day 1): Welcome – Here's Your Free Book (what to expect, whitelist instructions, give them a link to the free book)

2. Day 2: Did You Get [Book Title] Yesterday? (*only* to people who didn't open first email)

3. Day 4: Here's Another Free [Genre] Book (if you have another–don't send all your free books in one email) or How Did You Like [Free Book Title]?

4. Day 7: The Last Free [Genre] Book or What's Your Favorite [Genre] Book or My #1 Favorite [Genre] Book of All Time

5. Day 14: Want to Join the Review Team? or Can You Do Me a Quick Favor? (and ask them to review the book)

None of these dates or subject lines are set in stone; experiment. You can swap out elements at will; if you have more series, you can plug that in for Day 10's email instead of a book recommendation.

We can extend this to introduce our series by sending out an email on a specific day each week (the Netflix Strategy), a la:

1. Day 21 (Friday): Looking for your next weekend read? (Intro to Series #1)

2. Day 28 (Friday): Intro to Series #2

3. Day 35 (Friday): Intro to Series #3

And so forth, until you run out of series (you can also use it with standalones). If you have a lot of series or standalones, select your five or ten best-performing ones for the autoresponder instead of sending subscribers a neverending chain of emails.

KEY TAKEAWAYS

- The mailing list is the most critical part of your marketing arsenal and can drive hundreds of sales.
- Organic subscribers come mainly from your books and will be your most engaged subs.
- Non-organic subscribers come from sources like cross promos, giveaways, and paid ads. They are not familiar with your work, so they must be converted into readers via an autoresponder.
- Organic list building is mandatory; non-organic list building is optional, but helpful for authors just starting out.
- Once you reach 5,000 – 6,000 subscribers from cross promos/giveaways, you often hit a point of diminishing returns. At this point, switch to a different cross promo service, or give it three to six months to recharge.
- You can set up your organic list in six steps:

1. Get a mailing list provider. **MailerLite** is the best option for 95% of indie authors. If you're looking for more features, use **ConvertKit**.
2. Create a list for your fiction readers. If you write in multiple genres or have multiple pen names, create a separate list for each.
3. Create a form and install it on your website. The form should be the only thing on that page.
4. Create a compelling offer. I recommend an exclusive full-length novel or novella. The latter will be more realistic for most authors, time-wise, and is what I use. Make sure the book you're offering is **professionally formatted and**

proofread. **An excellent cover is necessary** to maximize its effectiveness.

5.   Put the link to your sign-up form in the front/back matter.

6.   Deliver the book via a welcome email with the subject line "Here's Your Free Book," using BookFunnel to provide the book download.

- Troubleshooting if you're not getting many subscribers: no traffic (#1 problem), the offer is bad/unappealing (#2), lack of clarity (#3).
- **A simple five-part autoresponder** can be remarkably effective.

1.   Immediate (Day 1): Welcome – Here's Your Free Book (what to expect, whitelist instructions, give them a link to the free book)

2.   Day 2: Did You Get [Book Title] Yesterday? (*only* to people who didn't open first email)

3.   Day 4: Here's Another Free [Genre] Book (if you have another–don't send all your free books in one email) or How Did You Like [Free Book Title]?

4.   Day 7: The Last Free [Genre] Book or What's Your Favorite [Genre] Book or My #1 Favorite [Genre] Book of All Time

5.   Day 14: Want to Join the Review Team? or Can You Do Me a Quick Favor? (and ask them to review the book)

ACTION EXERCISES

To get your first 1,000 subscribers (or add 1,000 more), do the following:

1. Set up your organic email list and put a link in the front/back matter of your books.

2. Set up your autoresponder.

3. Join two cross promotions in your sub-genre taking place in the next 30 days on Story Origin (**storyoriginapp.com**) or BookFunnel (**bookfunnel.com**). This will build your list to 1,000 subscribers (or close to it).

4. Repeat #2 each month until you hit 5,000 – 6,000 subscribers or the point of diminishing returns (e.g. you're losing more subscribers than you gain).

TEN:

NEWSLETTER ENGAGEMENT

After innumerable references to how critical your newsletter is to your career, we're finally ready to talk about using it to actually sell more books.

First, a little refresher on our Ultimate Book Marketing Formula, which is the heartbeat of this guide:

MARKET RESEARCH + 3 TRAFFIC SOURCES + PRO COVERS
+ GREAT BLURBS + NEWSLETTER + 4-6 NOVELS PER YEAR

CONSISTENTLY FOR 3-5 YEARS

↓

FULL-TIME AUTHOR

We've hit the most important part of the formula: building and engaging your newsletter subscribers. The email list is the backbone of your platform. In the previous section, we went over actually *building* our subscribers up via organic (front/back matter) and non-organic (giveaways and cross promos) means. So if you don't have any subscribers yet, make sure you review that stuff first.

Once you have some subscribers, however, your next mission is getting them interested in your books. Many authors think generating subscribers is the difficult part; it isn't. I understand why: getting your first subscriber (or couple hundred) can be an exercise in hair-pulling frustration. But once you crack that code, you'll find that the true test comes in getting them to read your next books.

Because having a bunch of subscribers who don't pick up your books is worth zip. You *need* **engaged subscribers** who will buy your work (preferably for full price). A list of 1,000 raving fans can catapult a new book into the top 500 of the entire store. A list of 15,000 people who barely know your name will do nothing.

I have personally seen both.

In this section, we'll cover:

- Email frequency: how often should you mail?
- Content and Tone: choosing what works
- Subject lines that actually work
- The Reactivation Campaign: How to re-engage inactive subscribers
- General engagement tips

In short, the choices you make regarding frequency, content, style, and tone comprise the entity that is "your newsletter." You want to establish these from the get go to set clear expectations.

These decisions become part of your overall brand. Make them wisely.

Before we hop into engagement, though, let's make sure you have three key pieces in place before continuing.

BEFORE WE BEGIN

This is a flight check of sorts. If you haven't done these three things yet, stop reading and go take care of them (they're all outlined step-by-step in the previous section):

1. **Set up your organic newsletter.**

2. **Set up a simple autoresponder.** This can just be a single "Welcome" email delivering a free book to new subscribers, or it can be longer. Longer autoresponders help increase engagement/sales when you have a large backlist or are using non-organic methods to build your list.

3. **Make sure your welcome email does three things**: (1) if applicable, delivers the free book, (2) asks subscribers to whitelist your email address and (3) establishes expectations in terms of newsletter frequency, content, tone, and style.

These elements will run passively in the background, regardless of whether you implement anything in this guide. *Plus,* it's easier to revise/fix what you already have using the ideas below than it is to try to build them from scratch *and* simultaneously remember everything we'll discuss here.

Remember: a platform is built brick-by-brick. Get the foundation down, then build on top of it.

EMAIL FREQUENCY

The fear of irritating readers is one of the main things that stops authors from starting a newsletter (or ever sending one at all). It's worth remembering that **readers specifically signed up to your list to hear from *you*.** If you don't send them newsletters, then you're doing them a disservice.

Rather than be paralyzed in fear as you wonder whether you should send an email, here are the three basic approaches to email frequency:

1. **The weekly or monthly newsletter.** This is sent regardless if you have a new book or new content to share. You'll also send newsletters when you have deals or new releases that fall outside the purview of the schedule.
2. **The release only newsletter.** Only email when you have a new book.
3. **The when I have interesting stuff to share newsletter.** This gives you more variety: you can share deals, new releases, books in the genre, and so forth.

There are variants of these, of course: you could do a weekly newsletter (appropriate in non-fiction, less so in fiction where you're unlikely to have enough news to justify that frequency). You could do a release only plus deals newsletter.

The idea here is to establish this frequency upfront, in your welcome email. **Tell people *exactly* what to expect.**

Then meet this expectation.

It's generally okay to move from *more* emails to less. The inverse poses a problem: if you tell people you'll only email them for releases, but then send them random emails about cross promos, cat pictures, and everything under the sun, you're break-ing expectations.

I do a monthly newsletter for my fiction books (around the 1st) and a weekly newsletter (every Sunday-ish) for my non-fic-tion. For the fiction, this actually ends up being once or twice a month with the other content (mainly release emails). I explain this in the welcome email to set their expectations accordingly.

Monitor click and open rates to gauge how readers are respond-ing to your email frequency. If you're getting a ton of unsub-scribes (1.5%+ per email) or lots of abuse complaints (0.5%+ per email), then you might be sending too many. Or you may not have sent an email in the past year...and no one remembers who the hell you are. Which leads us to a final point.

There is no best email frequency. The magic bullet, if there is one, is **consistency**. Pick a schedule that you're comfortable with, then deliver.

It's really that simple.

CONTENT & TONE: WHAT TO SAY (AND HOW TO SAY IT?)

Content is tied into email frequency. The more interesting content you have to share, the more frequently you can email people without having them ignore you.

Content-wise, here are some of the things you can share:

1. Slice of writing life stories.
2. Book recommendations.
3. Cover reveals.
4. Excerpts from upcoming books.

5.   Exclusive stories, epilogues, "lost" chapters, etc.

6.   New release info: dates, pre-order links, announcements, and, of course, the actual release day email.

7.   Podcasts, guides, blog posts, articles, etc. (for non-fiction).

These aren't mutually exclusive; in fact, you'll often weave these together in a single newsletter. In my monthly fiction newsletter, I add a brief update on the new book's progress and perhaps a little behind the scenes glimpse (i.e., I shared the illustration process one month). I also added a recommendation section, where I recommend books, shows, or movies that I've actually watched.

That last part is key. Your emails need to be valuable. Spending my *own* time to sift through stacks of books and recommend something in the genre that's good is useful. People have plenty of content to consume, but this abundance of choice makes it difficult to find *good* content. Shotgunning out recommendations because I swapped with other authors is the *opposite* of value.

Wasting the reader's time is the worst thing you can do.

Information is a commodity. You must further to keep readers engaged.

This is the same reason why my curated promo list is valuable (and it's shared frequently), and all the random lists on the internet are not. When you do the hard work *for* the reader by sorting through the maelstrom of BS, they appreciate that.

The other way to be valuable is by being entertaining or interesting. Glimpses into the writing process—which, while of little interest to you, can appear mystical from the outside looking in. Updates on a book that they're looking forward to qualify. Even pictures of animals can, provided you loop them back into your writing somehow.

You're only limited by your creativity. **Use your skills as a storyteller**. If you subscribe to any non-fiction lists, many of these newsletters are written like a piece of sales copy. This is a viable approach, but it demands different skills. Instead of developing an entirely new skillset, employ the one you already have.

Don't worry about length. There's an ongoing debate about the merits of long versus short copy. This extends to emails, where people make wild claims about readers being unwilling to read long emails.

I have sent out some very long non-fiction emails.

They got high open rates because they were interesting and relevant to the target audience.

Instead of length, follow this rule: **don't be boring**.

This rule dovetails nicely with our next consideration: *how you communicate with your readers*. That is, your **tone**.

While there are technically a million and one ways to approach this, let's whittle it down to two simple options: your natural email "voice" or whatever matches the tone of your target market.

For my fiction, I use the former, which happens to fit the sarcastic/laid-back tone of one of my target markets (urban fantasy).

For non-fiction, I used to strip most of this out in favor of a more *just the facts* tone. Readers of how-to non-fiction don't respond well to lots of expletives, and making things too voice-y can split your audience between people who *really* like it, and those who make it their mission to tell everyone that they didn't like how things were written and that everything inside is garbage as a result.

I still returned to my natural voice, though. Why?

Because this isn't about everyone who doesn't like you. Or is lukewarm. They're never going to share your content or books.

It's about the people who *really* like your stuff.

They'll stick around.

Share it.

Buy whatever you put out.

By straddling the middle, everyone is lukewarm to your stuff.

Polarization is a *good* thing. If you don't have a couple people who dislike your stuff (not because you're purposely an asshole, just because they strongly disagree), you're probably just getting lost in the market.

If your natural voice isn't a good fit for the market's preferences, you *may* limit your audience by leaning into it (this applies to the books, too). But the people who do connect with your voice will actually like what you do. Because they're connecting with your distinct author voice (your brand), rather than a milquetoast, watered down version.

Whichever option you choose, the tone should always be like addressing a friend. The inbox is a personal space. Think coffee shop rather than sales seminar.

Ultimately, with frequency, content, and tone, the format is less important than setting expectations early on during the welcome sequence and then being consistent. The people who naturally respond to your type of newsletter will stick around. **Don't try to please everyone.** Whatever format/tone you decide on will inevitably alienate other people. Trying to please *everyone* is a surefire way to crater engagement.

(And if you want to see what my book marketing newsletter's content and voice are like, check it out for free at **nicholaserik. com/newsletter**.)

FORMATTING

A brief interlude, but an important one. Keep the formatting of your emails *simple*. This should look like an email to a friend (as much as that's possible). Fancy templates resembling slick sales catalogs are terrible for two reasons: they get caught in spam filters and they look like advertisements.

We don't want either of those outcomes. So use one of the simple text templates. As a bonus, you'll save a ton of time on complicated formatting.

SUBJECT LINES

While I initially thought that clever subject lines would carry the day, extensive testing has demonstrated a clear trend: **obvious subject lines almost always outperform anything else**. This isn't surprising, given our oft-repeated marketing rule: **clarity trumps cleverness**.

It's also worth noting that direct-response marketing headlines like "one weird trick" should *not* be used here. You are not selling a get out of debt course. You can generate much better engagement (both short-term and long-term) with straightforward subject lines.

An example from the first email in my sci-fi autoresponder:

- "Your Free Novels & Novellas" produced a 79.2% open rate.
- "so, I heard you like science fiction..." produced a 62.2% open rate.

For new releases:

- [Title] is Now Available
- Drop Dead is Now Available
- Smoke Show is Out Now
- Bomb Shell is Out (and just $0.99)
- The New [Series Name] [Genre or Novel] is Now Available
- The Latest Jack Reacher Thriller is Now Available
- The New Tess Skye Novel is Out Now
- Ruby Callaway Returns Today (Just $0.99)

When in doubt, be obvious. It's hard to come up with something clever that will beat the direct approach.

You may see suggestions that subject lines that look like emails from friends a la "check this out" or "what's up" can generate high open rates. This can be true, but you want to be careful using these. They can feel *extremely* bait-and-switchy, and piss people off. If you're not a good copywriter, then don't use them. Even then, you'd only use them in *very* specific circumstances (like one of the tricks below).

WHAT SHOULD I DO ABOUT INACTIVE SUBS (REACTIVATION)?

Each subscriber you have on your list brings you *that* much closer to paying more per month. To be honest, while authors focus on that, it's a minor concern. We're talking about a couple hundred bucks a year, max, in most instances.

The reasons we want to engage inactive subs are two-fold: one, we'd like them to become readers if possible, since we went through the trouble of getting them on the list. Two, having a ton of inactive subs on your list can drag down the deliverability of your emails to *engaged* subscribers.

What to do about these inactive subscribers, then? Well, we don't just want to delete them out right. Click and open rate data, while useful, isn't 100% accurate. Some people will open every email, but won't appear in the stats for a variety of reasons. Just blanket-deleting them would be unproductive.

Instead, we want to send out what's known as a **reengagement or reactivation campaign**. A reactivation campaign is an email sent out specifically to inactive subscribers with the goal of getting those still interested in your content to essentially confirm that they want to stick around. It follows two steps:

1. Segment or tag all the subscribers who haven't opened your emails for a minimum of 90 days. You can go longer to be more conservative, like 6 months. Name this segment/tag "Inactive."
2. Send *only* these subscribers a reactivation email. Set up a link in the email that *removes* them from the Inactive segment/tag if they click on it.

Very important: no one will open every email. Even your biggest fans will occasionally miss an email. So don't boot people off for missing a couple emails. We only want to remove people who clearly aren't interested, *not* engaged fans who weren't interested in specific offers. Hence why we only send this out to people who haven't opened an email in 3 – 6 months.

The subject line should be "Do You Want to Keep Receiving My Author Newsletter?" Then the body of the email should be something along these lines:

Hey, my email service says you haven't been opening my emails. But sometimes that's a mistake, so I don't want to remove you from my newsletter list if you want to stay. Just click here to keep receiving my newsletter. If you don't click and don't want to stick around, you don't have to do anything. You'll be automatically removed in 7 days.

Then remove whoever doesn't click on the link. Generally speaking, you can expect about 10 – 15% of the inactive subscribers to stick around. That means you can chop *thousands* of subscribers if you do this. That can be a little disconcerting, but remember that these are dead-weight: they're costing you money, they're lowering your deliverability, *and* they don't want to receive your emails.

Removing them, then, is a win-win for everyone.

As for how often you should send these campaigns: I'd recommend doing them every six months if you're building your list via non-organic means and sending emails out on a monthly basis. Naturally, if you haven't sent a newsletter in six months, or have sent all of one, *don't* send out a reactivation campaign. You'll accidentally delete a ton of engaged subs.

And if you're exclusively doing organic list building, then I wouldn't worry about reactivation campaigns. Their engagement tends to be much higher, and there generally aren't enough inactive organic subs to be impacting your deliverability. In fact, I would exclude organic subs from any reactivation campaigns. They're too valuable to delete for any reason. If an organic subscriber doesn't want to stick around, they can unsubscribe.

Otherwise, keep them on the list.

GENERAL ENGAGEMENT TIPS

Here are a few tricks you can use to increase your open and click rates.

1. **Resend your emails to non-opens**. This can get you an additional 6 – 8% increase in opens (i.e., from 38% > 44 – 46%). Most email services can do this with a couple clicks.

   - Resend the second email with a different subject line.
   - Resend the second email at a different time. I.e., if you sent the first one at 7 AM, send the second one at 5 PM.
   - Choose the resend date strategically. If it's a launch, send it on the last day with a "last chance!" type of headline. If it's a general newsletter, maybe a week later (or not at all). You don't want to resend *every* email.

2. **A/B test your subject lines**. A good subject line can generate an additional 5 – 7% increase in opens (i.e., from 30% > 35 – 37%). Again, most email services can do this with a single click. This is typically only worthwhile once you have 1000+ subscribers; otherwise, there's not a large enough sample size.

3. **Double-check the first 50 – 100 characters of the email**. Basically the first two sentences. This is what pops up in the "preview" section of their email client. If neither this nor the subject line are compelling, they're probably not opening the email.

4. **Train subscribers to click**. Always have at least one link to click in your autoresponder and broadcast emails.

5. **Train subscribers to buy.** Don't give away only free stuff—or too much of it. Your unsubscribe rates will spike when you do ask them to purchase, and your click rates will be low.

6. **Send a "thanks" email on the last day of a launch or promo.** This one's simple, but wildly effective: when you're running a limited-time promo or launch, on the final day, you can send out an email with the subject line "thanks." Remember our discussion on using "real" subject lines? Here's one instance where it works. You kick off the email by thanking them for a great launch/promo, share some stats (readers especially love records), then add a mention that the deal hasn't ended a la "if you haven't picked up *Drop Dead*, you still have a little over 12 hours to grab it for the launch price of $2.99." This blends a classic "last chance" hard-sell into a *very* soft-sell email that can drive a ton of sales.

7. **Use your list for retargeting via Facebook.** If you don't know what this means, then don't worry about it. This is different than the other tactics listed, as it's exclusively used for selling books, not influencing open/click rates. You can reach subscribers who don't open your emails (or don't see them) via Facebook Ads by uploading your list as a custom audience.

WHAT SHOULD MY CONVERSION AND OPEN RATES LOOK LIKE?

The industry average open rates for music/musicians is 23%; media + publishing is 22.8% (according to Mailchimp). These are sad sack averages that you can trounce, however, by using the methods already outlined.

Here's what your open rates should look like:

1. **Landing page**: for non-organic traffic (i.e., from Facebook Ads), aim for 30%+ conversion. Organic traffic should convert at 40%+.

2. **Autoresponder**: aim for a 60%+ open rate for the first email. Click rate should be 40%+ (if you're giving away a free novella). These will both drop significantly over the next emails in the sequence.

3. **Basic broadcast email**: aim for an open rate of 25 – 35% from non-organic subs who bothered to actually download your initial freebie (i.e., the free novella); 35 – 60% open rate for organic subs. Click rates vary with news you're sharing. I'd aim for a 10 – 20% click rate for a new release.

All of this data is supplied automatically by your email service provider. You should have separate lists or segments for your organic/non-organic subs (along with separate landing pages) so you can compare the relative stats.

Most people judge the quality of their list based on open rates and click rates. Then they work on increasing those numbers. These metrics don't give you a complete snapshot of your engagement/list quality, however—ultimately the *best* metric is sales. If your list isn't generating sales, then actual engagement is poor.

A very important note on optimization: **make sure you're actually getting enough traffic through the funnel before spending a bunch of time tweaking stuff**. Stats get heavily skewed when you have seven subs—like 100% of people are reading your emails, or 0%. Open/click rate data is largely useless until you have a 200+ subscribers.

KEY TAKEAWAYS

- A well-engaged list can help you get reviews, sell books at full price during launch, and give you valuable feedback on your work.
- Having a well-engaged email list is far more important than having a huge mailing list.
- While open and click rates are useful, the ultimate measure of list engagement is **sales**.
- Frequency: choose a frequency that's appropriate for the amount of content you have to share. The true silver bullet is **consistency**. Pick a schedule and stick with it.
- Content and tone: rely on your storytelling chops to make your email content more engaging. You have two options for tone—your natural voice, or whatever is expected in your genre.
- Clean up non-openers/non-engaged subscribers to keep your email subscription costs down and click/open rates high.

ACTION EXERCISE

1. Decide on your newsletter frequency, content, and tone going forward.
2. Adjust your Welcome email and autoresponder to correctly set these expectations.

ELEVEN

OPTIMIZATION

Optimization is all about small tweaks you can make to your website and books to increase sellthrough and organic newsletter subscribers.

The essence of optimization is simple: find low to medium hanging fruit that you can apply across your backlist. Pay once, enjoy the benefits for years. This is a refreshing change of pace from active marketing. Ads require constant attention and maintenance. New books require new words.

Both of these are critical, but they demand hands-on time. Optimization shoulders some of that marketing load for us, saving our time and energy for more important things. Thus, to maximize our backlist, we want to find one-time simple tasks that pay big long-term dividends.

There are seven tweaks covered in the guide:

- **HOME PAGE**: optimize this so more visitors subscribe to your newsletter.
- **DOUBLE OPT-IN**: turn this off to stop losing 30%+ of your subscribers
- **AUTORESPONDER:** every week, have an automated email introducing readers to another series in your backlist
- **UPSELL:** make your "thank you for subscribing" page an upsell to the box set/Book 1 in the related series
- **FORMATTING:** limit fancy formatting and images to keep file sizes down
- **FRONT MATTER:** always include a link to your newsletter; can increase subscribers 2x or more.
- **BACK MATTER:** two CTAs on same page as THE END (newsletter and next book); put any additional info into an afterword or about the author etc.

All told, these adjustments will take you 5 – 10 hours to implement (less if you don't have a large backlist). But they could net you hundreds of sales and subscribers over the coming years.

A NOTE

We've covered most of these already. The reason for the repetition, then, is simple: there are not that many things that are truly effective in book marketing. This guide is information dense, which makes it easy to miss key points.

These optimizations are items authors tend to overlook or dismiss. A common author compliant is that they don't have time to market. **These things can carry part of the marketing**

load even when you aren't actively pushing your books. They're always working the background, 24/7, selling books passively.

None of these will take you from the Amazon cellar to bestseller status. But ignoring them in favor of shiny objects is ill-advised. Recall the principle of compounding from the very first section:

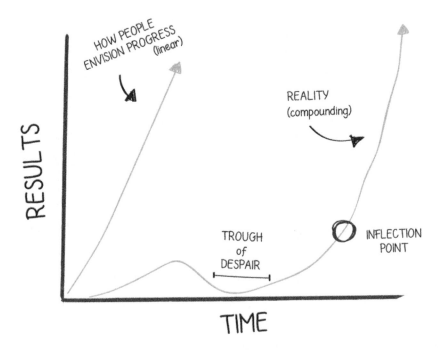

Note that compounding assumes you're *iterating* and *putting in the time.* Without making constant deposits into your skills account, so to speak, there will be nothing to build upon. You can make these deposits *actively—* by writing new books, running marketing campaigns, and so forth—or *passively.* The later involves getting your books and back matter to help you out in the background. Remember that we want to be building our platform brick-by-brick.

This is what these optimization tweaks are all about. As a simple example, let's say these changes add 10 subscribers a month. That's 100+ subscribers a year. That's an extra 5 – 10 sales per launch, which bumps you up *that* much higher in the rankings. Which gets you *more* sales and *more* subscribers from the ensuing visibility, getting you to that inflection point that much faster.

Convinced? Cool. Let's jump into the first tweak, which is to our website's home page.

THE HOME "LANDING" PAGE

A lot of people use aggressive pop-ups or other plugins to hound people to subscribe. Such methods can be effective when used correctly, but they also take time to set up and troubleshoot. You can get most of the benefits in a far less intrusive fashion by simply optimizing your home page.

How? Simple: make the newsletter sign up the *first* thing a visitor sees when they hit your site.

Here's the home page of my D.N. Erikson site:

This is the first thing you see when you type in **dnerikson. com** into your browser. It takes up the entirety of the screen (on both mobile and desktop).

Getting a reader on my email list is my primary objective. That has more value than them browsing my backlist or checking out any of the pages. After they've subscribed, they can explore further if they wish. But most people who visit a site once never return.

That's bad if we don't capture their email address, since it means we've lost them forever.

Here, I'm advertising my lead magnet on the home page. The majority of your traffic hits your home page at some point, ergo this maximizes exposure to your sign-up offer. The layout is simple: We have the cover on the left, a tagline/sign-up button on the right. There's only *one* core action to take, clearly drawing the visitor's attention with a contrasting blue button.

If people are intrigued by the cover and offer, they click.

Nothing flashy. It's not super aggressive. I don't make it so you *have* to sign-up, nor do I disable the top navigational menu (you can do both of these). You can also scroll down. I'm fine if people come to my author site, browse, and then *buy* books instead of signing-up. **It's always important to recognize that fans come in different forms**. In fact, I'm only on a few people's email lists (less than five). I don't join them, even if I really like the artist. Not my thing, which might sound funny given that I stress the importance newsletters throughout the guide.

But I don't design my marketing materials for *me*. I design them for readers. And that's why I use my prime real estate for the highest value item: getting them on the email list.

If you don't have an offer, you can just have the sign-up form. It works the same way. Note that here, the reason I use a button is not for some fancy marketing trickery. You may have seen information that having a two-step opt-in process converts better (e.g. having them click a button, *then* seeing the form). In my experience, that hasn't produced any improvement.

Instead, the reason I use the button is because my WordPress theme didn't allow me to easily integrate the sign-up form directly on the home page. Thus, when a visitor clicks the button, they're taken to a page on my website with the form installed (**dnerikson.com/bone**). This is an easy and effective workaround if you're struggling to get the technical side to play nice.

One final note: you might consider getting people to check out your new release as your highest value action. That's fine. The same principle applies: make sure it's the first thing people see when they visit your site, and ensure that the area is devoid of distractions. And whatever you do, **never use sliders on your home page**. Click data indicates people don't interact with them. They're also glitchy when it comes to device compatibility.

DOUBLE OPT-IN

Double opt-in is terrible from both an optimization and user experience perspective. Confirmation emails tend to get delayed or trapped in spam, wasting the reader's time. This is not an endearing first impression. As such, 30%+ of people never click the confirmation link. People erroneously believe that this filters out people who are uninterested or cuts down on spam complaints.

They are incorrect. There are people who will report the confirmation email for the list they *just* signed up for as spam. The only thing double opt-in does is kill your engagement and sub-scriber count.

The *only* reasons to enable double opt-in is if it's legally required in your country or you're having a significant problem with spam subscribers. The latter, however, can be mitigated by including a check box or CAPTCHA on the sign-up form itself.

THE WEEKLY AUTORESPONDER
(THE NETFLIX STRATEGY)

This is an easy one that most people skip for fear of "irritating" their subscribers or similar nonsense. Because yes, the people who *purposely* signed up to your list to hear more about your books will be annoyed when you tell them more about your books.

(that's sarcasm, in case it's not abundantly clear)

The real reason, of course, why authors refuse to set up auto-responders is simple: they're afraid. I get it. I've been there; for the first three years, I don't think I sent a single email to my list. I deleted my subscribers two or three times.

Being tentative did my career no favors. My sales reports from that time reflect this fact all too well.

An autoresponder that introduces your backlist to your readers is *not* an irritant. Instead, it's a *favor*. You're telling them about more books they might like.

Services like Netflix, Hulu, or HBO do the same thing. They have vast content libraries that can be overwhelming to navigate. To keep you engaged (and subscribed), these companies periodi-cally highlight shows or movies that you might enjoy via curated emails. This happens more frequently than you might expect.

Don't believe me? Do a quick search for their name in your inbox. You'll be shocked at the number of emails you receive.

Netflix sends me an email about new or backlist content every few days.

We can adapt this same idea to our own backlist by **sending subscribers an automated email every week introducing a new series to them.** All you have to do is schedule an autoresponder email every Friday (or a different day of the week) with a subject line like "looking for your next weekend read?" Want to do Wednesday instead? Try something like "Work sucks. This book doesn't." Obviously, you want to be on-brand: that irreverent tone might work for urban fantasy, but it's not going to fly for sweet romance. Calibrate things to *your* readers.

Have an email every week until you run out of series.

Don't lump all the series in a single email. This can be tempting, but it's overwhelming and counterproductive. Introduce one series at a time. If you write standalones, the same principle applies.

This strategy is an excellent, passive way to sell books without active promotion. Never assume your fans are familiar with all of your books—this won't be the case, especially if you're prolific.

UPSELL: SELL SOMETHING ON YOUR THANK YOU PAGE

You'll see the upsell thank you page referred to as a "tripwire" in eCommerce. The idea is simple: after someone signs up to your newsletter, you direct them to webpage with a relevant offer. In our case, this offer is simple: we can sell them one of our books or box sets.

When it comes to author websites, however, I'm generally not taken anywhere. Or the page just says "thanks for subscribing." This is a missed opportunity. Turn that thank you page into an upsell. You can see an example at dnerikson.com/rc-box (a screenshot is also posted below). When a reader signs up to receive the Ruby Callaway novella *Bone Realm*, they're sent to this page, where they can buy the entire series at the retailer of their choice.

Most people will ignore this, but you will pick up some extra sales as people sign up for your newsletter.

More importantly, you're introducing the series and the box set to the reader. So even if they *don't* purchase right away, you still make them *aware* that more books exist.

An important caveat here: you still need to include the "thank you" and tell them that their subscription is confirmed/their free book (if you're offering one) will arrive shortly. Put that first. Otherwise people will be confused, and you will receive emails from folks asking their sign up went through. Remember: **clarity trumps cleverness**. Always spell things out.

LIMIT IMAGES AND FANCY FORMATTING

You probably know that KDP charges you a delivery fee on books that receive 70% royalties. What you may not have checked is how much this can impact your bottom line. Delivery fees are not static; they're based on the book's file size. So while it's pretty much unavoidable to get charged $0.03 - $0.05 for a full-length novel, by limiting the number of images and any fancy formatting, we can greatly reduce the delivery fees and thus boost our take-home royalties with a few simple tweaks.

There are three things to keep in mind here:

1. Any image you include is likely going to cost you an additional $0.01 - $0.02. If you're embedding your book cover (or all the book covers, if it's a box set), consider removing these for a quick win.

2. Assess whether other images, like covers for your free novella, or images of your backlist, are pulling their weight. In theory, showing an attractive cover image of your free novella *can* increase the number of subscribers you generate. But each of those additional subscribers comes at an increased cost.

3. Custom chapter breaks and headers take up less space, but add up because they're repeated throughout the book. While there is an argument to be made in favor of branding (e.g. a distinct header will make your book look different than the hundreds of other titles using the same Vellum template), that's impossible to quantify. I prefer to go with numbers I can quantify. As another plus, you save on commissioning the custom graphics.

It's especially important to optimize your files if you plan on running Kindle Countdown Deals. These offer you a 70% royalty rate at $0.99 and $1.99. But you're still charged your standard delivery fees. Thus, if you're running a box set, having a number of unnecessary images like book covers inside can drop your effective royalty rate from about 55% (typically a large set, even without images, will cost $0.10 - $0.20 in delivery fees) to 40% or even below 35%. In which case you'd be better off *not* running the deal, since you'd make more money (at the 35% royalty rate, you're not charged delivery fees).

In general, my rule of thumb is simple: unless the image is **absolutely necessary, cut it out**. If you have a map or image that's vital to the story, don't remove that. That's idiocy. Everything else, however, should be likely removed.

FRONT MATTER: INCLUDE A NEWSLETTER LINK

Always include a link to your newsletter in the front matter; it can increase subscribers 2x or more. This applies even if you have nothing to offer in exchange (e.g. "sign up to my newsletter for updates"). It will still help.

The reason is simple: readers consume your book in different ways. By placing the newsletter link in the front *and* back matter, you maximize the number of eyeballs on it. People who read your sample can also see the newsletter link, which means they might not immediately purchase your book - *but* they might sign up to get your free novella to try one of your complete works. This is also a win.

The approach? Just put the newsletter link on its own page in the front matter, like one of the three options below:

Keeping this link on its own page is crucial. I often see authors bury the link on their copyright or also by page, thus effectively making it so no one will ever see it. You want to give it a page unto itself, with a heading so that it appears in the table of contents. This way, readers browsing through the TOC will see "Get the Free Prequel Novella" or "Get [Book Title] for Free." Make sure this heading clearly describes the offer.

From our previous discussion of file sizes and delivery fees, you'll know that I recommend the text-based option over the images. However, if you do want to include an image, just make it the book cover. A graphic like the one in the center, while eye-catching, will cost you additional money to commission, and should you need to make any edits to the text, will require additional funds and time to adjust.

Finally, as a general rule, I try to limit my front matter. Just the copyright page (which can probably go to the back), the table of contents, and the newsletter link page. That makes it easier for readers to spot, which in turn increases the chance of them signing up.

BACK MATTER: LIMIT OF TWO CTAS

Fear drives a lot of bad marketing decisions. Nowhere is this more prevalent than in the back matter, which is your book's most valuable real estate. Someone just liked your book enough to finish it. That's a *big* win. Now, instead of keeping that excitement going, what do most authors do?

They overwhelm them with thirty-six different links that make the person immediately put down their Kindle. Authors are deathly afraid of leaving anything out. What if the person who only likes Twitter doesn't see a Twitter link? What about that Bookstagram reader who might blast their book out to ten thousand followers?

Meh.

You should be more afraid of freezing excited readers into inaction through sheer informational overload.

Here's an example of stripped down back matter:

Put the upsell to Book 2 and the link to the newsletter on the same page as THE END. By placing these items right after THE END, instead of on a separate page (e.g. using a page break), you avoid triggering Amazon's automated end-of-book pop-up. This pop-up appears on most devices, asking the reader to review the book and also presenting them with other titles they might be interested in. If your books are linked in the series, this will include the next title, but it can also include other books in the genre. These distractions will decrease sellthrough, which is why we want to direct the reader to focus on our most valuable actions (buying the next book or signing up to the newsletter) ourselves.

You'll also notice that I include the *actual* link, and not just a hyperlink. This is important because web pages won't display properly on certain devices (e.g. e-Ink Kindles). Thus, the reader will need to enter the link on their smartphone or computer. By including a URL that they can easily enter, you make it easy for these readers.

If you do include a hyperlink, make sure the CTA text is clear, a la **TAP HERE TO GET [TITLE] BOOK 2 NOW**. You'd think that including language like "Tap Here" would be superfluous, but such instructions do help. Never underestimate the power of absolute clarity.

You can see here that streamlining the back matter generated an increase in sellthrough of about 40% (this was for a perma-free, hence the low sellthrough numbers).

Two notes: if you're just starting out and need reviews, you might include a review request instead. If you do this, make sure you link directly to the Amazon review form. That will increase the number of reviews you get beyond just the standard request. Once you have ten reviews, however, I'd generally remove this request in favor of the newsletter and next book.

Finally, you'll see here that I only have *one* CTA: a link to the next book (and a link to the box set). If you do strip things down to a single CTA, that item will naturally get more attention. Here I have sacrificed some mailing list sign-ups to encourage more sales. This was a calculated decision. In most instances, however, I'd make sure you have both links.

HOW TO RUN YOUR OWN OPTIMIZATION TESTS

You might want to run your own optimization tests in the future. Here's a list of things you can test:

1. Front Matter
2. Back Matter
3. Autoresponder: length, email subject lines, emails included
4. Price
5. Covers
6. Blurbs

And more. If you have control over a specific element, you can probably test it. You're only limited by your imagination.

Here's a basic framework for performing tests.

1. **PROCESS:** A/B testing. This means we compare our data from version A (our control) to a Version B to see which produces better results. Change a *single* element per test. We want to isolate a specific change. Thus, you might choose to change the back matter *or* the front matter— but you wouldn't do both at once. If you want to change your cover, don't change the blurb at the same time. When

you change more than one thing, you can't know which adjustment produced the impact.

2. **RECOMMENDED TIME FRAME**: 30 days. Note that tests may take longer if you're not selling many books. Two weeks is the lowest I'd go, since many items have second order effects—i.e., your price can increase the number of sales, but might decrease sellthrough, which will take longer to show up in your tracking.

3. **IMMEDIATE FEEDBACK**: Occasionally you may see an *immediate* negative impact; in this case, it's okay to change things back sooner and end the test. Be sure this isn't related to an outside factor, however.

4. **TRACKING DATA**: Tracking may involve daily tracking or simply comparing the stats to the original variation at the end of the test run.

5. **ANALYSIS**: Compare final data of challenger to the original (known as the "control" or "winner"), looking for big changes. When dealing with smaller amounts of data, small changes can just be regular variance or randomness. With large changes, there's a higher chance the result is reliable.

6. **SAMPLE SIZE**: The more data you have during that time frame (i.e., sales/visitors/subscribers—whatever is related to the item you're testing), the more reliable your results will generally be. E.g., if you're trying to assess the impact of changing the back matter on sellthrough, selling 500 copies of Book 1 during a 30 day test will give you a much better idea if the new back matter is better/worse than if you only sell 5.

7. **CHOOSING A WINNER**: If change is largely in favor of the new version, make the switch. If the original wins, keep the control. If uncertain or the difference is small, stick with the control. **You don't want to go backward.**

Here's how you can set up a back matter test, for example:

1. Calculate current sellthrough for the existing back matter during a recent 30 day period. Make sure you didn't run any outside promotion or launch a new book in the series, as these will skew the sellthrough numbers.

2. Make the change to the new back matter, upload the new file, and mark the start and end dates of your test on the calendar.

3. Wait 30 days, then compare sellthrough data for that 30 day period to the original 30 day period.

4. Determine the winner.

5. Repeat with a new version of the back matter, or test something different.

I try to have one optimization test in the fire at all times. Many of them end up making no difference, but if you do find something that moves the needle, you can apply it across your entire catalog.

For tests where you're not tracking daily, you can set up a calendar note, or use a service like Follow Up Then (**followupthen. com**) to automatically drop a reminder that the test is ending.

KEY TAKEAWAYS

- Optimization is all about one-time investments (i.e., low-hanging fruit) that produce long-term dividends
- This passive marketing helps increase your sellthrough and organic newsletter subscribers, thus accelerating your rate of progress.

- **HOME PAGE**: optimize this so more visitors subscribe to your newsletter.
- **DOUBLE OPT-IN**: turn this off to stop losing 30%+ of your subscribers
- **AUTORESPONDER:** every week, have an automated email introducing readers to another series in your backlist
- **UPSELL**: make your thank you for subscribing page an upsell to the box set/Book 1 in the related series
- **FORMATTING**: limit fancy formatting and images to keep file sizes down
- **FRONT MATTER**: always include a link to your newsletter; can increase subscribers 2x or more.
- **BACK MATTER:** two CTAs on same page as THE END (newsletter and next book); put any additional info into an afterword or about the author etc.

ACTION EXERCISE

1. Take one item from the list and optimize it.

TWELVE

LAUNCHING

It's finally time to put together everything we've learned into a flexible launch framework. New releases are the lifeblood of your author career; without them, your earnings will dwindle and die.

Too many authors try to rely on their backlist, or skate by without releasing for too long. That doesn't fly in 2020; if you're not releasing 3 – 4 books a year, you're going to have a *really* hard time. The reason? Amazon is set up to churn. They know that their customers like new content, and that new books convert better than old books. This is because we, as human beings, are wired to like *newness*—even if, with something like a hundred million books written over the centuries, we technically don't need any more.

None of that matters. We like new stuff. Amazon's data no doubt backs this up, which is why they've fine-tuned their recommendation systems to offer a plethora of visibility advantages to just-released titles.

And naturally, we want to leverage this visibility for our own benefit.

Which is where this guide comes in.

However, there are so many ways to approach a launch that any blanket recommendations would be nigh useless or, worse, detrimental to your overall success (due to fitting square pegs into proverbial round holes). Instead of ready-made templates, then, you need the tools to customize a launch strategy for yourself. That way, you can calibrate the variables based on the situation at hand.

Crafting a launch strategy requires answers to the following questions:

- **GOAL**: Profit or rank? If rank, what are you aiming for?
- **BUDGET**: Budget for actual launch window? Budget for first 30 days?
- **PLATFORM**: Your existing platform (mailing list subs, followers, etc.)
- **RELEASE SCHEDULE**: When is the next book coming out?
- **EXCLUSIVITY**: Launch in KU or going wide?
- **PRICING**: $0.99 or $2.99+?
- **PRE-ORDERS**: Pre-orders or no pre-order?
- **TIMEFRAME**: 5 – 14 days? (launch window)
- **STRATEGY**: Rapid release? Multiple simultaneous releases? discount prior books via KCD? Free run for a prior book? Rank push the new book to Top 250/100? Box set at $0.99 pushing toward Top 100 for page reads?

Answer these on a sheet of paper or in an Excel sheet. Eventually, you'll just automatically cycle through each point mentally as you craft an upcoming launch. But I still write them out, so I can refer back to them when analyzing the numbers months or years in the future.

WHY LAUNCH?

Some suggest that launches no longer matter in indie publishing.

I strongly disagree.

While Amazon's algorithms can (and do) change without warning, they currently provide substantial visibility boosts for titles released in the past 90 days. In practice, this means **each advertising dollar is worth anywhere from 1.5x to 3x normal during the launch period**. This is just a rule of thumb based on anecdotal observation, *not* based on data analysis. But the core takeaway is thus: since you're essentially playing with house money, there's no reason *not* to use the launch window (the first 30 days of your book's life) to your fullest advantage. Marketing aggressively during these initial 30 days is often more beneficial than spending a similar amount six months later.

Visibility doesn't completely fade after these first 30 days; **you actually get 90 days of new release visibility from Amazon**. However, this visibility starts to decay at Day 30, when books are no longer eligible for the Hot New Release chart. Another drop-off follows at 60 days, before new release visibility finally vanishes at the 90 day mark. At that point, your title is "backlist" on Amazon, and receives no special visibility benefits. In the indie community, these are colloquially referred to as the 30/60/90 day cliffs. The cliffs have become more pronounced in recent years, particularly the 30 day cliff; in hyper-competitive genres, you might lose effectively all of your new release juice after Day 30.

However long that extra visibility lasts, you want to use it to sell more books. In fact, launching a book is *so* powerful that you could theoretically ignore many of the marketing tenets in this guide and simply release a book a month in a hot genre. While you by no means have to release anywhere close to a book a month to succeed (recall the Ultimate Book Marketing Formula), this speaks to the power of a new release. Launches are one of the best opportunities you have as an author not just to make money, but also to build your platform (e.g., newsletter and fanbase). Remember that no promo or marketing campaign is a one-off effort; approaching them as isolated events is a major mistake. Instead, each marketing piece is a brick in your publishing career.

The launches are your biggest bricks of all. And when properly used, they rapidly accelerate how fast your publishing career progresses.

GENERAL APPROACH

A launch is all about hitting critical mass. **The more firepower you stack up, generally speaking, the better**. There are limits to the scope of this firepower, of course, as you can incinerate skyscraper-high stacks of cash with incredible ease during a poorly optimized launch. But if you don't move the sales needle high enough, then you're not going to get any help from Amazon's algorithms.

To that end, the three traffic sources concept often flies out the window during an aggressive launch. This is because of synergy: when your book is *everywhere*—promo sites, Facebook, your newsletter, other authors' newsletters, FB Ads, BookBub Ads, Amazon Ads, and so forth—it gives readers the impression that it's *important*. That it's *big*. It also reminds people *constantly* that it's available. They turn around and *boom, there's your book again*. If they don't buy the first time, it doesn't matter; you're hitting them from three other angles later in the week. Eventually, after seeing your book five, six, ten, or even twenty times—over multiple venues—a reader's brain goes *I have to check this out*.

This type of synergy is, of course, only possible with higher budgets. With more modest spends, you'll want to focus on your core three traffic sources. Spreading yourself too thin will limit the critical mass you can achieve; you only want to go far and wide should your budget risk exhausting your core three options.

Now that we've talked about the principles underpinning the launch, let's get into that list of questions we started with at the beginning. First on the agenda? Setting a launch goal.

GOAL

This boils down to a simple question: **are you gunning for profit or rank?**

While these are not mutually exclusive goals—indeed, one only aims for high ranks in the hope that this visibility transforms into profit somewhere down the line—they easily can be. That is because, absent a large platform, you will need to spend a substantial amount of money to push your book high in the Amazon ranks. This will usually demand that you lower your price to $0.99; at this price point, you earn only $0.35 a sale in royalties. Thus, if you don't get your book very high—say, the top 250 or Top 100—and then *hold* it there for a few days (recall that Amazon's algorithms prefer sustained sales rather than transient one day spikes), this ephemeral visibility can wear off very quickly indeed.

Gunning for rank is a Kindle Unlimited only strategy. Chasing rank is pointless when you're wide, since there is no Kindle Unlimited pot of page read gold to chase. A wide book, since its rank is not propped up by borrows (which count the same for ranking purposes as a sale), will have trouble making a push toward the Top 500 on the strength of advertising and a modest platform.

A Top 100 run for a Kindle Unlimited book costs anywhere from $1,200 – $3k, depending on the genre. This is assuming the book in question is $0.99; at $2.99, it becomes much pricier (and harder). You're banking on this massive visibility turning into page reads some 4 – 14 days after the end of the launch window. If you can get the book high enough, and sustain that rank for long enough, these page read rewards can be massive.

But if Amazon doesn't push your book, or you fail to hit lofty ranking heights?

You'll be left with a heap of $0.99 sales, a massive advertising bill, and little tail to show for it.

Thus, instead of playing rank roulette, I'd recommend aiming for profit in 99% of cases. The absolute ceiling is going to be lower, but it's a more reliable way to build a career.

BUDGET

More modest budgets will produce more modest rewards. That much is fairly obvious. It is, however, worth mentioning that the days of spending a few hundred dollars, organizing some newsletter swaps, alerting your platform, and potentially riding the Amazon algorithmic lightning are all but gone. These cases were always isolated, but they've become even more rare. As Amazon pushes their own advertising platform (Amazon Ads) store-wide, this will only become truer. After all, why give away visibility that authors are happy to pay for?

This doesn't mean organic visibility has dried up, only that it requires more of an advertising push than it used to.

I don't have specific suggestions for budget. Instead, bear in mind that no launch is a career making silver bullet. If you *need* any book or series to be the one that saves you, you're in a poor position. Never bet the house on a single release. Glitches, mistakes, and flops abound, even for savvy marketers.

Whatever budget you choose, make sure you can live to play another hand. If that means spending very little, or saving your powder for next time at the expense of the current launch, then that's fine. There's always a next time; your job is to make sure, financially, that there is a *next* time. Without being so conservative that you never give yourself the opportunity to succeed in a competitive industry at all.

PLATFORM

It's easy to focus on paid advertising options like promo sites or pay-per-click ads. While these are important, the foundation of your launch will be your existing platform. A large existing fanbase can carry the brunt of the marketing load, allowing you to save time and money on the paid options. Or, if you prefer, you can leverage this fanbase and combine it with paid advertising to launch your book into the stratosphere.

The core of your platform is your **newsletter, social media** (if you're active), and **relationships you have with other authors.** The first two have been covered in other parts of this guide, so I won't rehash them here. The last is fairly simple, but worth a little expanding: if you cultivate quality relationships with other authors in your sub-genre, this can be a tremendous asset come launch-time. This not only helps you hit critical mass (by tapping into *their* fanbase), but it also teaches Amazon's algorithms by funneling the *exact* type of reader you're looking for. If a popular author in your sub-genre recommends your book, it will become tied to their catalog in the also boughts, and Amazon will recommend it to the same general audience.

This is powerful.

It's also a part where many authors go wrong. Cultivating genuine relationships is *hard*. It is fairly easy to set up some newsletter swaps with other authors; these can help, but they're quickly becoming oversaturated. Readers are wise to newsletters filled with "recommendations" that the author hasn't even purchased, let alone read. As such, genuine refers to *not* just your relationship with other authors, but with your readers, as well. Sharing books from other authors that *you* enjoy is much more valuable than a hundred random titles to fulfill your swapping obligations.

Thus, I'd recommend, should you seek outside help with your launch, to do so carefully and methodically. That will serve you better long-term than blasting authors (and readers) with requests that put them in an awkward position.

RELEASE SCHEDULE

It was already said but 1,000 words ago, but it bears repeating: launching a book is *so* powerful that you could theoretically ignore many of the marketing tenets in this guide and simply release a book a month in a hot genre.

Most authors can't release a book a month (I certainly don't). This doesn't leave you DOA. But whatever your release pace is, you want to have an idea of what books are coming down the pike—and *when*. This will dictate all your decisions for your current launch, from the budget to the pricing.

For example, if you release a book a month, you don't have to go as heavy on the advertising. Since one of your titles will always be on the Hot New Release chart (provided you get it visible enough), you can simply ride this from month-to-month, reigniting the momentum with each subsequent release. If you release twice a year, on the other hand, you'll probably want to go as big as possible, because that book needs to carry more of the load.

As a rule of thumb, the quicker you get books out (particularly if they're in a trendy Kindle Unlimited genre), the less time and money you have to spend on each launch. That being said, this is optional: even if you release fast, the more high quality marketing firepower you can put behind each release, the better things will generally turn out.

EXCLUSIVITY

Choosing whether to launch your book in Kindle Unlimited or wide is one of the biggest decisions you'll make, and heavily dictates what launch strategies are available to you. Kindle Unlimited has much higher upside, since each borrow counts the same as a sale in Amazon's ranking algorithm, thus allowing you to get significantly more visibility on your books. Tools like KDP Free Runs and Kindle Countdown Deals make generating visibility easier for exclusive books as well.

When you're wide, *you* need to bring the visibility. If you're just starting out, your skills and also your platform are unlikely to be up to the task. Even when you're experienced, if you don't have a solid platform to launch from, pushing a new release wide can be a sobering endeavor.

I recommend launching every new book into Kindle Unlimited for at least one 90 day cycle. If it doesn't perform well, then you can always move it wide later. This gives you two bites at the apple, granting you exposure to the upside of KU while also keeping the flexibility of wide in your back pocket for later. Note: If you're a wide-only author, then you would simply launch wide from the get-go.

PRICING

I'm not a fan of launching at $0.99; it brings you only $0.35 a sale, which makes profitability tricky to achieve. However, the real reason I don't like launching at $0.99 is simple: it devalues your brand. Consumers expect new media properties, whether they're video games or movies, to be *most* expensive upon release. This extends to the book market as well. Pricing at $0.99 from the get-go, then, puts you in a bargain-basement category with straight-to-video movies and other commodities. It instantly makes readers suspicious: why is this *new* book so cheap? Is there something wrong with it? Price is a quality signal, and this sends the wrong ones. Those people who do shop for new releases in these bins tend not to be author loyal, but price and genre loyal; they're looking for $0.99 urban fantasy books first. The name on the cover is essentially irrelevant.

This is fine and not a judgement regarding these readers. It is merely important to understand, as a business owner, that such readers are unlikely to turn into hardcore fans in great numbers.

Remember that our overarching goal is to build our platform long term. Readers seeking new release deals, on balance, aren't author loyal. If you raise prices, many of them will seek cheaper books. In short, it's difficult to survive long term as a commodity. Instead, I'd recommend cultivating a premium brand, where readers are buying *your* books specifically, rather than simply the cheapest available title in their genre of choice.

Generally, unless you're trying to push a KU book into the Top 100 overall during the launch (see our discussion of rank v. profit above), you're better off launching at $2.99+. You get the 70% royalty rate, but $2.99 is still enough of a discount to remain in semi-impulse buy territory. This makes getting people to pick the book up cold via Facebook or Amazon ads a realistic option (whereas pricing at $4.99 or $5.99 makes that extremely difficult). You also maintain your brand as premium and high quality.

In certain hyper-trendy KU genres, long-term branding is less of a concern; immediate visibility is *much* more important. In these circumstances, the calculus shifts, and it can be better to come out pushing your new releases *hard* at $0.99 to wring every last bit of visibility you can while the sun is shining. You're not playing for tomorrow; you're playing for right now, and the couple months thereafter. While this can be a highly lucrative game to play, it requires deft navigation of current trends; stick around a chilling sub-genre too long, and you'll find your earnings in a similar deep freeze. I believe building a brand in a well-established sub-genre is a better (and easier) long-term play, although it can demand greater patience.

I want to be very clear about one thing: I am not against discounting. In fact, discounting earlier backlist books in the same series is an effective way to use lower prices to snag new readers during a launch without devaluing your new release. This is a tried-and-true practice across many industries: older products are discounted as they get further along in their lives. Consumers expect this, and don't see it as a negative quality signal. Instead, they take it as a positive: *wow, I'm getting a good deal on a great book*.

And that's a win-win for everyone.

PRE-ORDERS

If you're wide, then do a pre-order on non-Amazon retailers. It will benefit you.

On Amazon, I used to recommend against long pre-orders. The reason was simple: pre-orders only counted toward rank when they occurred. Thus, a pre-order spread these out over time. The ultimate consequence was often not generating enough visibility to get Amazon recommending your book.

However.

While pre-orders still count toward rank on the day they occur, Amazon seems to have mitigated the effects on launch day. I'm not entirely sure how they've tweaked things, but pre-orders no longer seem to negatively impact your launch day visibility. This shift occurred around the same time that Amazon changed the max pre-order period from 90 days to a full year.

Thus, I'd recommend pre-orders, assuming you have the book finished for four key reasons:

1. Getting the also-boughts to populate. If you do have an existing fan base, a few people will pre-order the book, thus getting the ball moving on the also boughts. Anyone who has had the also boughts delayed for a new release knows how that can ruin a launch; this largely prevents that from happening.

2. Requesting for the new book to be added to the series page. This is especially vital when using Kindle Countdown Deals on earlier books—Amazon gives the series page a new URL every time a book is added, so you need to make sure this link is correct in any ads you're directing to the series page.

3. Linking paperback and audio editions to the eBook. If you have any ARC reviews that people left on the paperback, those will appear on the eBook version.

4. Setting up ads, social media posts, and your newsletter in advance. Since you'll have the Amazon link to your new book, you'll be able to schedule all of these items for launch day.

They're especially useful if you set up a pre-order for Book 2 (or a later book in the series) to capture that Book 2 sale right away while doing a big launch push for Book 1. Include a link in the back matter of Book 1 to the pre-order for the next book. In this way, you can "daisy-chain" your books together. And if you're a slower author, putting the next book up for pre-order can demonstrate to potential readers that you plan to keep writing—and keep them more engaged in the series.

Finally, if you do a pre-order of 30 days or more, and check the Kindle Unlimited exclusivity box when you submit your pre-order, your book will be eligible for a Kindle Countdown Deal when it launches. This can be useful if you plan to launch at $0.99. Note that if you plan to run a Kindle Countdown Deal on a just-released title, you can't actually schedule it until the book is live. Thus, the earliest you can schedule a KCD is 2 days *after* the actual release date; I'd give yourself 3 or 4, just to build in a buffer.

LAUNCH WINDOW TIMEFRAME

An all-out marketing blitz can generally only be sustained for 3 to 14 days, maximum. I prefer 5 – 7 days for three reasons:

1. This gives you ample time to activate the Amazon algorithms, while being short enough to realistically sustain visibility (and your full attention) throughout the duration of the launch.
2. It matches the max length of a KDP Free Run (5 days) or Kindle Countdown Deal (7 days).
3. At 10+ days, things generally become far too expensive and stressful to manage from an administrative perspective. A launch is a lot of hands-on effort, and every minute you spend making ads and managing spreadsheets is one that you can't spend writing.

STRATEGIES

The section on promotional strategies covers approaches that you can adapt to launches. There are, of course, a nearly infinite number of ways to structure your launch. Such is the beauty of marketing: as you learn more, and your skills develop, you unlock a creative canvas that surpasses even writing the books themselves. If you're skeptical of this statement, I'll gently posit (as an author and a marketer) that you probably haven't done enough marketing to explore its full creative potential.

With that being said, let's cover one launch strategy *not* covered in the guide above: **rapid releasing**. This comes in multiple flavors, the two most popular being **one book a month** and **multiple simultaneous releases**. The basic reason in favor of the rapid release approach is simple: Amazon's algorithms like new releases. If you go longer than a month between them, your visibility fades from its peak. Thus, if you release a book, say, every two months, or three, part of that launch's job is to recover visibility ground that you've ceded since the previous book came out.

Rapid releasing solves that problem, in that you're never losing ground. You consistently build on your momentum from month-to-month. Multiple simultaneous releases ups the ante further: dropping two or more titles on a single day, then usually following that up with another book 30 days later.

It's probably self-evident why such approaches are hyper-powerful. They feed Amazon's algos exactly what they like: more books. And readers dig the fast releases too, since it allows them to consume the story at a rapid pace, a la Netflix binges.

What's less obvious at first glance are the downsides. There are only two, but they're substantial:

1. **Capital**. If you're releasing multiple books in rapid succession, this often requires a block of cash upfront to secure editing, covers, and other services related to production. You don't want your cover designer to be all booked up in the month before Book 2's release, which means shelling out months in advance. This can be difficult if funds are tight.

2. **Time and patience**. It's hard to carve out the hours necessary to write a book a month, or have the patience to stockpile multiple books. Note that some authors who can't write a book a month choose to stockpile releases, then push them out 30 days apart. After they've emptied their book bank, there's a few months until the next rapid release.

Number one is surmountable with some basic financial planning. Managing your psychology, and accurately assessing your productive output is another matter entirely. While rapid releasing is simple on paper, it is *extremely* difficult in reality. Most authors are not capable of writing a book a month or withholding releases until they're ready.

These are not problems.

The problem, then, is when you convince yourself that you are a faster or more patient author than you currently are. To be clear, you can build these skills, but that takes time. If you're writing two books a year, you can't suddenly write 12 because you "want it really bad" or decide to do so. You must build up that capacity. This can take years, *if* it's possible. Most writers max out at a far lower level of production. In the meantime, however, forcing yourself to write much faster than you're capable of results in two things: missed deadlines and burnout.

Thus, trying to rapid-release, while the most effective launch strategy in the business, ends up *hurting* most writers. People set unrealistic goals for themselves, inevitably miss their deadlines, then end up writing *less* than they would have. This is how a four book a year writer becomes a two book one.

Meet yourself where you are and build your skills from there. If you want to rapid release, that's fine; just know that getting to that point is a process. And it might not suit your strengths. For some, it takes months; for others, it never becomes possible. Ultimately, most authors are better served simply releasing books at their own pace (while trying to improve their writing speed gradually) instead of chasing rapid release fool's gold.

PUTTING IT ALL TOGETHER

How you design your launch depends on the decisions you make regarding the factors above. These are but two sample templates that you can build from, or simply use as examples of how to apply the previously discussed concepts.

Since launching a completely new book differs vastly from launching a book in an existing series, we'll cover each separately.

FOR A NEW BOOK 1 OR SERIES

If you have a new Book 1 fresh off the presses and ready for publication, you *do* want to support it with a launch. There is no reason to squander new release visibility. After all, you never know: Book 1 might be a smash hit out of the gate. You wouldn't want to cut things off at the knees by not giving it a shot. But you don't necessarily want to come out guns blazing, either. Reason being, even if Book 1 is highly successful, readers have nothing else to buy until Book 2 arrives.

As an example, if a book is ranked #1,000 in the store, it's generating approximately 100 – 125 sales + borrows a day. Let's say for the sake of argument that this is split 50-50. Here's how the data breaks out (KENP is the official term for Kindle Unlimited pages):

Daily #s	Price	KENP	Rank	Sales	Borrows	Page Reads	Sales $	Reads $	Total Daily Revenue
Book 1	$ 2.99	300	1000	50	50	11,250	$ 104.65	$ 50.63	$ 155.28

*Assumes 75% of borrowers finish book and page read rate of $0.0045

$155/day is excellent money—about $4,500 a month and $56,000+ a year.

However, there are three caveats: one, you can't sustain a book in the Top 1,000 forever. After 30 days, that high-flyer will begin an inevitable trek down the rankings. Two, propelling a book into the Top 1,000, unless you write in a super-trendy genre or have a sizable existing fanbase, is an expensive endeavor with ads alone. Revenue is not the same thing as *profit*. It's likely you're *spending* close to $155 a day (if not more) just to maintain this sort of visibility on a $2.99 release. And three, it's really hard to get a book into the Top 1,000 and keep it there for even 30 days.

There are seven million books and counting on the Kindle Store.

The Top 1,000 is rarefied air. Achievable, yes. But when you take those three caveats under advisement, *holy shit, I'm making $155 a day* becomes, *holy shit, I'm doing something this hard and only making $155 a day?*

Thus, you typically want to be a bit more conservative with the first book—if it's responding really well in the first few days of launch, you can push harder with your advertising efforts. If it's not, lay off the gas a bit and focus on writing the next book. Then, you can put the resources you saved toward the *next* launch. Because if you can get Book 1 to #5,000 (which requires a far less herculean effort) with, say, six more books in the series, *that's* where the real money is:

Daily #s	Price	KENP	Rank	Sales	Borrows	Page Reads	Sales $	Reads $	Total Daily Revenue
Book 1	$ 2.99	300	5000	20	20	4,500	$ 41.86	$ 20.25	$ 62.11
Book 2	$ 3.99	300	7500	10	10	2,250	$ 27.93	$ 10.13	$ 38.06
Book 3	$ 4.99	300	10,000	8	8	1,800	$ 27.94	$ 8.10	$ 36.04
Book 4	$ 4.99	300	15,000	6	6	1,440	$ 22.36	$ 6.48	$ 28.84
Book 5	$ 4.99	300	20,000	5	5	1,152	$ 17.88	$ 5.18	$ 23.07
Book 6	$ 4.99	300	25,000	4	4	922	$ 14.31	$ 4.15	$ 18.45
Book 7	$ 4.99	300	25,000	3	3	737	$ 11.45	$ 3.32	$ 14.76
Total				57	57	12,801	$ 163.73	$ 57.60	$ 221.33

*50% readthrough from Book 1 to Book 2; 80% readthrough from Book 2 onward
*Assumes 75% of borrowers finish book and page read rate of $0.0045

Now, at first glance you may say, *wait, I'm only making $65 more after writing six more books?* Perhaps. But remember that our first example was an absolute best case scenario. It is far more realistic to get a quality Book 1 to the 5,000 mark and have it hang around there for a few weeks, than it is to stick it in the Top 1,000.

It also costs far less. Once you get your ads dialed in, it's possible to keep Book 1 "pinned" in the Top 5,000 – 10,000 following a launch for as little as $50 – $75 per day. So our take home profit here is $150+, whereas on our single title, we might be spending every shred of profit (and then some) to merely keep the book visible.

And one final note: this is but one series. Let's say we have 21 books—three seven book series. Perhaps they're not all as illustrious as our example above; maybe the others only achieve half those heights following a launch. That is still $440+ in revenue and about $300 in profit.

Which would put us right around the six-figure mark annually.

See what I mean about building things brick-by-brick?

With that in mind, then, let's talk about releasing a new book in an already established series.

FOR A NEW BOOK IN AN EXISTING SERIES

Since your launch approach will differ slightly depending on whether you're releasing Book 2 or 20, here are three basic ideas:

1. For Book 2's launch, consider offering the first book for $0.99.

2. For Book 3's launch, consider making Book 1 free or $0.99 and Book 2 $0.99.

3. If this is the fourth book or later, you can consider discounting *all* the previous titles, or just the first three (free/$0.99/$0.99 or $0.99/$0.99/$0.99).

Note that you don't *have* to discount earlier books. But I like doing so because it lifts the series from both ends: you get people into the backlist titles (and boost their visibility) while also pushing the latest release. This is especially effective when you have books that don't have to be read in order (e.g., mysteries/thrillers a la Reacher, or romances in the same world that star different couples). Naturally, it can still be used to great effect with series that must be read from the beginning.

When discounting, I like using Kindle Countdown Deals. I recommend reviewing the promotion section, which covers a KCD strategy you can use for both regular promotion *and* launching. While you can simply discount the books manually, doing so via KCD generates better results for two reasons:

1.   You get 70% royalties (instead of the normal 35%) on those $0.99 sales, which makes an *enormous* difference in your earnings. It's not uncommon for promo sites and PPC ads to be profitable or breakeven solely from the sales of the discounted volumes alone (not counting other non-discounted later books in the series, the newly launched book, or page reads).

2.   The ticking clock that readers see when they hit the page increases the number of sales produced by your advertising. This timer isn't present during a non-KCD discounted $0.99 promo.

A lot of people sleep on Kindle Countdown Deals. Don't; they're a super-effective way to jumpstart a series and massively boost your launch (hat tip goes out to David Gaughran, who I first learned about them from). I won't review the whole strategy here; go read that section for information on how to execute it. The same framework applies regardless of whether it's for a standard promo or a launch.

As a final note, I would only do *really* aggressive series discounting (i.e., all books at once) if you're exclusive to Amazon and using Kindle Countdown Deals (even then, discounting everything often doesn't make sense). Keep the discounts to Books 1/2/3 if you're wide. Getting $0.35 in royalties for each book on your entire series kills profitability.

LAUNCH SCHEDULE

Again, this is just a framework you can (and should!) adapt for your own purposes.

1. **1 MONTH BEFORE LAUNCH DAY**: pre-order up.

2. **1 MONTH BEFORE LAUNCH DAY**: schedule promo sites on Book 1 (or Books 1, 2 & 3 box set) for free or $0.99.

3. **1 MONTH BEFORE LAUNCH DAY**: send your newsletter/social media followers an announcement that a new book is coming, along with the release date. You can reveal the blurb/cover at this point—or involve them in the process and have them vote on their favorite. Ask subscribers if they want to join your ARC team if you don't have one already.

4. **2 WEEKS BEFORE LAUNCH DAY**: release the paperback version. Don't announce the paperback release anywhere. Send out review copies to your ARC team. Include the link to the paperback review form so ARC members can post their review before launch day.

5. **1 WEEK BEFORE LAUNCH DAY**: set up an eBook pre-order. This allows the Amazon also-boughts to populate, lets you link the print/eBook editions on Amazon, and makes sure everything is ready to go for launch day. If the new book is part of an existing series, also email Amazon to add the new book to the series page; this usually doesn't happen automatically, and if you're using the Kindle Countdown Deal strategy outlined above is absolutely critical, since you'll be directing a lot of the ads to the series page.

NOTE: only set up a pre-order this close to launch day if the final version of the book is done. You need to upload the final file three days before the launch date, but sometimes the pre-order process appears as "publishing" in your dashboard for a few days whenever you put through an update. You can't edit your pre-order when it's in this status. Thus, you don't want to be locked out of your book with a placeholder file still uploaded.

6. **1 WEEK BEFORE LAUNCH DAY**: start testing Facebook and BookBub ads. You can direct these to the pre-order page. Note that you want to keep your budgets *extremely* modest at this point, because people are unlikely to pre-order from an ad. This is about nailing down your best ad creatives (the images, headlines, copy, and so forth) and audiences.

7. **1 – 2 DAYS BEFORE LAUNCH DAY**: schedule your best Facebook and BookBub ads to go live the day after launch. Launch any Amazon Ads you plan on running, since these can take a few days to warm up and start seeing significant impressions.

8. **1 – 2 DAYS BEFORE LAUNCH DAY**: schedule your newsletter to go out the day after launch.

9. **LAUNCH DAY (DAY 0)**: check to make sure the book's formatting is correct (buy a copy) and that everything on Amazon is also in order. Don't announce anything yet; this gives you a small buffer to fix anything that's wonky.

10. **LAUNCH DAY (DAY 0)**: send email to ARC team reminding them to review.

11. **AD PUSH BEGINS (DAY 0 or 1 DAY AFTER LAUNCH)**: if everything is in order, now you send out your newslet-

ter. Split it into multiple parts if you have more than 2,000 subscribers: i.e., half get it on Day 1, half on Day 2.

- Use a simple subject line like "The New [Character Name] Novel is Now Available" or "[Title] is Out Now and $0.99 for a Limited Time." These outperform clever subject lines.

12. **DAY 2 or 3**: free run or Kindle Countdown Deals start if you're discounting earlier titles.

13. **DAY 2 or 3**: depending on when you sent out your newsletter, post to your social media sites. You can stagger them across multiple days—i.e., Day 2 is Twitter, Day 3 is Facebook, and Day 4 is Instagram.

14. **LAUNCH WEEK**: monitor your various PPC ads (Facebook and BookBub in particular). Scale the good ones if your budget allows; scale back or kill the ones that are performing poorly. Create new ones to replace the ineffective ones.

15. **LAUNCH WEEK**: if you're typically active on social media, occasionally mention the launch and interesting things related to it.

16. **DAY 7**: last chance email to newsletters saying that this is the last day to get the deals. However, you don't want this to be a hard sell email; instead, you want to use a softer subject line like "Thanks" and then genuinely update them on the launch (readers love to hear about this) and thank them for the support. After this, you can mention and link to the deals one more time.

17. **DAY 7**: last chance posts to social media.

18. **DAY 8**: scale back ads, return the launched book to full price, and other books to regular prices (if not doing KCDs, which automatically readjust the price).

Whew. That's it: by the end, you'll probably be ready for a break from marketing. But don't ease off the gas completely—you should still be doing some marketing stuff to keep momentum going. Keeping some money in reserve for advertising to maintain visibility when the books return to full price generally helps the tail. And, of course, you should be writing that next book!

One final note: track your sales numbers day-by-day in Excel for the first 30 days of release. You want to know how the launch went—not only so you can tweak things like your ads during launch week, but also so you have a record of what worked (and what didn't) for your *next* launch.

KEY TAKEAWAYS

- Launching is not a paint-by-numbers exercise; you must create a custom strategy for each specific book that considers:
- **GOAL**: profit is recommended over rank
- **BUDGET**: the more money you can spend *effectively*, the greater your potential upside
- **PLATFORM**: your existing platform (mailing list subs, followers, etc.) increases the upside of your launch
- **RELEASE SCHEDULE**: the more frequent your releases the less important/less you have to spend on any one launch to maintain momentum

- **EXCLUSIVITY**: at least one 90-day cycle in KU per book is recommended unless you're a wide-only author
- **PRICING**: $2.99+ on new releases is recommended to establish a premium author brand and get 70% royalties. Can discount backlist titles.
- **PRE-ORDERS**: yes for non-Amazon retailers. On Amazon, a pre-order is extremely useful for taking care of administrative tasks like linking paperback edition, getting series page updated, scheduling ads/newsletters.
- **TIMEFRAME**: 5 – 7 days, since longer requires additional time and substantially more money.
- **STRATEGY**: rapid release? Multiple simultaneous releases? discount prior books via KCD? Free run for a prior book? Rank push the new book to Top 250/100? Box set at $0.99 pushing toward Top 100 for page reads?

ACTION EXERCISE

1. Create a launch plan for your next book.

THIRTEEN:

THE ULTIMATE WRITE TO MARKET STRATEGY

Now that we've covered everything, I'm going to show you how I'll be applying the guide's principles to my own books during 2020.

The purpose of this last section is two-fold:

1. To demonstrate how productivity, craft, and marketing dovetail to form a cohesive strategy with a clear action plan.

2. To show you my thought process and how I adapt this guide's principles to my books. While this guide has been very methodical and presents everything in step-by-step fashion, it is your job to apply the concepts to your own situation. Not everything will line up 1:1 with your career. I'm showing how I do that, so you can take those ideas and use them to create your own strategy.

Curious how things turn out?

I'll be doing monthly progress updates on my site for the rest of 2020; follow along at **nicholaserik.com/start**.

MY STRATEGY

Way back in Part 1, I had you sketch out a rough draft of your strategy for the next year. You needn't re-read that part right now, however; I've copied and pasted the strategy template here and filled it out. Here's what my final draft looks like:

- **CORE OBJECTIVE**: hit $25k net a month (between non-fiction/courses/consulting/fiction)
- **LAUNCH WIDE or KU**: all in KU
- **SERIES? PLANNED # of TITLES?**: yes. One 5 - 6 urban fantasy book series and (potentially) finishing the final books in two sci-fi trilogies.
- **LENGTH**: 40,000 – 60,000 word novels
- **NEW TITLES IN 2020**: 4 – 8
- **SUB-GENRES**: urban fantasy, post apocalyptic, space opera
- **CORE TRAFFIC SOURCES**: Facebook Ads, Amazon Ads, BookBub Ads, promo sites
- **NEWSLETTER BUILDING PLANS**: organically only via a reader magnet novella specifically written for the 5 – 6 book series. Not actively building sci-fi list.
- **PRODUCTION BUDGET PER TITLE**: $750 – $900
- **ADVERTISING BUDGET PER TITLE**: variable

Everything fits on a single page. That's by design: this format takes the last 70,000 or so words of this guide and crunches the key questions you need to answer into something you can process without being totally overwhelmed. Simplicity always trumps unnecessary complexity.

My situation is unique in that I obviously have a non-fiction component to my business that includes guides such as this, along with courses. This will not be most people's situation. But that's kind of the point of the guide, right: *your* situation is unique. There is no one-size-fits-all plan.

Let's break down the rationale behind these decisions. I'll focus on the books side, since that's what's relevant to 99.9% of people.

The core objective is simple: I want to hit $25k, net, in a single month.

All the other decisions flow from here.

I do have revenue coming in from the non-fiction side, but this is still an aggressive earnings target given that I haven't released a book in the last 18 months. Thus, I need to maximize my potential upside. Building up my catalog in a single popular KU subgenre (urban fantasy) will make my backlist **highly correlated**. This increases my upside, but also lowers the earnings floor, since there's risk in placing all your eggs in one genre/retailer basket. If my books don't resonate with Kindle Unlimited readers (which they haven't in the past, at least not to the degree I was hoping), or my Kindle Unlimited strategies need work, then I'll be buried beneath authors who have advantages in those areas.

I'm confident that my books hit the right urban fantasy notes; the existing ones have solid reviews and one series hit the *USA Today* Bestseller list. Kindle Unlimited strategies aren't a problem. To date, however, I've struggled with Kindle Unlimited read-through on my urban fantasy titles, which is part of the reason

I took my backlist wide. I believe these struggles, however, are largely due to missing pre-order/release dates and releasing relatively slowly. Many of the most popular urban fantasy authors are prolific. To stay visible, you need to release books at a solid clip.

Many authors are worried about Kindle Unlimited being a risk from an existential standpoint (e.g. you can be arbitrarily banned). I believe that's less of a risk than the program's structure suddenly changing. This has happened multiple times, most recently in 2015, when the borrow system was replaced with the current page read system (you used to get paid ~$1.30 per borrow after someone read 10% of your book).

Despite that inherent risk, I've placed the rest of my books back into Kindle Unlimited. If one of my upcoming books is even a modest hit, its success will massively lift the entire backlist by virtue of the aforementioned correlation. Should I have a solid KU hit while the rest of my books are wide, the upside is far lower. Kindle Unlimited readers are unlikely to purchase non-KU titles, whereas they'll gladly borrow multiple backlist books.

Mitigating some of the risk, however, are two factors. One, I know the ropes and what to expect after taking the existing books wide. It's steady if unspectacular money with some marketing elbow grease. So if I double my urban fantasy backlist over the coming year, and things don't shake out in Kindle Unlimited, that isn't the worst fallback plan. Two, I don't actually have all my eggs in one basket, anyway. Since I do client work and marketing courses for authors, this gives me another income stream, smooths out cash flow, and hedges against any massive flops.

As for the remaining decisions: For the past year and a half, I've been trying to release a book a month.

While releasing quickly is necessary to stay visible in urban fantasy and build momentum, this pace exceeded my current writing capacity.

Similarly, I was aiming for the higher end of the word count listed here (60,000+). While I may reach that on occasion, my natural word count trends more toward the 45k range.

By working with my strengths and tendencies, rather than against them, I think I should be able to release 4 – 8 books during 2020, which puts me on a solid book every two months pace. I have released seven books in a year before, so this is a realistic output.

One key change is series length: while I prefer writing trilogies, I've found that it's challenging to advertise these profitably via Facebook, BookBub, and Amazon Ads. Hence writing 5+ book series to make it easier to market. A second planned series (down the line in 2021 or later) might turn into an extension of this series should it become a solid hit. No strategy is set in stone; it should be flexible, since divining the future is impossible.

On the traffic front, I'm comfortable with all the PPC Ad platforms and promo sites, and prefer using paid advertising, since I have full control over the results.

I've done quite a few cross promotions to build my newsletter in the past (along with Facebook Ads), but I have no plans to continue with non-organic methods of list building. I already have over 7,000 subscribers. Instead, I have novellas for each current series (and will write a novella for my upcoming series) to continue to grow my organic subscriber base.

In terms of production costs, I've found from commissioning 80+ covers at a wide range of prices that, above $200 – $300, you hit a point of diminishing returns. I've found plenty of quality designers in this range; spending more doesn't seem to produce additional sales or benefits (an obvious exception would be if your genre requires illustrated covers, which start at higher price points). Keeping the production costs lower limits my risk—I can swap out the covers if need be without much hesitation. When you sink $700 or $1k into a cover, that becomes a much more bitter pill to swallow.

One thing I'm doing is testing the first in series covers via Facebook Ads before releasing anything. This isn't perfect, but it does reduce the chance of picking a dud cover that doesn't resonate with the target audience (or perform well with ads).

Commissioning three covers for my upcoming series cost the same as a single expensive cover (total for the three was $800) and mitigates the risk of missing the target audience. Once I have a cover I'm comfortable with for Book 1, I can be confident that the remaining covers in the series will also resonate with my target audience, since they'll share similar branding.

The remaining production costs are for proofreading. I've found that getting two proofreaders is usually required to squash the majority of typos in my novels, even though I write fairly clean.

Finally, the advertising budget will vary. I'm going to spend less at the beginning, as I focus on writing. I'm okay with this being a slow burn where I spend the first half (or even first three-quarters) of 2020 building the series and working on my craft. Consistent production has been my biggest problem (as mentioned previously, I haven't published a novel in 18 months), so I want to concentrate on dialing that in before I worry too much about complicated marketing plans. Babysitting ads and logging numbers are both more interesting to me than writing at this point, so they'll definitely take attention away from getting words down. I also need more books to effectively employ some of the promotional strategies, so it doesn't make sense to come out wallets blazing from a profit maximization standpoint, anyway. I expect that to change; for the first couple books, I'll probably spend a few hundred bucks on the launches, whereas come November 2020, it's conceivable (if things are going well) that I'll be spending $5,000 - $10,000+.

One important note: I'm focusing on my urban fantasy pen name; I just have a couple trilogies that I want to wrap up under my sci-fi pen name. This is not really related to the strategy; in fact, strictly speaking, finishing those books is probably a bad business move (those series never sold well). But I'd like to close those trilogies out, and they'll also give me additional case studies and material for my courses. Thus, from an overall business and learning standpoint, they *do* make sense. If I was strictly writing fiction, however, finishing those trilogies would be a poor use of time, since I have no current plans to build up my Nicholas Erik pen name past those books.

EXECUTION

Now that I have my high level strategy, I need to translate that list of abstract items into actual tasks I can execute. Recall from Part I that execution flows from strategy. The two are inseparable. When you have a bad strategy, your execution inevitably suffers. As a simple example, consider this "strategy": drink eight beers and then try to write your daily words. For most, this results in unbelievably poor execution. No one would use this as a strategy. But people make "big, audacious" goals that effectively do the same thing—disempower them through their sheer ridiculousness.

Then they compound this by trying to fix everything at once—making huge goals in *all* areas. Lose 100 pounds, write 12 novels, become a marketing guru. This year will be the year that *everything* clicks.

I'm as guilty of this as anyone.

Life doesn't work that way, unfortunately. Not that you can't make great progress. You can. But remember this when you're setting up a strategy for any part of your life: **adherence is number one**. If you can't show up to execute your strategy, it doesn't matter how great your diet, book launch, job plan, schedule, or productivity hack looks on paper. You need to scrap it, and then revise it into something that you can actually do.

That means you need to be *really* selective. Focus on one thing at a time. Why am I not worried about marketing out of the gate? Because I need to get the writing production back up to speed. That's going to be rocky. I know that. The first book will not be particularly fun. I've already tried to finish it a couple times with no success. So generating enough momentum to get over that obstacle will require most of my energy.

And that, really, is the key ingredient of this strategy: it's designed *for me*, based on reality. Which means my plan for the year essentially boils down to:

1. Read 12 urban fantasy, sci-fi, or craft books in 2020.
2. Publish 1 full-length novel (40k+ words) every other month with an emphasis on practicing **dialogue** and **scene structure**.
3. Do a large launch or promotion on a backlist series every month (this will start later in the year, when I have enough content to advertise in a rotation without burning out promo sites/ad options).

Obviously, I'm not starting from scratch, so it's worth noting that I have these elements already established:

1. **PPC**: I've probably run 2,000+ ads at this point between my own books and working with other authors.

2. **PROMO SITES**: I know what sites work and have tested things across multiple genres.

3. **BLURBS/ADS**: I've hand copied many blurbs and written 100+ in a variety of genres.

4. **COVERS**: I have professional covers and now employ a testing process to shore up previous misfires in this area.

5. **BACKLIST**: I have 9 existing urban fantasy books (three trilogies) with solid reviews.

6. **BRAND**: from reader reviews/feedback, I've determined that my overall brand can be summed up as: Anti-heroes with a touch of philosophy. Darker edge without being bleak. My books are dialogue heavy and move fast.

7. **AUTHOR WEBSITE**: I have this already set up, with newsletter sign up forms, a list of books, series pages, about, and contact pages.

8. **NEWSLETTER**: sign up forms, lead magnet novellas/stories for existing series, autoresponder, all set up.

Basically, my entire marketing infrastructure is in place. All that I need to do is focus on writing and then execute the marketing strategies that I've already been honing over the past couple years.

As for the plan itself: reading 12 books is for market research and craft purposes. I want to get a feel for what's selling (both long-term and in Kindle Unlimited *right now*) and get a better understanding of how bestselling authors write their books.

The specific emphasis on dialogue and scene structure is because "get better at craft" is too broad a goal 24+ books in. There are eight core areas of craft: character, plot, setting, scene structure, story structure, voice and style, theme and dialogue. For the first few novels, it's possible to improve all of these skills at once. Once you've hit an intermediate level of proficiency, however, making significant strides often requires narrowing your focus to a single area.

This does not mean ignoring the other areas, merely being content with allowing those skills to remain at the same level for the time being. Often you'll find that improving one area dramatically will lift the others as well, however; more compelling dialogue creates more engaging characters, and also moves the plot along at a faster clip, for example.

I'm starting with scene structure, because my Kindle Unlimited readthrough stats suggest that people aren't finishing books at the rate that I'd like. I believe this is a scene structure issue (although it may be a plot structure issue, which is why I'll be examining that area as well). This could end up taking the bulk of the year, or it could be done and dusted after a novel or two. I'm prepared to dedicate whatever amount of time it takes.

Finally, the large launch or monthly promotion will mostly be comprised of launches. If I hit the book every other month target, then it could conceivably be *all* launches, as I'll also have content like box sets to fill in gaps where I don't have a brand new novel available. But if I miss a release, hold a few books back for a rapid release, or see an opportunity to push some of my backlist, a promotion may carry the load that month instead of a launch. The ultimate goal here is maintaining momentum: I want my books to remain visible and for my royalties to not jackknife downward. Some downswings are inevitable, particularly in non-release months. But hopefully this approach can mitigate the most precipitous dips.

Anyway, if you've read my stuff on productivity, you know that I'm actually *not* a fan of yearly goals (or goals in general). They're artificial, constraining, and largely ineffective, since they focus on the end. The ultimate result is that even if you achieve them, you spent the entire year in a state of failure, save for the one moment where you crossed the finish line. Then it's back to failure once you set the next batch of goals.

No wonder no one actually achieves their goals. They suck.

So we need to reverse engineer all of these to figure out what we need to do on a daily basis:

1.   Read for twenty minutes.
2.   Write 1,200 words.

Yes, that's all it takes to read 12 books and write 8 books in a year:

- 50k words x 8 books= 400k words = 1,095 words a day.
- 12 books = 1 book a month @ 6 hours per book = 19.7 minutes a day of reading.

Then we throw in a little slack for rest/days off/general life stuff and you have your daily habits. About one hour of work. You'll notice that I don't have anything marketing related listed. That's because, in my case, I'm pretty much knee-deep in various marketing stuff all day, and the tasks/workload vary considerably. So I'll be doing quite a bit of marketing over the next year. But at this stage of my career, it doesn't break down into a neat daily habit. Which is fine: you'll find some things don't fit into that structure.

And, as it turns out, nor do my writing and reading tasks.

I am not a super consistent person on a day-to-day basis.

Trying to establish a daily writing habit has been one of the reasons I haven't published anything for 18 months. I'm a burst writer, spurred to the finish line by hard deadlines (i.e., pre-orders; I'm writing this very sentence two hours before this guide is due for pre-order on Amazon).

Habits work for me when it comes to exercise.

They don't work here.

That's okay. It means some days I'll write for four hours to meet a deadline. And a lot of days I won't write at all. Accepting this about myself is key to tapping into productive capabilities.

So it's a good exercise to reverse engineer things.

It means I know that this is a realistic plan.

An hour of work a day, on average, is doable.

I just need to make sure I distribute the workload so it matches my strengths.

THE ULTIMATE STRATEGY

This section is called the Ultimate Write to Market Strategy, so I should probably lay that out, right? Well, it's pretty similar to what I outlined in the previous section, just with four key differences: higher word counts, more releases, more books read, and picking a popular KU sub-genre.

- **CORE OBJECTIVE**: five figures a month
- **LAUNCH WIDE or KU**: all in KU

- **SERIES? PLANNED # of TITLES?**: yes. 5 – 6 book series, minimum.
- **LENGTH**: 60,000+ word novels
- **NEW TITLES IN NEXT YEAR**: 12
- **SUB-GENRES**: popular in KU
- **CORE TRAFFIC SOURCES**: Facebook Ads, Amazon Ads, BookBub Ads, promo sites
- **NEWSLETTER BUILDING PLANS**: both organic and non-organic
- **PRODUCTION BUDGET PER TITLE**: $750 – $900
- **ADVERTISING BUDGET PER TITLE**: variable
- **BOOKS READ**: 50 in the sub-genre to nail down tropes.

Why the differences? Releasing 12 novels in a hot KU sub-genre combined with ads is like nitro fuel. Writing longer means more potential page reads and more revenue. And reading 50 books in a year will drive the tropes and expectations deep in your bones.

While this is probably the fastest route to building a career, it's also one of the most difficult. Not from a workload perspective; if we reverse engineer it, we get the following daily habits:

1. Read for one hour.
2. Market for one hour.
3. Write 2,500 words.

That's about four hours of work. But most authors can't sustain this workload for long without burning out. It's hard to write 2 novels in a year, let alone 12. Writing the novels may not be hugely time-consuming, but it is *intense* from a focus perspective. And doing it back-to-back-to-back each month wears most authors down, which means that instead of being a recipe for success, the ultimate strategy is a roadmap for burnout.

I outline it for two reasons: one, for the right author, it *will* be useful. But for most, it's simply to free you from the tyranny of unrealistic expectations. You don't have to write a book a month to succeed. If you can't do it, you're not screwed. To sustain for years, it demands innate production capabilities that most authors don't have. And remember that this level of production is relatively new. Ten years ago, publishing a book a year was considered wildly prolific.

GENERAL STRATEGY

Okay, so not everyone has time to write 12 novels (or even 8) along with all that other stuff. What about a more widely applicable strategy?

Let's take a look at the Ultimate Book Marketing Formula again:

MARKET RESEARCH + 3 TRAFFIC SOURCES + PRO COVERS + GREAT BLURBS + NEWSLETTER + 4-6 NOVELS PER YEAR

CONSISTENTLY FOR 3-5 YEARS

FULL-TIME AUTHOR

And then let's reverse engineer the Formula into a strategy for a hypothetical new author:

- **CORE OBJECTIVE:** break $1,000 net a month
- **LAUNCH WIDE or KU:** all in KU
- **SERIES? PLANNED # of TITLES?:** yes. Two series of 4 - 6 books, alternating releases.
- **LENGTH:** 60,000 - 70,000 word novels
- **NEW TITLES IN NEXT YEAR:** 4
- **SUB-GENRE:** contemporary romance
- **CORE TRAFFIC SOURCES:** Facebook Ads, Facebook, newsletter swaps, and promo sites
- **NEWSLETTER BUILDING PLANS:** cross promos until she hits 5,000 subscribers and organically via epilogues after the happily ever after.
- **PRODUCTION BUDGET PER TITLE:** $750
- **ADVERTISING BUDGET PER TITLE:** $1,000

Here, we've adapted pieces of the guide to fit contemporary romance. Our hypothetical author has chosen to release her books in KU, since she's new and figure that Amazon's marketing tools like free runs and KCDs will be useful for generating visibility. Oh, and about that visibility: she knows it's a little bit easier to attain, since each borrow counts the same as a sale in Amazon's sales rank algorithm. Finally, from a little poking around and talking with successful authors, she knows that contemporary romance does well in Kindle Unlimited.

Our author here writes a little bit longer than I do at 60,000+ words, plus has a day job and a family that take current priority over writing, so she hashes out a plan for four releases during the next year. If she only hits three, she's okay with that, but she doesn't want that to drop to one or zero by overextending herself chasing unrealistic expectations.

On the ads front, she's heard Facebook Ads and Facebook are important pieces of the puzzle for most romance authors; a significant portion of the audience hangs out on that platform, which makes it a good place to focus. She's saved up a bit of money from her job over the past months to put toward production and advertising costs to give her books a professional polish and launch push. And since she's outgoing, and has less cash to play with for each new release than some of the heavy hitters in the genre who spend 5-figures per launch, she's decided to focus on networking with other authors and doing lots of cross promos/newsletter swaps. Our author understands that these can burn out her list, so she plans on being careful and choosing swap partners wisely (and she also will only share the swaps with non-organic subscribers, rather than her organic subscribers). But for now, she feels like the trade-off is worth it to build up her readership.

Instead of novellas, the author has settled upon writing 2,000 to 3,000 word epilogues for each book, which romance readers love and will gladly sign up to the list for. This saves time and words for actual full-length releases, which also make this tactic a fit for our author's busy schedule.

Our author doesn't have any of the infrastructure like a website or newsletter set up, and she doesn't yet know the nuances of writing a blurb or working with a cover designer. So she's set aside some time in the first year to build these things and learn the ropes. In the future, she expects that, with these skills under her belt, she might be able to write 5 – 6 books a year, even with a full-time job and family time.

Finally, this author has read hundreds of contemporary romance books. So she's a huge fan of the genre and understand the tropes. But she still wants to stay up on what's popular/hot in Kindle Unlimited, particularly on the indie front to make sure her own books match the marketplace's expectations.

On a yearly basis, her plan looks like:

1. Read 25 Top 100 contemporary romances in the next year.
2. Publish 1 full-length (60k+) novel every three months.
3. Complete one major marketing project each month: website, newsletter, autoresponder, etc.

She reverse engineers that to the following daily habits:

1. 1,000 words per day.
2. 30 minutes of reading per day.
3. 1 marketing task per day.

Our author knows that she thrives on consistency and is not motivated by external pressure; in fact, things like pre-order deadlines stress her out and reduce her word counts. Thus, she sets up a place to track her daily habits and checks them off as she finishes them for the day.

With this method, within a few short years, our new author will already have 12 – 15 books in their catalog. Maybe she'll be a full-time author by that point; maybe she'll be earning a decent side income. Whatever the case, she'll be well positioned to keep growing and building their career brick-by-brick into the future.

And that, really, is the ultimate goal. Each day, you put another brick down. It can be a tiny brick. But always be building toward whatever it is you want. Consistency is an unbelievably powerful force.

ACTION EXERCISE

1. Review the rough draft of the strategy you designed in Part
    1. Then take out a new sheet of paper and revise it:

    - Your core objective
    - Whether you'll launch your books wide or in KU
    - Whether you'll write in a series and, if so, the planned
      # of titles
    - What length they'll be: novels, novellas, serials, or short
      stories
    - The number of new titles you'll release over the next
      year, with approximate word counts
    - The sub-genre(s) you plan to write in
    - Your core three traffic sources
    - How you plan to build your newsletter
    - Your production budget for each title
    - Your advertising budget for each title

2. Break that down into yearly production, reading/craft, and
    marketing targets.
3. Break those yearly targets down into daily habits. Then tear
    up the yearly targets (keep the strategy, though! you'll be
    referring to it) and get to work right now.

FOURTEEN:

AUDIO

udio is a tricky format to market. I don't profess to be an expert here; I'm still experimenting myself. But these strategies should provide you with some ideas for pushing more copies of your own audiobooks. The operative word here being *more*, not "suddenly crushing it to an absurd degree."

An important note: unlike most of this guide, this bonus section comprises of a great many ideas that I have either not directly tested or have limited direct experience with. Audio is still a fledgling area when it comes to indie marketing, and the landscape will likely look very different in a couple years as more options become available to us.

The little information that *is* available is scattered across blog posts, forums, Facebook groups, and a myriad of other assorted places. Thus, consider this section a compilation of the most promising ideas I've found for selling more audiobooks.

MAKE SURE IT'S WHISPERSYNCED

If you release an audiobook—whether that's for a single novel or a box set—make sure that it's linked to the corresponding eBook version and Whispersynced. Amazon will then automatically upsell the audio version when someone purchases the eBook version. This extends to $0.99 promotions and free downloads as well, which means that when a reader picks up your three book box set for $0.99, they can Whispersync the audio version for $7.49, which is an excellent deal.

BOX SETS

Speaking of box sets, one of the best tools at your disposal as an indie is the trusty box set concept—simply applied to audiobooks. One of the main challenges when it comes to audio is the price. If you publish through ACX, you don't have control over your price, which means that your audiobooks are sold at retail price. And $25 or a precious Audible credit is a hard sell for an author (or narrator) that a reader isn't already familiar with.

However, if you package three books (or more), listeners suddenly get 20 or 40 hours of audio for a single Audible credit. This effectively discounts each audiobook in the set to around $5 – $10 apiece.

As mentioned above, you can pair the audio box set with a $0.99 eBook set (I've personally tested this with the $0.99 Kindle Unlimited box set strategy outlined earlier in the guide, and it was very effective) to supercharge audio sales. The visibility on the eBook set—particularly if you hit the Top 1,000 or 500 in the Kindle Store—can shift an enormous number of audiobooks, both through Whispersync *and* people simply seeing that the audio is available when they visit the discounted eBook set's Amazon page.

GET A POPULAR NARRATOR

Many audiobook listeners are fans of certain narrators—and will follow them across series, authors, and even genres. That means that by hiring a popular narrator, you can tap into this person's existing fanbase and bring these listeners to your books.

Popular narrators can be both expensive and in-demand. They are not a necessity, and oftentimes the expense can outweigh the benefit. But if the right opportunity arises, booking a popular narrator who is perfect for your book could help you reach a whole new group of listeners.

CHIRP

Chirp is BookBub's new audiobook deals newsletter. It works much the same as their famed Featured Deals: you submit your audiobook for consideration at a discounted price and their editors select the ones they believe will appeal most to their listeners.

This is one of the only marketing opportunities outside of pay-per-click ads where we can directly push traffic to our audiobooks. And while it's still in its early stages, Chirp looks extremely promising (I've never run a deal, so I can't speak to results).

The only caveat?

Your book must be published via Findaway Voices. Most authors publish through ACX (Amazon's audiobook platform).

Why is Findaway Voices a requirement to be eligible for Chirp? Because it allows you to set your price.

ACX does not, and thus you can't discount your audio for a Chirp deal.

With that in mind, it's worth considering—as Chirp and the audio market both evolve—whether you should publish via ACX or a different platform going forward. ACX certainly has benefits, as we'll get to in a second, but as more promotional opportunities develop that revolve around discounting, the benefits of alternative options may continue to grow.

ACX: BOUNTY LINKS AND PROMO CODES

If you publish your audiobook via ACX, you receive what's called a bounty link. This is essentially a special kind of affiliate link that, when someone signs up for Audible through it (and stays a certain amount of time), you receive what's called a bounty. This bounty varies depending on whether you've done a royalty split with your narrator, but it can total up to $75 per person who signs up.

The best part? You can use it *anywhere* at the time of this writing (double-check the ACX terms to make sure you're up-to-date). This includes locations like PPC ads or emails where normal Amazon affiliates aren't allowed.

Make sure you're using your Bounty link everywhere you can.

The other main perk of ACX is the promo codes. They give you these codes to dole out as you see fit. They're great for audio ARCs and freebies for your newsletter.

Not only do you get to give your book away for free, but each promo code counts toward your Audible rank.

FACEBOOK ADS

Sending cold traffic (people unfamiliar with you as an author) to an expensive audiobook is a tough sell, as previously mentioned. It's generally ineffective to try to push the audiobook directly via Facebook Ads.

Instead, I prefer to focus on selling the Kindle edition. I've found selling more copies of the Kindle version is more effective for selling audio than trying to sell the audio directly. Selling the Kindle version raises its visibility in the Kindle Store, which in turn brings more eyeballs to the audiobook. Buyers of the Kindle version will also sometimes Whispersync the audio.

Additionally, instead of making the ad focus on the audiobook, you can make the focus and main link to the Kindle version—then add a link to the audio (using the bounty link) at the bottom of the ad copy.

NEGOTIATE

If your eBook is doing well, you might be approached by an audio-only publisher interested in publishing the audio version. This can be a good alternative to self-pubbing the audio; while you'll have to split the royalties with the publisher, they take care of the production, including the associated time and costs. You get a professional product, without having to lay out a bunch of extra hours and dollars.

If you're approached by a publisher, know that any royalty rates or advances they toss out are often more flexible than they first appear. Most authors are so surprised to get an offer at all that they simply accept the first one that comes. But don't be afraid to negotiate for more.

EXCERPTS

One of the main reasons authors struggle to move audio is a failure to apply the same marketing techniques they've already learned for eBooks. Asking your narrator to include a short excerpt of the next book at the end of your audiobook can be a great way to encourage people to pick up the next title in the series.

This works even *better* in audio than it does in print because of the differences in how each format is consumed. People often listen to audiobooks in settings like the car, cooking, walking the dog, and so forth, where their hands aren't free or near their device. When a book ends, your excerpt will autoplay unless they *actively* turn it off. Most won't, thus you instantly hook them on the next book in the series. Just make the excerpt isn't super-long (first chapter, max); having too much extra content that isn't the actual book can get you in hot water with ACX.

Finally, you'll want to put your audiobook samples up on Soundcloud, and embed them on that book's page on your website. That way prospective audio listeners can listen to it while they're browsing your backlist.

FIFTEEN:

WRAPPING UP

We've reached the end of the *Ultimate Guide to Book Marketing*. Thanks for reading. If you've read this front to back, you might be overwhelmed by the sheer amount of information. That's okay. Take things one task and one day at a time. And if you've been at this for a while and are just as overwhelmed by the sheer number of things you already have to do as an author and small business owner, just remember the 80/20 rule: chop most of the BS out of your day.

It only takes about two to four hours a day to publish and market 4 – 12 novels a year, depending on how long your books are and how fast you write. Often, the path forward is not through addition, but through subtraction. Cull things to the essentials, hone those to a fine point, and then use the rest of your day to cook, walk your dog, play an instrument, volunteer, hang out with your family, or however you like to spend your time.

Or crank things to eleven and work 12 hours a day on your core 20%.

The choice is yours.

If you remember just one thing from this guide, make it this: always build brick-by-brick. This is a long game. Much longer than even people who think of themselves as patient imagine. In the short-term, you have little control over what happens. You'll have wins, losses, and feel like you're stuck in neutral a lot of the time.

But if you dedicate yourself to honing your craft over years, the odds start to tilt in your favor. And when you get impatient, never forget that this is not a one month or one year game. Over five, ten, or twenty years, skill will win.

You just need to keep writing.

For more information like the stuff in this guide, subscribe to my free marketing newsletter at **nicholaserik.com/newsletter**.

If you'd like to double down on implementing the marketing principles you've learned in this guide, check out the **30 DAY SPRINT**—it bridges the gap between productivity and marketing with the aim of starting a solid habit and getting your core mar-keting system up in just 30 days. Check that out at nicho-laserik.com/sprint.

And if you're ready for a deep dive into Facebook, Amazon, and BookBub Ads, check out **80/20 AUTHOR ADS** at **nicholaserik.com/ads**.

That's it.

Now go sell some more books.

ACTION EXERCISES

CHAPTER 1: PRINCIPLES

1. **Devote time to taking action.** You can go through the guide exercise by exercise—they're specifically designed to help you apply the keystone points—or pick and choose whatever is useful based on your current situation. A simple system is doing one marketing task a day OR up to one hour of marketing each day.

CHAPTER 2: BUSINESS FUNDAMENTALS

1. Make sure you have a website and mailing list.
2. Calculate your net profit for the past year.
3. Calculate your average monthly burn over the past year.
4. Set up a spreadsheet and start tracking your net profit and organic subscribers on a weekly or monthly basis.

5. Set a timer for 10 minutes. Then map out a rough draft of your strategy for the next year by writing out the following on a sheet of paper:

- Your core objective
- Whether you'll launch your books wide or in KU
- Whether you'll write in a series and, if so, the planned # of titles
- What length they'll be: novels, novellas, serials, or short stories
- The number of new titles you'll release over the next year, with approximate word counts
- The sub-genre(s) you plan to write in
- The format(s) you plan to publish in
- Your core three traffic sources
- How you plan to build your newsletter
- Your production budget for each title
- Your advertising budget for each title

Answer as best you can, but *don't* spend hours deliberating, researching, or otherwise worrying about making it perfect. This document is not set in stone. Rather, it's something you'll update as you learn more about marketing.

If this guide does its job, by the end you'll have the necessary tools to confidently answer *each* of these questions, thus giving you a personalized marketing strategy to work from going forward.

CHAPTER 3: THE ULTIMATE BOOK MARKETING FORMULA

1.   Make sure your Amazon Author Central account, Amazon Affiliate account, and your Amazon series pages are all in order.

CHAPTER 4: MARKET RESEARCH

1.   **Research your sub-genre on the Amazon bestseller charts (nicholaserik.com/top100).**

- Write down the ranks of the #1, #5, #10, #20 and #50 book in two sub-genres that fit your series.
- Write down ten indie authors and ten traditionally published authors who represent your target market (i.e., authors who can realistically complete the statement, **my book is for fans of [Author X]**).
- Write down character names instead, if the character is more recognizable than the author.
- You'll use this list of authors and character names for PPC (pay-per-click) ad targeting, your blurb, cover inspiration and more down the line, so save it (Excel tends to work best).

CHAPTER 5: AMAZON'S ALGORITHMS

1. Design a promo stack that properly leverages the organic visibility from Amazon's charts + recommendation engine.

CHAPTER 6: TRAFFIC

1. **Choose your three traffic sources and write them down.** Be realistic about your time and budget constraints as well as your personal preferences. If you're never going to post regularly on Facebook, don't lie to yourself. Just pretend that Facebook doesn't exist, rather than wondering what could have been.

CHAPTER 7: 7 PROMOTIONAL STRATEGIES

1. Choose one strategy, adapt it for your series, and execute it.
2. If you don't currently have money to advertise, either design and execute a low cost (or free) option, or outline a hypothetical strategy with a budget of $3,000.

CHAPTER 8: BRANDING

COVER: ACTION STEP

1. **Find 3 – 5 covers that you like on your sub-genre's Amazon Top 100 bestseller list.** Identify a mix of traditionally published books and indie titles. Readers have voted with their dollars that they prefer these covers in this genre. Maybe you're getting sick of me mentioning the bestseller charts; too bad. These charts are like the ultimate focus group that definitively answers the question "what do readers want?" totally free.

2. **Find a cover artist with a portfolio matching your desired style and book genre.** Visit my resources (**nicholaserik. com/resources**) if you're stuck. I only list designers that I've personally worked with and recommend.

3. **Send your 3 – 5 sample covers to the designer and tell them to MAKE IT LOOK SIMILAR TO THE EXAMPLES.** It is crucial to provide your designer with clear visual expectations, as text can be easily misinterpreted. Be specific regarding the design elements you do or do not want. The more clearly you communicate expectations, the better your final cover will be.

4. **Ensure that the typography is consistent in terms of font/ placement across your series.** This is critical for branding and to signal that books are in the same series.

BLURB: ACTION STEP

1. Write a new blurb based on the principles and the formula that best fits your book.

BACK MATTER: ACTION STEP

1. Reduce the number of CTAs on same page as THE END to two: a mailing list link and a link to your next book.

CHAPTER 9: NEWSLETTER BUILDING

To get your first 1,000 subscribers (or add 1,000 more), do the following:

1. Set up your organic email list and put a link in the front/back matter of your books.
2. Set up your autoresponder.
3. Join two cross promotions in your sub-genre taking place in the next 30 days on Story Origin (**storyoriginapp.com**) or BookFunnel (**bookfunnel.com**). This will build your list to 1,000 subscribers (or close to it).
4. Repeat #2 each month until you hit 5,000 – 6,000 subscribers or the point of diminishing returns (e.g. you're losing more subscribers than you gain).

CHAPTER 10: NEWSLETTER ENGAGEMENT

1. Decide on your newsletter frequency, content, and tone going forward.
2. Adjust your Welcome email and autoresponder to correctly set these expectations.

CHAPTER 11: OPTIMIZATION

1. Take one item from the list and optimize it.

CHAPTER 12: LAUNCHING

1. Create a launch plan for your next book.

CHAPTER 13: THE ULTIMATE WRITE TO MARKET STRATEGY

1. Review the rough draft of the strategy you designed in Part 1. Then take out a new sheet of paper and revise it:

- Your core objective
- Whether you'll launch your books wide or in KU

- Whether you'll write in a series and, if so, the planned # of titles
- What length they'll be: novels, novellas, serials, or short stories
- The number of new titles you'll release over the next year, with approximate word counts
- The sub-genre(s) you plan to write in
- Your core three traffic sources
- How you plan to build your newsletter
- Your production budget for each title
- Your advertising budget for each title

1. Break that down into yearly production, reading/craft, and marketing targets.
2. Break those yearly targets down into monthly milestones and daily habits. Then tear up the yearly targets (keep the strategy, though! you'll be referring to it) and get to work *right now.*

CALCULATIONS & TARGET METRICS

This is a reference list of key metrics from the *Ultimate Guide to Book Marketing*. These are rules of thumb, not set in stone; many factors affect the numbers below. As you become more advanced with your marketing, you'll better understand the factors responsible for deviations— either positive or negative— from these benchmarks.

Generally speaking, if your numbers are *way* above these, you're probably not getting that much traffic (or only dealing with organic traffic, like people coming from the back of your books) or you've miscalculated. Open rates for 200 subscribers are wildly different than those for 20,000.

If your numbers are far below these, something is usually very wrong. A quick fix (i.e., no complicated A/B split-testing) to a major element can often return things back to normal ranges.

A final note: metrics are useful, whether that's Amazon rank, Facebook likes, a certain conversion rate or whatever. But they are not the ultimate arbiter of success; **profit is the king metric, and will be until the end of time**. If you're getting an 80% conversion rate on your landing page, but none of those subscribers are buying your stuff, that doesn't mean shit.

NET PROFIT

NET PROFIT: the amount of money you get to put in your pocket after all expenses are paid. The entire point of being in business.

CALCULATION: royalties – expenses
EX. $26,731 royalties - $9,024 expenses = $17,707 in net profit

SELLTHROUGH

SELLTHROUGH: the percentage of people going on to read Book 2, 3, etc. after picking up Book 1. To maximize accuracy, measure during a period where you weren't running any promos on the series, had no price changes in the series, didn't launch a new book in the series, and optimally had at least 100 sales of Book 1 (or 1,000 downloads for a perma-free). Note that sellthrough varies based on retailer (i.e., your sellthrough on Amazon will differ from Barnes & Noble) and traffic source (i.e., Facebook ads will produce different sellthrough than promo sites). This is not possible to factor into the calculations, but it is important to be aware of.

The four best ways to increase sellthrough are:

1. Cliffhangers (when used properly, otherwise can irritate readers; not appropriate in all genres, e.g., crime/thriller/mystery)

2. Improved craft (scene and plot structure influence pacing the most)

3. Limiting the number of CTAs on same page as THE END to two (link to next book with one to two sentence teaser and newsletter sign-up link).

4. Include an excerpt of the next book (helps when wide, little to no impact in Kindle Unlimited).

FROM BOOK TO BOOK: (# of sales of Book 2 / # of sales of Book 1) or (# of sales of Book 3 / # of sales of Book 2)
EX. 22 sales of Book 2 / 45 sales of Book 1 = 48.9% sellthrough

FOR THE TOTAL SERIES: (# of sales of Book X / # of sales of Book 1) (where Book X is the last in the series)
EX. 12 sales of Book 5 / 45 sales of Book 1 = 26.7% series sellthrough

FOR KU: # of borrows of Book 2 / # of borrows of Book 1
BORROWS: total pages of Book 1 read / total KENP in Book 1 (this is found in the KDP Dashboard)
EX. 12,627 Book 1 pages read / 323 Book 1 KENP = 50.36 borrows (round down to 50)

REVENUE PER SALE

REVENUE PER SALE (RPS): the total series revenue a sale of Book 1 generates when factoring in sellthrough to the other books in the series.

SALES: total series sales revenue / Total Book 1 Sales
EX. $10,240 revenue / 702 sales = $14.59 revenue per sale

BORROWS: total series KU revenue / Total Book 1 Borrows
EX. $5,467 revenue / 589 borrows = $9.28 revenue per borrow

NOTE: like sellthrough, this should be calculated during a period where data was stable. Price changes, big promos, and new books in the series will throw off the RPS and make it an unreliable estimate. Optimally, aim for 100 sales of Book 1 (or 1,000 downloads for a permafree) during the period you choose. Also, revenue from box sets can sometimes skew RPS; you can exclude them.

COST PER SALE

COST PER SALE (CPS): the total amount of ad spend it takes to produce a sale of the advertised book.
CALCULATION: ad spend for that book / sales of that book
EX. $58 in ad spend / 8 sales = $7.25 per sale

Cost per sale is more accurate when factoring in the **baseline**, which is the average number of daily sales your book produces organically without any advertising.

> **CALCULATION**: # sales / # days during baseline measurement period
> **EX**. 82 sales / 16 days = 5.1 baseline sales per day.

Incorporating the baseline into cost per sale, we get:

> **CALCULATION**: total ad spend for that book / (total sales - total baseline sales)
> **EX**. $58 in ad spend / (8 sales - 5.1 baseline sales) = $20 per sale

CONVERSION RATE

Conversion is impossible to accurately calculate, as Amazon doesn't give us granular enough data. Further, our stats are corrupted by KU borrows, which we can't measure. However, it's still useful, even as a rough estimate:

> **CONVERSION**: the percentage of clicks resulting in a sale.
> **CALCULATION**: sales / clicks
> **EX**. 45 sales / 967 clicks = 4.7% conversion

Like cost per sale, conversion is more accurate when factoring in the **baseline**, which is the average number of daily sales your book produces organically without any advertising.

CALCULATION: # sales / # days during baseline measurement period

EX. 42 sales / 7 days = 6 baseline sales per day.

Incorporating the baseline into conversion, we get:

CALCULATION: (sales – baseline) / clicks

EX. (45 sales – 6 baseline sales) / 967 clicks = 4.03% conversion

TARGET METRICS

CONVERSION

1. Landing Page mailing list sign-up conversion rate (organic traffic): 40%+

2. Landing Page mailing list sign-up conversion rate (paid traffic): 30%+

3. Thank You upsell page sales conversion: 1 - 3%

4. Facebook Ads conversion (free book): 25%+

5. Facebook Ads conversion ($0.99): 5%+

6. Facebook Ads conversion ($2.99+): 1 – 5%

7. Amazon Ads conversion ($0.99+): 4 – 12%

8. BookBub Ads conversion (free): 25%+

9. BookBub Ads conversion ($0.99): 10 – 20%

10. BookBub Ads conversion ($2.99+): 1 – 5%

EMAIL

1. Open Rate (welcome email): 60%+

2. Open Rate (regular email, organic): 35%+

3. Open Rate (regular email, non-organic): 25%+

SELLTHROUGH

1. Sales readthrough (full price Book 1 > Book 2): 30 – 40%

2. Sales readthrough ($0.99 Book 1 > full price Book 2): 15%

3. Sales readthrough (free Book 1 > full price Book 2): 2 – 5%

4. KU readthrough (Book 1 > Book 2): 50 – 60%

RESOURCES

Here's a list of the main resources mentioned within the guide, so you don't have to hunt page-by-page to find them.

- Curated promo site list: nicholaserik.com/promo-sites
- Designers/resources: nicholaserik.com/resources
- Marketing newsletter: nicholaserik.com/newsletter

EMAIL & WEB SERVICES

- Google Domains: domains.google.com
- Google Custom Email: gsuite.google.com
- Flywheel Hosting: getflywheel.com
- Pressidium Hosting: pressidium.com
- Astra Theme: wpastra.com

- Elementor Builder: elementor.com
- MailerLite: mailerlite.com
- ConvertKit: convertkit.com

AUTHOR SERVICES & SOFTWARE

- BookFunnel: bookfunnel.com
- StoryOrigin: storyoriginapp.com
- Vellum: vellum.pub

THE
ULTIMATE
GUIDE TO AUTHOR
PRODUCTIVITY

THE 80/20 SYSTEM FOR
DOING WHAT MATTERS

NICHOLAS ERIK

80/20 your productivity step-by-step with *The Ultimate Guide to Author Productivity*. Now available in eBook and paperback at **nicholaserik.com/productivity**.